Two week loan

Please return on or before the last
date stamped below.
Charges are made for late return.

IS 239/0799

INFORMATION SERVICES PO BOX 430, CARDIFF CF10 3XT

MICHAEL ROSE

INDUSTRIAL BEHAVIOUR

THEORETICAL
DEVELOPMENT
SINCE
TAYLOR

PENGUIN BOOKS

Penguin Books Ltd, Harmondsworth,
Middlesex, England
Penguin Books, 625 Madison Avenue,
New York, New York 10022, U.S.A.
Penguin Books Australia Ltd, Ringwood,
Victoria, Australia
Penguin Books Canada Ltd, 2801 John Street,
Markham, Ontario, Canada L3R 1B4
Penguin Books (N.Z.) Ltd, 182–190 Wairau Road,
Auckland 10, New Zealand

First published by Allen Lane 1975
Published in Penguin Education 1978

Made and printed in Great Britain by
Hazell Watson & Viney Ltd, Aylesbury, Bucks
Set in Monotype Ehrhardt

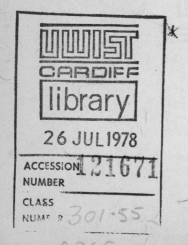

For
Glenys and David
and
in memory of my father

7

Contents

OH THAT MINE ENEMY
WOULD WRITE A BOOK!

From several points of view the aims of this study are rather modest, and though the notices which the Allen Lane edition received were gratifying it seemed that some reviewers took this book as an effort to accomplish rather more than to stimulate reflection and debate about teaching and research in the domain of industrial studies. It is, then, necessary to repeat here, with a certain emphasis, that the study does not set out to propose in a systematically argued fashion any strikingly novel approach to the study of industrial behaviour. What I hope it does provide is some encouragement and equipment for critical thinking, and some outline suggestions for ways of building up a larger stock of fruitful studies and interpretations in this field.

My personal ideas about how this best may be done have naturally evolved since the text was originally written, and there are certain restatements or revisions that I would wish to make if it were technically possible. This applies in particular to the sections on the socio-technical approach, where some of the judgements are somewhat brusque, and to the brief chapter on Alain Touraine, which abstracts this writer's work excessively from its context and fails to discuss other important industrial researches in post-war France.

9

But there is nothing of a major kind that I would wish at this moment to retract. My accounts of the work of others can be checked beside the original material; and as for post-war French industrial sociology, a separate monograph is at present under preparation.

In a more general way, I wish to reiterate some of the opening remarks of the Allen Lane edition, with some amplification. Firstly, many readers of this book are likely to be managers or students of management, and I hope it will provoke in them a more thoughtful attitude about the managerial role and the social position of the manager in contemporary society. Managers face changes in the nature of their work of a thoroughgoing kind, and a wider perspective will make these upheavals more comprehensible and perhaps more acceptable. Managers have a positive right to understand the context in which their work is executed, which is typically frustrated in practice; and this deprivation of the instruments of analysis is even more pronounced amongst other employee groups. Acquisition of a wider perspective would never of itself eradicate the conflicts which register the process of change, but it can aid identification of the real sources of these confrontations.

Next, it seems to me that the crisis that began about ten years ago in sociology is already much less severe than it was. Excessive expectations of sociology as a comprehensive theoretical science (plus, sometimes, excessive claims about its potentialities in this respect), which accompanied its expansion, were bound to produce certain types of over-reaction once they were frustrated. Thus, the various 'alternatives' which began to attract support were often embraced with a distinctly fideist zeal. Most regrettably of all, the anti-rationalist element in these responses was directed frequently against sociology's most enduring asset: that is, its vocation and technical apparatus for investigating and describing social structure. Undeniably, this research technology can introduce systematic and unrecognized misinformation into the collection and presentation of material; equally, however, researchers are now more alert to this risk, and efforts to improve the technology continue. As sterile criticism (and fashion) exhaust themselves, more adult attitudes prevail.

On a second front the position remains more enigmatic. What relation is sociology to have to Marxism? Evidently such a question cannot be answered properly here, for it seems that an answer must depend somewhat on wider economic and political developments. Is it possible for anyone to make real sense of the continuing crisis of the western socio–economic system without some resort to the methods and perspectives adopted by many marxists? How is it possible to study and explain most social phenomena in these countries without reference to that crisis? What degree of reason remains in the dismissal, *en bloc*, of Marxism as a rigid (and alien) ideology, at a moment when it is being reappropriated and developed as the flexible theoretical guide of the democratic labour movement in advanced countries, to the evident dismay of totalitarian doctrinaires? But this said, any claim that Marxism constitutes a ready-made alternative to sociology remains implausible to me, especially when it is chanted with evangelical fervour. Marx himself sought to create a science whose propositions were to interact with experience and not to be incanted like a litany or invoked like a talisman. Events themselves will continue to aid the determination of the value of these propositions, as the need to remodel our industrialized societies is increasingly matched by our opportunities to do so.

In closing this foreword, I must thank once more those people mentioned in the Allen Lane edition, those who have given me their views in the last three years, and Jill Norman in particular.

Milan, February 1977

INTRODUCTION: INDUSTRIAL SOCIOLOGY A TERM IN SEARCH OF A MEANING

This book is about industrial sociology – at least, that is the least misleading description. It is not a textbook on industrial sociology but deals with the development of the subject area. (What this area covers will be discussed presently.) It is *not* an exhaustive chronicle but focuses on certain stages of this development which have been widely identified as the most interesting or important. I do not wish to suggest that the resulting pattern could not be improved; but, provisionally, it is convenient for purposes of exposition. In the course of this exposition it will certainly be necessary to present studies widely accepted as important additions to our knowledge of industrial behaviour. It will be equally necessary to suggest criticisms of them. Finally, it will be useful to examine the pattern of criticism and revision itself, and ask what morals can be drawn from it.

There are three questions which must be explored immediately. First, what is industrial sociology? Second, what are the agreed key stages of development? Third, what are the main available interpretations of the resulting pattern?

WHAT IS 'INDUSTRIAL SOCIOLOGY'?

There are two ways of answering this question, neither entirely satisfactory. One is to examine the doings and statements of persons who have called themselves industrial sociologists. We shall do this shortly, but some objections to the method are immediately obvious. The second alternative appears more logical; i.e., first define 'sociology', then define 'industrial'. The logic here may be faultless, but the results of trying to follow it are likely to provide rough going for the reader; and it does not really answer the question.

A vast literature debating what sociology is, or should be, awaits anyone with a taste for running round in intellectual circles, and I am reluctant to add what may be merely another loop.[1] What I believe sociology *should* be will emerge from the text, and is tackled more squarely in the final chapters. At this stage all that needs saying is that by the understanding adopted, most 'industrial sociology' is not sociology at all.

The term 'industrial' raises comparable problems. Special sociologies are largely artificial creations, which result partly from careerism amongst academics, partly from tidy-mindedness amongst teaching administrators and partly from a sloppy kind of common-sense thinking. Of course, a degree of specialization in empirical study is necessary and this may result in some inevitable fragmentation in substantive theories. For example, a theory which explains why working-class schoolchildren perform less well than middle-class children (when intelligence is matched) and a theory which accounts for the greater propensity of workers in a certain industry to strike will obviously call attention to varying factors (parental encouragement or the attitude of teachers on the one hand, for example, versus the prosperity of the industry or the nature of union leadership on the other).

But, if it is a valid one, the basic sociological method will be identical in both cases, and permit the linkage of the findings and substantive theories at a higher conceptual level. (After all, working-class educational 'under-achievement' and the pattern of industrial conflict are certainly not unconnected phenomena.) We shall find that until fairly recently few industrial sociologists have bothered themselves unduly over such considerations.

None the less, granting the convenience of some specialization, why should industry be chosen as a distinctive sector of social life as a whole? An evident reply, and an increasingly respectable one in professional circles since the rediscovery of Marx's early writings, is grounded in philosophical anthropology. Man, the basic premise runs, is necessarily an active being: he must feed, house and clothe himself; in other words, to live he must work. Under modern conditions this generally means that he must obtain money to buy necessities (and luxuries) by selling his labour. Other parts of his life may *together* absorb a greater proportion of his time, energy or thought; but none of these is, singly, as important as work – and indeed none could occur unless he worked. Whether work is a central *life-interest* or not, it is emphatically a central *life-fact*.

Now this is all true, though like other unchallengeable existential verities (for example, that we all die one day) it lends itself to a number of elaborations which are as vacuous as they are ideological. However, the fact is that industrial sociologists have in the past paid little attention to it, though recently fashion has changed.

A comparable reason for selecting industry as an analytical focal point is the evident differences between industrialized and non-industrialized societies. Philosophy (though not ideology) is discarded in favour of fact here. If industry can be taken as the dominant institution of modernized societies, then industrialism as a way of life can be compared with traditional modes, and differences and similarities between industrialized societies enumerated.

However, study at this level of analysis is a comparatively recent preoccupation – or rather, a reversion to concerns which were central to the work of the classical grand theorists of sociology.* As with them, there are good historical reasons for its revival (and

* Above all Marx, Durkheim and Weber. It is somewhat inaccurate to characterize Marx as a sociologist, for reasons briefly indicated in the final chapter of this book.

for its ideological content: much of it could be crudely characterized as a sigh of relief over the unexpected resilience of Western society after the Second World War). We shall examine this work again below. But for the moment the point should be made that this type of study forms little of industrial sociology as commonly understood, and widespread interest in the questions it addresses is very recent.

But the simplest way of accounting for social scientific interest in industry, and especially in workers' behaviour, is as an effort to obtain knowledge which can be used to augment labour productivity, i.e., as an aspect of economic exploitation. In the most abstract sense, the notion of exploitation carries no necessarily perjorative overtones, since any overall economic growth implies that on balance some labour is not compensated by immediate consumption; and it is possible to conceive of circumstances in which producers themselves would seek scientific aid, or even attempt spontaneously to apply scientific knowledge, to increase their productivity. But the 'historical reality of exploitation, in which unrewarded effort has been exacted through physical violence, psychological terror and – most effectively of all – the operation of free markets in labour and commodities, inevitably conditions our view of it.

The themes which I have outlined here reappear regularly in the lengthy debate in academic circles over the nature and status of industrial sociology. As a prelude to the main body of this study, it is worth looking briefly at this controversy.

For other branches of social study boast a literature comparable to that in which, at great length, industrial sociologists have struggled to define industrial sociology and come to a conclusion about what they should be doing.[2] A review of this discussion reveals certain patterns. Contributions embody aims which are both critical and cartographic, and there appears to be some historical distribution in the nature of the arguments put forward, which allows us to distinguish two phases of the debate.

Tremors presaging phase one were recorded just before the Second World War, built up shortly after it, reached a peak in the late 1940s of truly seismic dimensions, and gradually subsided into a more interspersed series of rumblings distributed over a wider zone, though at least one of these (its epicentre appropriately enough located on the American West Coast) was sufficiently severe to send some of the more nervous members of the threatened population racing for the protective shelter of defiant polemics.[3]

This disturbance was associated with the assault on 'human relations'. Since it is dealt with in more detail later in this account (see Part III), we shall notice here its main outline only. Contributors to phase one were mainly concerned to show that the majority of those describing themselves as industrial sociologists at that period were probably not true sociologists at all; if they did merit the title they were excessively narrow in their research interests and theoretical thinking, and/or over-involved in the practical application of their work. The human relations group were accused, amongst much else, and not without justification, of focusing undue attention on work-groups in large factories, of ignoring the essentially conflictual nature of industrial relations, of overlooking the influence of union and community affiliations on work-place behaviour and attitudes, of picturing the worker as irrational, of under-emphasizing the influence of economic incentives and wider economic events, and of providing managers with a spuriously 'scientific' prop for their authority. In sum, industrial sociology was no more than an elegant fancy-dress to disguise scientific incompetence and moral subservience to the industrially powerful.

The phase-one critics were a rather heterogeneous brood, embracing sociologists, social critics, economists and historians of labour; their known or deducible ideological affiliations covered the whole spectrum with the exception of the radical right. It is therefore not surprising that, in the event, their remarks about human relations were more effective in putting a brake on what industrial sociologists had been doing than in providing a clear alternative line of advance.

In view of this critique, which gave the impression that industrial sociologists had sold out to business interests, it is remarkable that so many people in the United States, and in an increasing number in Western European countries, continued to refer to themselves by the title. But while these people became more assiduous in avoiding the errors of the human-relationists (or at least, claiming to), they do not appear to have been entirely sure where any specialist competence they possessed could or should begin and end.

Phase two of the debate continues sporadically into the present and is articulated with phase one by a celebrated article of 1957 by Kerr and Fisher, 'Plant Sociology; the Élite and the Aborigines'.[4] This phase has been much more concerned with the cartographic issue, with whether there really is or can be a branch of sociology concerned with industry; and, if so, with exactly where it can rightfully place, or get away with placing, its boundary posts. There are several background factors to this dispute. Two – the human relations stigmata, and the continuing insistence of many that they wished to be known as industrial sociologists – have already been touched on. There are at least three others which should be mentioned.

One is the emergence of the branch of study, originating with E. C. Hughes in Chicago in the 1940s, known usually as the sociology of occupations. While most of those who have claimed the title of industrial sociologist have traditionally been concerned primarily with behaviour in the work-place, the occupational sociologist has explored such matters as the subjective consequences of work for the individual, its meaning to him, its effects on his attitudes and relationships in other social contexts, and the tactics which members of an occupation adopt to increase their rewards, security and prestige – a clearly more sociological concern than all of the preceding ones. Generally speaking, however, occupational sociology can be regarded as complementary to traditional industrial sociology.

This cannot so easily be said of the second new factor – the explosive growth of organization theory. This set of studies is one of the most extraordinary features of contemporary intellectual life. From the outside, and at a distance, one could easily form the impression that a mighty and subtly planned edifice is in the course of construction. Reports from the architects themselves assure us that this is indeed what is happening. On closer inspection we find something more closely resembling a shambles.*

Some of the builders are clearly working as speculative developers on the grand scale, while others seem to be hand-carving exquisite statuary with little idea where eventually it will be sited. Some have the openly entrepreneurial intention of selling off the finished pile at a handsome price, while their more otherworldly colleagues would be happy to bequeath it to posterity as a monument to the theoretical art. One group of craftsmen must be picked out for special mention here. These are the organizational sociologists. Increasingly, they have demanded the incorporation of industrial sociology within their 'more comprehensive' scheme.

The academic boom in organizational sociology was manifested largely in the second phase of the squabble over the definition of industrial sociology. Perhaps over-reacting, in their liberal pluralist wrath, against the human-relationist assault on economic man, Kerr and Fisher pressed for a highly restricted field for industrial sociology. Far from being a sociology of industrial phenomena in general it should become a sociology of the factory ('plant sociology'); and, in as much as industrial sociologists had shown themselves inclined to dabble in other areas, their extra-plant concerns should be redistributed amongst other specialized sociologies – of occupations, the community and politics. Plant sociology itself should be a branch of organizational sociology.

These recommendations, which were probably intended as little more than a form of kite-flying, were in fact taken up fairly promptly by Amitai Etzioni.[5] Industrial sociology still had a useful part to play, he affirmed, but it should indeed be incorporated in the much more promising field of organizational sociology. As a concession, however, he would expand Kerr's specifications. Industrial sociology might be the sociology not merely of factories, but of all economic organizations. And there was a period in the early 1960s when such an absorption seemed imminent, as more and more literature which would previously have announced itself as industrial

---

* This can be verified by comparing the contents of any two books, taken at random, whose titles include the terms 'organization'. A larger sample illustrates the heterogeneity more or less in constant proportion.

sociology appeared under some kind of 'organizations' label. Several veteran industrial sociologists, such as W. F. Whyte and F. J. Roethlisberger, adopted the new title with enthusiasm.

In Europe, adoption of the new label – and of the structural-functionalist outlook which soon seemed to accompany the sociological approach to organizations – was less ready. In some respects this was paradoxical because during this period British students of industry at the Tavistock Institute were in the process of creating an analytical model (the *socio-technical system*; see Part IV) which has proved immensely influential amongst American organization theorists. However, one productive group of students, mainly though not exclusively empirical in orientation, under the leadership of W. H. Scott at the University of Liverpool, clung to the title 'industrial sociologist' and produced work which only with some difficulty could be incorporated into any organization theory framework then available.[6]

In France, likewise, the large number of students reared under the influence of Georges Friedmann soon proved themselves hostile to the waning human relations tradition and indifferent to the supposed advantages of the organizations approach. The title of their main forum, *Sociologie du travail*, is some indication of their outlook. This probably approximated most closely to that of the Chicago occupational sociologists amongst the increasingly heterogeneous Anglo-Saxon 'schools', though like the Liverpool group much of their early work was strongly empiricist. They were also far less shy of exploring Marxian insights than their Anglo-Saxon colleagues. In the person of Alain Touraine this unique blend of influences was to produce a theorist whose general form of thought is particularly tantalizing.*

It would be wrong to overstress the significance of the preservation of industrial sociology on the eastern side of the Atlantic in the late 1950s and the 1960s. After all, many American students continued to employ the label, and several unambiguously titled (if not unambiguously structured) textbooks published there at the

---

* See Chapter 28 below. The amount of this French work translated into English, or read by English-speaking students in the original, is rather small.

time remained the only ones available in English.[7] However, it was in Britain that the most persuasive plea for the resurrection of industrial sociology was eventually to originate.[8] The proponent (D. Silverman) seems to have modified his views a little since his 1968 statement; but his complaint that organization theory is leading towards sterility in theory and research (and has discernible obscurantist ideological undertones) remains largely valid despite Silverman's own recent attempt to ventilate the theory of organizations with the breeze of 'actionalism' (see Part V) and the agreeable, though somewhat heady, incense of phenomenology.

At roughly the same time we find a statement in an introduction to a collection of readings from an unreconstructed American industrial sociologist which, in its attempt to define the field, shows a good deal more fight than one has come to expect from adherents of the old faith in the land of the *Administrative Science Quarterly*.[9] Indeed, Faunce's remarks are not merely defiant but can be construed as a reverse takeover bid:

> The concerns of industrial sociologists have been rapidly changing during the past decade. Some would maintain that the field has suffered the 'ultimate transformation' and no longer exists as a viable subdiscipline . . . and that much of what is relevant is best incorporated into other subdisciplines, such as the sociology of organizations . . . one of the purposes of this reader is to suggest (paraphrasing Mark Twain) that reports of the death of the field have been greatly exaggerated.[10]

If editors of readers on the sociology of organizations will include sections on work behaviour, then editors of readers on industrial sociology will have sections on organizations, as Faunce does. In each instance the impression created is that the major concern of the rival is a mere aspect of the 'senior' subject.

Such antics would be of no interest to us if they did not reflect a problem of genuine theoretical importance. The fact is that both organizational and industrial sociologists have at last been forced to recognize, though they have not solved, a common problem of levels of analysis. This has been washed ashore by new currents of thought which have already been briefly alluded to: namely, the sudden popularity of macro-theoretical speculations about industrialized societies as wholes.[11] The impact of these inquiries can rapidly be made apparent if we examine three fairly recent works from self-declared industrial sociologists.

1. Faunce has himself analysed the content of major American texts on the subject. Common to them, he asserts, are treatments of certain substantive areas: the work-group, industrial bureaucracy, union–management relations, work-roles in industry, the industrialization process, the organization of trade unions. For him, majority vote is decisive. Some other areas (he mentions the sociology of occupations and industry–community relations) are not included in his reader for strictly pragmatic reasons: 'Although these areas were once regarded as part of the field, the rapid growth of knowledge has made it impossible to do justice to them all in a single college course.'[12] However, what justifies industrial sociology as a separate field, and links together the substantive areas selected, is the 'common thread of interest in some central features of industrialism as a way of life that runs through industrial sociology'.

2. Parker *et al.* view the general enterprise as involving 'the application of sociological theories and methods to one segment of society, that is, the one concerned with the economic function . . . Industry is sometimes narrowly defined as what takes place in factories, but in this book we shall use it to mean the world of work.'[13] In practice this results in their applying sociological theories at three levels: functionalist theory to analyse the relations between industry and the family, education, etc.; organizational theories at the 'organization-role level'; and various social–psychological and other approaches at the 'role-person level' (a quick tour through the study of occupations).

3. Burns, in making his selections for a recent reader, declares that he has been guided by three major themes. These are: 'industrialism as a major force in social change'; 'organization as a developing social technology'; and 'the consequences, for individual working members of society, of the organization of work under industrialism'.[14]

From this it is clear that some kind of institutional or societal analysis, or a declared set of assumptions about industrial society, is increasingly regarded as an essential accompaniment to the study of concrete patterns of relationship and behaviour in the work-place – the traditional concern of industrial sociologists, and certainly of the majority whose work is reviewed in this book. This is a welcome extension of scope, which we shall return to and assess in later chapters. But it is a further illustration of the difficulty of adopting 'industrial sociology' as a term of reference.

In fact our troubles on this score are by no means over. A good deal of theorizing about industrial behaviour originates with management thinkers (or ideologists) and psychologists, and self-declared industrial sociologists have inherited many of the problems they raised. This sometimes gives the impression that the work of figures such as F. W. Taylor – to take the most obvious case – forms part of industrial sociology. But there is no sense at all in which Taylor can be considered a sociologist.

Since some work from these sources must be evaluated here, the comment made earlier, that to claim this book is about industrial sociology may be misleading, should now be quite plain. However, I would still maintain that this characterization is in the circumstances the *least* misleading. Those engaged in many different kinds of enterprise have claimed the title, certainly, and have often drawn their problems and methods from non-sociological sources. Yet it is possible to trace a historical path through them which brings us, in the present time, to the threshold of a *genuine* social science of industry.

For this reason the term will be retained in much of the text. The general policy will be to adopt it when referring to the work of persons who have called themselves industrial sociologists, or to those who did not but whose work may be considered as real contributions towards a true sociology of industry. In other instances the term 'industrial studies' will be used.

Let us now take an over-view of the general pattern of development of the subject.

STAGES OF DEVELOPMENT

At the core of industrial sociology as conventionally understood is, firstly, a concern with industrial behaviour, particularly with that of manual workers. Associated with this there has usually been a readiness to utilize findings to increase the productivity of labour or to further harmonious relations between labour and management. This concern with applications, which are always in principle primarily for managerial benefit, has repeatedly aroused the concern of liberals and radicals. But there is a sense in which it has worked to benefit, and perhaps advance, intellectual variety. For where policies based on an inadequate theory have been introduced they have failed conspicuously, thus stimulating renewed search for the real bases of motivation and behaviour.

It is this cycle of research, theorizing, application, disappointment and renewed research which a student with an encyclopedic capacity and taxonomic inclinations should discover in the field of industrial studies as a whole. Much of this activity, it should be said, has produced nothing of any genuine interest to science – this can quickly be confirmed by glancing through practically any textbook of management theory. (As moral weaponry, such material can be rather more important.)

We shall follow only one possible path through the maze of management thinking, industrial psychology, organization theory and industrial sociology. This takes us through five principal stages of development, each constituting a *relatively* distinct approach. (That is, relative to each other; most of them can be seen as variations of a single and much larger intellectual orientation.) An approach is distinguished by its disciplinary origins, its methodological assumptions, the social philosophy of its exponents and their choice of specific problems.

These stages are, in order: scientific management; human factor industrial psychology; human relations industrial psychology and sociology; technological implications industrial sociology; and industrial sociology employing an actionalist perspective.

This categorization is not mine. Parts of it appear in, for example, Baritz's attack on the managerial entanglements of American students of industry, in Friedmann's classic critique of technicism and in Bendix's exploration of managerial ideologies, as well as in many textbooks on industrial (*or* organizational) sociology.[15] It was suggested most explicitly in an early paper by J. H. Goldthorpe, which unfortunately has not been published.[16]

Goldthorpe pointed out that the division is an illuminating one not only because the exponents of a given stage had different methodologies and theories from the immediate predecessor, but because they set out consciously to attack it. Indeed, he argued that the dialectical form of the development of industrial sociological theory is apparent.

The precise connotations of the term 'dialectical' here are not made clear, though the notion is certainly present that a later approach refined elements of an earlier one in contradicting it, thus leading to a higher synthesis. As a *description* of what has happened this certainly seems to fit the facts very well. But to what extent Goldthorpe is also proposing an explanatory *theory* of social scientific advance is not quite clear. (It probably was not his intention to do so.) None the less, this aspect of the matter is a crucial one, and, in view of the recent upsurge of the 'sociology of sociology' and revival of controversy over the methodology of the social sciences, a highly topical one. The material in this book may be useful to those engaged in these disputes. Several kinds of explanation are available, and readers may find it convenient to consider their plausibility as they go through. In a later chapter a general assessment of their applicability is given.

INTERPRETATIVE POSSIBILITIES

Social scientists hold, or have held, a wide variety of theories of self-understanding. Other observers of these studies have often challenged what they regard as the extravagantly self-complimentary, if not erroneous, nature of these models. Any reduction of the large variety of explanations thus generated is bound to appear a somewhat oversimplified schematization. Unfortunately, the scope of this book demands such oversimplification. However, the following schedule discriminates roughly between the main alternatives.

Orthodox positivism. Those who believe that the social sciences are able to emulate the procedures of natural science will naturally seek a pattern in the development of a social science which reflects that imputed to 'hard' science. The general pattern will be one of the gradual cumulation of positive knowledge resulting from careful observation, the construction of testable hypotheses, the collection of empirical data· to enable such verifications to be made, and a resulting refinement of theories which organize and explain discovery in an economical and meaningful way.[17]

Those engaged in these activities do and should regard themselves as the dispassionate investigators of an objective reality. As value-free scientists their aim is to understand the world. Others can change it, making use of their new knowledge, but that is not the scientist's concern. This viewpoint will picture industrial studies as a legitimate attempt to create new knowledge about an important area of human activity.

Vulgar-Marxism. But, leaving aside the question whether the social student can *in principle* copy the procedures of the natural scientists, what guarantee can he give us that his choice and treatment of problems, and the theories which he creates, are in fact value-free? Does he recognize that society is divided into antagonistic strata, the rulers and the ruled; that these classes are created by the historically evolving forces of production; that they are engaged in an underlying struggle for power; that social theory and philosophy are justifications for the hegemony of the owners of property; and that unless he recognizes these verities his theories will merely reflect the changing needs of the ruling class for new 'ruling ideas' as the precise constitution of the material base evolves towards the conditions for a final revolutionary convulsion?

For those who hold such opinions, all bourgeois social science is merely an item in the ideological apparatus of capitalism.[18] Industrial studies must then be seen as one branch, though a rather important one, of ideological production. Since such a viewpoint has usually been put forward by self-proclaimed 'Marxists', but does not require any great grasp of Marxist theory, it will be characterized as vulgar-Marxist.

Kuhnianism. The orthodox positivist model of scientific advance, with its stress on the workaday cumulation of knowledge, has been attacked by T. S. Kuhn.[19] Kuhn is mainly concerned with the physico-chemical sciences where he claims advance consists in an oscillation between normal and revolutionary periods of inquiry.

During a period of 'normal' science, the work of established investigators and the training of young scientists is guided by an accepted paradigm – a model or a set of concepts and theories which is believed to organize knowledge within the field in the most coherent manner. Acceptance of the paradigm is vital for admission to an appropriate 'scientific community'. Anyone who refuses to do so is regarded as an incompetent, an impostor or a crank. Eventually, however, findings which conflict with the paradigm accumulate, and theorists put forward revolutionary alternatives to it.

The new paradigm is rarely accepted peaceably, and the revolutionary period may be marked by fierce partisanship. Once a substitution is made, however, the incoming paradigm redefines reality and thus alters the choice and handling of problems – Kuhn calls them 'puzzles' – as the science subsides into a new period of normality.

One or two commentators have suggested the adaptability of Kuhn's very sociological theory to sociology itself, and on the surface this has great plausibility. Friedrichs has recently added an elaboration. He suggests that, in the social sciences, a submerged paradigmatic dimension must be considered in addition to the more substantive one. This depends on the social scientist's self-conception – whether he views himself as a value-free 'priest' or as a 'prophet' committed to changing the world.[20]

Both the 'classical' and Friedrichian variants of Kuhnianism should be borne in mind in assessing its applicability to the following material.

Gouldnerism. In his *The Coming Crisis in Western Sociology*, Gouldner is concerned with sociology as a whole.[21] One of his aims is to show that sociology is ambiguous politically *in principle*, although in practice the dominant structural-functionalist mode of theorizing can be seen as a response to the socio-economic problems of capitalism (or 'middle-class society' to use Gouldner's euphemism). This aspect of Gouldner's analysis need not detain us here, though we shall take it up in a later chapter. More important is his idea that a social theory is related to a theorist's 'domain assumptions' (unverified and unrecognized conceptions of the nature of man and society), which are emotively grounded in 'sentiments' acquired from his social background and sustained in maturity by association with sympathetic minds. To some extent these domain assumptions are historically specific products. Thus theory is not merely a reflection of the 'state of the art' but the state of society itself, mediated by the theorist.

In some respects this is vaguely reminiscent of vulgar-Marxism. Gouldner, however, is rather less hospitable to the direct influence of economic forces on social theory. Moreover, he is certain that, ideologically contaminated though it may be, sociological theory can be salvaged as a branch of social science in its own right. This is because sociologists can acquire insight into their own domain assumptions, and neutralize their effects.

In so far as Gouldner intends his analysis for sociology alone, it obviously cannot be applied to some of the stages of development of industrial studies reviewed here. But it may be tested against some of the more specifically sociological approaches – after all, Mayo, the founder of human relations, belonged to the same circle at Harvard in the 1930s as the sociologist Talcott Parsons (the chief target of *The Coming Crisis*).* And we shall need to ask to what extent the latest styles of industrial sociology embody opposing currents to orthodox theory. What signs are there, too, that 'reflexive sociology' is possible and productive in this field – indeed, in any?

Possibly none of these alternatives will be adequate. But that matter can be dealt with later.

* See Chapter 12 below.

PART I

TAYLORISM

RATIONAL WORKMEN
AND
INCOMPETENT MANAGERS

It is difficult to discuss the 'contribution' of F. W. Taylor to the systematic study of industrial behaviour in an even-tempered way. The sheer silliness from a modern perspective of many of his ideas, and the barbarities they led to when applied in industry, encourage ridicule and denunciation. This tendency is accentuated if one concentrates on Taylor personally, rather than as the representative figure of a certain historical movement – 'scientific management' – which itself can be situated in an even larger tradition – 'technocracy'.

Unfortunately, however, a satisfactory account of this tradition has still to be written; and though scientific management has received a good deal of attention, some important aspects of it remain untreated. One of these is its relation to 'classical' nineteenth-century economics – and indeed even to the thought of Ricardo and Marx: Taylor's own amateurish economic assumptions project something rather like a distorted labour theory of value, argue the importance of organization as an independent force of production, and embody a weird variant of the materialist conception of history.

The present treatment must be restricted to establishing why Taylorism initiated the systematic study of industrial behaviour and how its content and course influenced in a decisive way the problems upon which later industrial students were to focus so much of their attention. For much of later work, until thirty years after his death, was unquestionably a 'debate with Taylor's ghost' – or rather a remonstration with it – and his opinions about the effect of incentives on industrial behaviour are a hare which is still being chased with dogged, and well-financed, scholasticism.

A review of Taylorism is also an instructive reminder of how 'scientific' theories of workers' behaviour which fail when actually applied in industry can none the less acquire a substitute vitality as managerial ideologies. Further, we must remember that, to an extent which it is difficult to assess, experience of the type of managerial devices which Taylorism promoted – in particular work-measurement and job-fragmentation – decisively modified the 'subculture' of the manual working class. In this respect, if in no other, Taylorism possesses historic significance.

At the core of any theory of industrial behaviour lies an image of the typical worker. Formal students of industrial behaviour spell this out systematically, and relate it logically to conceptions of management–worker relations and of the enterprise as a social organization. These propositions, ideally, should be linked to explicit assumptions about the total form of socio-economic relations. How far this is done varies enormously. Not surprisingly in Taylor's case, since he in no sense saw himself as a social scientist, this systematization was never undertaken. Rather, it must be inferred from contrasting his diagnosis of the general industrial ills of his time with his prescriptions for curing them.

Taylor's diagnosis of the industrial situation reduces to one simple theme: inefficiency. For him, the waste of resources, especially the waste of time, was morally appalling. Inefficiency stemmed from both labour and management. On the worker's side, the principal vice was 'slacking' and 'soldiering'. On the manager's side the complementary evil was incompetence. It is clear that he did not regard these failings as altogether of the natural order of things. They were pathological deviations for which he offers informal sociological explanations.

Take 'soldiering'. It has two forms: 'First, from the natural instinct and tendency of men to take it easy, which may be called natural soldiering. Second, from more intricate second thought and reasoning caused by their relations with other men, which may be called systematic soldiering.'[1] It is clear that he regarded this second form, the group control of output, as the more important kind. He did so not because it shows any inherent 'group instinct' towards sociability and solidarity but because it 'results from careful study on the part of the workmen of what will promote their best interests'.[2] It was a rational strategy.

Why had they made this discovery? Because of managerial incompetence. Managers lacked information about workers' abilities and the time which is reasonably required to perform industrial tasks. Times allocated for a set of given tasks were arrived at by guesswork. When this resulted in easy jobs managers arbitrarily altered the times if workers were tempted to complete them too quickly. Workers therefore colluded to ensure the maximum economic returns all round without having to exhaust themselves.

But why were the managers incompetent in the first place? Firstly, the growth in the scale and technical complexity of industry had to be taken into account. Secondly, however, in line with these structural changes, the traditional entrepreneur was becoming displaced by men 'spiritually aloof from the mass': financiers on one side, professional managers on the other. Taylor revered the captains of earlier nineteenth-century American industry. As his biographer Copley reminds us, these folksy pioneers 'jollied their men and joked with them; bawled them out and beat them up in man-to-man fashion; dealt with them, no matter how roughly or savagely, on a plane of simple human relations, of perfect social equality'.[3] Taylor himself longed to be a muscular six-footer like William Sellers, his boss at the Midvale Company, instilling a 'fearful' loyalty by his mere physical presence, and not afraid to 'joke with the apprentice boy one minute and give him a spanking the next'. But these halcyon days, when indiscipline or idleness could be settled promptly by manly fisticuffs in the yard, were passing.

Without any question Taylor regarded the average manager of late-nineteenth-century America as an incompetent, and therefore lacking a legitimate basis for his authority. Since his prescriptions had more severe consequences for the worker in practice, the punitive element in them for managers is easily overlooked. Taylor's scorn for managers, in fact, was almost hysterical. They are portrayed as ignorant, arbitrary, selfish and blind to their own real interests, i.e. largely *irrational*. His assertion late in life that nine-tenths of the opposition to his managing system (in its complete version) had come from management was more than a rhetorical sop to his critics in the labour movement.

Taylor's technical proposals – his system – was, then, a set of devices which sought to capitalize on workers' rationality and suppress managerial irrationality. It would eradicate inefficiency and arbitrary managerial prerogatives (and thus the workers' rebellious response to them). In sum, it would create an authentic industrial partnership. But why should either party accept it? And who would form the vanguard which could secure its adoption? Taylor's reply to the first question was, because it was *scientific*: impartial, universal, *lawlike* in both the scientific and juridical senses. To the second his response was, the production engineer.

Both of these answers reflect crucial aspects of a contemporary social reality. The first, the Victorian faith in science as the material embodiment of irresistible human progress. The second, the emergence of engineers as a profession indispensable to technically advanced industry; a stratum increasingly conscious that its indispensability rested on science-based expertise, and with a vague sense (which later was to become more definite) that its interests were not indivisibly linked to any particular form of ownership of productive capital.

Taylor's technical prescriptions form a logically consistent package of devices for an efficiency-minded production engineer, which can be divided into three broad classes.[4] The first set comprises recommendations about organizational structure and routine. The second revolves around the measurement of work and the design of tasks. The third deals with the selection and motivation of workers.

The organizational prescriptions must be dealt with briefly. The best-known is an insistence on 'functional foremanship'. This would make the worker responsible to four first-line supervisors simultaneously – the 'gang', 'speed' and 'repair' bosses and an inspector. But they also demanded a central and powerful 'Thinking Department'. This would oversee the optimal routing of materials and sub-assemblies in the factory and the preparation of job order tickets for operatives. It would also take care of pay-calculation, engagement and discipline.

Attempts to apply functional foremanship have usually been unsuccessful because the gains from supervisory specialization are offset by role-conflicts and ambiguities of jurisdiction. The call for a 'Thinking Department' is much more interesting, and not only as an illustration of the drift of Taylor's personal thought. It represents a demand for the extension of industrial 'bureaucracy' and as such is highly symptomatic of its times, when the scale and complexity of operations were outstripping traditional administrative technique.

The second set of proposals is more important. Taylor, rightly, is regarded as the founder of work-study. He aimed to relate to each other in an ideal way the methods adopted, the time taken, the tools used and the fatigue generated by any task. The most generous remark that can be made about his procedure is that, as a pioneering contribution, it was uncluttered by the refinements which later followers brought to the craft.

Essentially it took the following form. Pick 'ten to fifteen' men (from different establishments, if convenient) already skilled in the work whose 'science' is to be discovered. Observe them at work and define the elements of the sequence of operations they employ. Time each element, for each individual, with a stop-watch. Identify those operations which seem to contribute nothing towards the completion of the task and eliminate them. Select the quickest methods discovered for each element and fit them into a sequence. Teach the workman this sequence, forbidding any deviation or the introduction of unnecessary operations. Add up the times for each element, and include an allowance for resting. The result will be the 'quickest and best' method for the task. Because it is the 'best way' all workers selected to perform the task must adopt it and meet the time allowed.[5]

Further study might be needed to determine the right length and spacing of rest-pauses, and they were certainly needed to permit the design of better tools. In his studies at the Bethlehem Steel Company, Taylor discovered an optimum load in shovelling. Since the materials to be shovelled varied in their density an entirely new range of shovels and forks had to be designed to ensure that this weight of material was always lifted. In such labouring tasks physiological fatigue could be warded off by tactically timed rest-pauses, their timing and duration depending upon the work. Study could thus determine the maximum amount of work possible in one day short of physical collapse.

The final set of prescriptions, for labour selection and motivation, is encapsulated in two formulae. First, every task should be performed by a 'first-class man' for that type of work. Second, 'first-class' men should be given 'a fair day's pay for a fair day's work'. What is a 'first-class' man? He is both born and made. Taylor never systematized his selection techniques completely, except for pig-iron handling, where they are clear: 'Now one of the first requirements of a man who is fit to handle pig-iron as a regular occupation is that he shall be so stupid and phlegmatic that he more nearly resembles in his mental make-up the ox than any other type.'[6] A second guide is less positive. Those workmen initially judged well-adapted to a task who fail to maintain a 'fair day's work' should be sacked.

It is worth noting in passing that these selection procedures could be applied equally well to horses. In 1903 Taylor purchased a mansion, Bloxley, on the outskirts of Philadelphia, and set about the redesign of an extensive classical garden laid out by one Comte Jean du Barry, a French émigré occupier of the 1800s. These operations demanded the removal of a hill. The horses used were time-studied: 'We found out,' Taylor wrote excitedly, 'just what a horse will endure, what percentage of the day he must haul with such a load, how much he can pull, how much he should rest.' As Copley notes: 'His standard was set by the best heavy-draft horses of the locality, and he used his keen eyes to chase all others off the job.'[7]

Taylor recognized, however, that men can be trained to a higher level and for tasks beyond the aptitude of horses. Training a 'first-class' man implied the inculcation of a perfect grasp of the routinized movements of a given task. Considerable managerial resources should be devoted to this purpose. And since some workers tended to relapse into bad habits once trained, refresher courses should be provided. One prerequisite for successful training was to convince the worker that he could not know better than the scientific manager how a job should be done. As Taylor saw it, the worker should perceive this as an advantage. He is reported to have told workers that they were not supposed to think, since other people were paid to do that for them. This was meant kindly.

Defining a 'fair day's work', Taylor asserted, is a purely technical matter. It is laid down by production engineers after work-study and is therefore not a matter of opinion but science. A 'fair day's pay' is more elusive, but Taylor felt that it should be substantially above the going rate for similar kinds of work in the locality. Its critical feature, however, was that the level of reward should be tied closely to output, through the mechanism of the *differential piece-rate* system. Under this system, a worker who failed to produce a 'fair day's work' should suffer a proportionate loss of earnings. If he exceeded the target he would receive a bonus. However, bonus-payments would be so adjusted that they would reach a ceiling between 30 per cent and 100 per cent above normal. (The ceiling of 60 per cent usually mentioned in this respect was intended to apply to heavy manual work only.) The ceiling was advocated, Taylor claimed, for the benefit of the worker, since if men 'got rich too quick' dissipation, drunkenness and absenteeism would increase. Originally, it was *not* to protect management from 'excessive' wage-bills.

It is interesting to note here that Taylor recognized the possibility that the supply of labour might decrease. Hence, although Taylor's conception of worker motivation is essentially 'economistic', he did recognize the possibility that workers might be subject to other motivations – the hedonistic use of leisure in particular.* Moreover, since the ceiling for bonus payments was to vary with different kinds of task, and therefore, following *ex hypothese* his demand for selection, with different kinds of workers, one can detect here some

* J. H. Goldthorpe seems to have been first to notice the theoretical importance of this aspect of Taylor's thought.

implicit recognition of a varied ordering of priorities in different segments of the labour force. And his recommendation that bonus earnings should be communicated to workmen as soon as they could be computed, preferably daily, is a psychologically sound insight.

It hardly needs stressing, however, that nearly all of the foregoing ideas are seriously flawed. The whole notion of the 'quickest and best way', and the means of determining it, are technically faulty. First, it derives from a study of operatives who are already skilled at the task in question: in statistical terms, from a *purposive* not a random sample. If a rationalized task is then imposed on a whole work-force (and that frequently happened – indeed still does), some workers will inevitably be outpaced. Taylor thought such displaced workers could become 'best men' at some other task. In the real world there was, and is, no certainty that this would happen.

Second, there is a more fundamental objection to the procedure. Since the 'best' way is a compilation of the movements of *several* workers it ignores the psychology of individual differences: a particular movement may be rapid and economical for one man, within the context of his total set of techniques for performing the whole task; but there is no guarantee that it will be so for others, or even for the original subject himself when he is forced to fit it between other movements foisted upon him from the total technical repertoires of other workmen. Likewise, the removal of 'wasteful' movements can be self-frustrating. We have since learnt that many such movements, although 'useless' when viewed in isolation, are in fact essential to the rhythm of an overall efficient working motion.*

One can hardly condemn Taylor for ignoring the psychology of individual differences, since it was only very poorly developed at the time he was preparing his system. And it is true that he did make genuine discoveries about the more efficient performance of certain tasks. These were, however, simple labouring operations in which the psyche is not importantly engaged. When one turns to more complex tasks, such as machining, where dexterity and attention are important, the crudity of Taylorian work-study is evident. And

---

* This point will be taken up in Part II below.

there is little doubt about the source of Taylor's fallacies here. Despite his informal recognition of social and psychological factors, he saw the worker from an engineer's standpoint; that is, as a machine.

That a 'fair day's pay' may be determined *scientifically* is a contradiction in terms.* Taylor's reasoning seems to have been that a production engineer who studies the capacities of men and machines in a systematic, quantifying way, with a view merely to increasing productivity (not profit), is being scientific; that science is impartial and objective; and that therefore when the 'scientific manager' decides on a price for a job this sum must somehow be objectively right. But the very use of the term 'fair' introduces notions of social equity. Taylor's simple-minded conception of science did not include the notion that propositions in the imperative mood cannot be deduced from those in the indicative, but its truth is here given a back-handed recognition. Fairness in payment clearly demands some social reference-point. But whose reference-point should this be? Certainly not the worker's; the worker is not a scientist. In theory, it should be that of the scientific manager. But of course, in practice, the reference he will be obliged to adopt must also take into account the ability of the enterprise to continue showing a profit.

Fairness here, then, is not some abstract equity. Given a continuance in labour and commodity markets, it simply could not be much more than a rhetorical device. The most one can say is that Taylor was asserting a managerial right to operate an arbitrary and unilateral wages policy within the confines of the enterprise.

For 'fair day's pay' one should really read 'opportunity to earn higher pay' – higher than the workman earned before, or than local averages – 'for doing much more work in the same time'.

There is no doubt at all that Taylor himself did want workers to earn much higher wages than previously. This was absolutely necessary to make his system viable as a whole. Here he adopted

---

* Unless *complete* consensus about the level of equitable rewards for varying kinds of work exists in a society, or some (so far undiscovered) technique is evolved for applying broadly agreed 'objective' criteria to establish a set of rewards.

virtually undiluted the postulates of individual rationalism, hedonism and atomism of Victorian economics. The worker was overwhelmingly instrumental in his approach to work. Social rewards in work, as opposed to social safeguards, were of no account beside the wage-packet. The social safeguards – group restriction of output, and trade unions – had come into being to further economic objectives. Once scientific management could meet these objectives the social bonds would dissolve.

Or would they? Rather, a new, and needless to say much 'healthier', bond would replace them: that linking the worker to the scientific manager in 'willing, hearty collaboration'. In other words, scientific management was also an exercise in social engineering, the primary objective of which was to remove the cleavage between management and workers and replace it with a harmonic fellowship. If conflict were to remain in industry, it would rather be between the workers and scientific managers on one side and the financial controllers of industry and the 'outmoded' trade unions on the other. (This redirection is mainly implicit in Taylor's writings, but the division of interest between owners and their employees as a whole was stressed by some of Taylor's explicitly 'technocratic' followers.)[8]

A second element in Taylor's thought which can be seen as an additional attraction of his system for workers was his conviction that practically everyone could excel at some task or other, given sufficient training and the proper design of work. This constituted a repudiation of contemporary socio-economic wisdom in its extreme form as 'social Darwinism'. This ideology had raised the labour market to the status of a sacred human evolutionary vehicle. Those unfortunates who found no work and starved were the necessary sacrificial victims of Progress. Taylor's faith in selection and training constituted an oblique attack on the labour market as a natural, and naturally selective, phenomenon with which only rogues or fools would tamper.

As we have seen, Taylor entertained grave doubts about the virtues of unrestricted markets. The economic process had led to an unnatural situation, the artificial restraint of productivity. Large-scale industry could only be made efficient and fair by massive intervention and redirection. For this to happen a revolution was necessary. And to secure this revolution, he correctly concluded, the consciousness of key groups must be transformed.

But the last thing that Taylor had in mind, of course, was anything as upsetting and concrete as a political revolution. What was required was The Great Mental Revolution. This would be signalled by workers and managers abandoning their squabbles over the division of the product and agreeing to collaborate on maximizing its size. Dynamic energies straining at the leash of tradition and mistrust would be released by this shift of consciousness.

Taylor believed that his system could produce such a shift; and that it was the historical destiny of the most progressive elements of the managing class – the production engineers – to recognize and propagate the mind- and world-transforming verities of scientific management. How did things actually turn out? By answering this question we can further highlight the properties of the Taylorian approach to industrial behaviour.

3

THE THEORY
AND PRACTICE OF A
TORY RADICAL

Reference to Taylor's biography cannot explain either his view of the industrial worker, the content of his system or the course of the scientific management movement. But it illuminates them all, and does draw attention to some general features of American industry and society of his time which were more potent influences.

The linkage between experience, thought and deed in Taylor's life was particularly direct. They came to cohere in a world-view which, stripped of its subjective idiosyncrasies, important groups in early-nineteenth-century America passionately shared. This 'technicist' vision, apparently timeless and politically neutral – so much so that both Lenin and Mussolini expressed enthusiasm for scientific management – remains very much alive today.[1]

This should be borne in mind. Taylor's biography illuminates particularly clearly the central heresy of technocratic thought: that by systematically overlooking the social context in which it subsists it can claim impartiality to any social grouping or philosophy. In other words, it purports to be non-ideological. Yet it is this self-misconception which precisely renders it ideological; and, as such, particularly servile to the interests of the dominant groups of whatever society its adherents belong to. In Taylor's case, and that of his closest followers, scientific management permitted the pleasure of an apparently radical confrontation with his society while leaving that society not only intact, but stronger, in its essentials.

With rare perceptiveness, Taylor's biographer Copley characterized him as a 'Tory radical'. This indicates neatly the underlying nature of Taylor's overall project – of which, of course, he was quite unaware: the succour of American society in a period of stress and the reassertion of New England puritan virtues, particularly that of hard work. With a family pedigree as authentically Yankee as a plank from the Mayflower, and a comfortable upper-middle-class Quaker family upbringing in Philadelphia, the source of Taylor's deepest personal values seems evident enough. Of more interest for present purposes, however, are the experiences which led him to concoct his system.

The proximate cause of Taylor's attempt to devise a novel managing system was his own use of dictatorial supervisory practices at the Midvale Steel Company in the early 1880s, in an attempt to eradicate 'soldiering'. This caused great bitterness with his subordinates (although it doubled their output) and brought Taylor close to nervous collapse.

Originally, Taylor had been set to follow his father in a law career, but instead of going to Harvard he took up apprenticeships in pattern-making and machining. In 1878 he joined the Midvale Company (one of whose owners was a close family friend) as a labourer, refusing to take an office job, and was allowed to become a machinist. He soon became a 'gang-boss' or foreman, and for three years waged his 'mean' and 'contemptible' struggle – his own words – to double output. Since he had 'soldiered' before his promotion he knew all the tricks, and he cut piece-rates, sacked 'slackers' and brought in blackleg labour to speed production.

Although this had the immediately desired effects, Taylor realized that such supervisory weapons were wasteful, if not counter-productive, in the long run. The arbitrary powers of management, especially to cut piece-rates, were themselves one of the causes of output restriction. If managers knew the true capacities of men and the machines 'fair' piece-rates could be established in the first instance. But they did not. Setting a rate depended upon guesswork and bluffing, as it still largely does. Although it might seem that managers, through their autocratic actions, and workers, through output restriction, were registering a vote of no confidence in each other, and by extension, in capitalism, in fact they were both victims of ignorance. If working capacities, both human and mechanical, could be determined accurately, and production planned and administered more precisely, wages could be made fair and managerial autocracy thrown on the scrap-heap. Management 'science' would replace 'rule-of-thumb'. This would recast industrial authority relations (while naturally leaving property relations intact, indeed more secure).

At this stage, Taylor was not sure where or how to begin. Nor had he concluded that the form of the reward system would be crucial. However, a series of experiments with metal-cutting machines which he originated at this time decisively shaped his thinking. These experiments were to continue for about twenty years, but soon yielded astonishing findings – for example that some steels could be cut a hundred times faster than others. A mathematician, C. G. Barth, whom Taylor recruited to help him – and who later became a leading disciple – invented a slide-rule which enabled a semi-skilled worker to calculate quickly how to set and run his machine for any metal-cutting job.

Along with this went 'shop order cards' drawn up by a special department which told a worker precisely what work he was to do. On completing the task the worker returned the card, thus enabling the planners to compute average times and costs for any job.

But this was a slow process, and Taylor did not publish his results until 1886, in a paper read to a conference of the American Society of Mechanical Engineers (A.S.M.E.).[2] This body had been founded as recently as 1880, but rapidly grew in membership and influence, reflecting the suddenness of industrialization in the United States after the Civil War and the increasing technical complexity of manufacturing. Industrial engineers were eager to assert their identity and extend their jurisdiction in management. In fact, a paper which caught this mood better than Taylor's was entitled 'The Engineer as Economist', which advocated the involvement of engineers in work-costing and accountancy.[3]

Nor was Taylor to be first to outline a more general integrated managing system. Numerous engineers put forward their pet schemes in these years, but all stressed the importance of linking wages directly to output. However, by 1895, Taylor, now Chief Engineer at Midvale and best known professionally for his steel-cutting experiments, had shaped his ideas into a coherent whole. At the centre of his proposals, too, was a payment-by-results formula – the 'differential piece-rate' – which was intended to be sharply discriminatory against slow work. But this was to be linked with all his other organizational and scientifically managerial innovations: as he constantly stressed, the package had to be implemented in its entirety if it was to work.

Its efficacy *as a whole* still had to be demonstrated. The chance to do this came in 1898 when Taylor was appointed as a management consultant to the Bethlehem Steel Company. In his contract he insisted upon sweeping powers, and almost certainly the controllers of the company did not expect that he would exercise them. In this, they were very much mistaken. Taylor's belief in his methods – in their moral no less than their technical rightness – had become almost messianic. In one of his more extreme passages, Copley once more comes somewhere near the truth:

Let us consider what Taylor was contending for. Essentially it was this: that the government of the Bethlehem Steel Company cease to be capricious, arbitrary and despotic; that every man in the establishment, high and low, submit himself to law. A far cry down the centuries since the days of Latimer and Melville and their demand for one law for kings and scullions. A greatly different scene. Yet in Frederick Taylor, the descendant of those Puritans, the same old spirit flaming up anew; as bold as ever, and as stern, as uncompromising, and as imperious as ever.[4]

Indeed so. Taylor had fought workers on the shop floor at Midvale and won. Later he was to take on the trade unions and the American Congress. During his stormy stay at the Bethlehem Company he took on management. And he lost. This organization was an altogether different firm from Midvale. It was very much larger, and controlled not by locally rooted family bosses but by finance capitalists who viewed it less as a testing-ground for new administrative techniques than as a counter in a high-level economic game of mergers and trust-building.

It is probable that Taylor had been hired partly as a publicity gimmick and for his reputation as a *mechanical* innovator. (He continued his metallurgical experiments there and had a part in inventing a process which brought spectacular economies.) When he was sacked after a couple of years it was possibly part of a secret deal for the sale of the firm. At one point in his stay, in protest against top management double-dealing, Taylor in effect went on strike for three months. In sum, at Bethlehem Taylor was treated in essentially the same way as any other employee of such a company, and he responded in many ways similarly.

None the less, it was here that his methods of work-study and rationalization were first operated with impressive results. It had been hard to determine a 'fair day's work' at Midvale owing to the preponderance and variety of machining tasks. At Bethlehem a much larger section of the work-force were engaged in straightforward heavy labouring, and Taylor successfully 'systematized Schmidt and his fellows', first in pig-iron handling, and then in shovelling – 'a great science compared with pig-iron handling'. Schmidt, a remarkably avaricious and thick-skulled little Dutchman, has become legendary in industrial history. Taylor trained him to load about fifty tons of pig-iron a day, four times his base output.* For this he was awarded a bonus of just over half his previous pay, a rise which impressed Schmidt and the local workers who besieged Taylor with job applications no less than it should impress theorists of surplus value.

But only one-eighth of Schmidt's fellows possessed such a capacity. True to his promises, Taylor redeployed the remainder of the gang to other tasks in the yard. None the less, the local press carried out some basic arithmetic and forecast that eventually three quarters of the labour force would be made redundant. This poor publicity, and the risk of labour trouble, not to mention the con-

* F. W. Taylor, *Testimony before the Special House Committee*, Harper & Row, New York, 1947, pp. 47ff. Rumour later spread that Schmidt died prematurely as a result of his exertions. Taylor went to great pains to trace him and obtain a medical report; see Copley, op. cit., vol. II, pp. 55ff.

sequences of widespread unemployment for the company's heavy investments in housing and stores around the plant, did not help the Bethlehem bosses in their financial jiggery-pokery and they ordered Taylor to slow the pace of change.

Taylor, waving his almost *carte-blanche* mandate to implement his system, not only refused but paraded his independence. (A favourite provocation was to arrive at important meetings an hour late in golfing clothes, swinging a club and chattering breezily about his handicap.) The shovelling experiments proceeded; but things went from bad to positively appalling when the company president, Lindemann, blocked a previously agreed rise for Taylor's assistants and upheld a head bookkeeper who refused to implement a new accounting system. Eventually Taylor had his way over these matters, but in early 1901 he was dismissed (in a one-sentence letter). Although he could have contested this legally, Taylor, close to another nervous collapse, announced his retirement from 'money-making' and withdrew to his mansion at Bloxley.

The rest of his life was spent propagating and defending his management system. But it is ironic that he had never actually installed scientific management at Bethlehem; and his own response to the emerging logic of advanced capitalist industrialism there had been remarkably analogous to that of the labour leaders whom he increasingly castigated for attacking it. True enough, his denunciations of financial manipulators and *rentiers* also grew in ferocity. But even in them there was a major ambiguity, for Taylor himself now lived off the proceeds of a share portfolio astutely purchased during the economic recession of the early 1890s.

In fact, the experience from Bethlehem that seems to have stuck hardest in Taylor's mind was his successful 'systematization' of Schmidt, and the apparent potency of modest bonuses as motivators. This confirmed his earlier ideas, which now became an obstinate conviction that the 'science' of any work could be propounded and workmen motivated to follow it. Inside all workers a Schmidt was struggling to get out. The belief that more skilled work might defy universal systematization was a heresy to be stamped out of un-scientific sentimentalists. The refusal of skilled workers to trade their principal asset, their skill itself, to the scientific manager in return for a specialized task and an uncertain monetary gain was a sign of a determined opposition to Progress created by unscientific managers and sustained – a growing theme in Taylor's middle age – by the 'irrelevant' trade unions.

From 1903, when his *Shop Management* was published, Taylor became an increasingly public figure.[5] He was elected president of the A.S.M.E., and his 'On the Art of Cutting Metals' (why not 'Science', one wonders) crowned his engineering fame in 1905.[6] But he now led a growing number of disciples. His old protégé Barth began introducing the full version of the 'Taylor System' – as others called it, to Taylor's disgust: it was a *science*, he insisted, and therefore distinct from any individual – into the Link Belt and Tabor Manufacturing companies from 1903, and these firms became the show-places of 'genuine' scientific management.

The qualifier 'genuine' is important. As public fascination with efficiency grew, so did the corps of 'fakirs and charlatans' who claimed to be followers of 'Speedy' Taylor.[7] Often they were simply the plausible adventurers which management consultancy typically attracts. But some had read their *Shop Management* and concluded that work-study alone could speed up production and there was no need for management to bother with bonus payments. This seemed very good sense to management. Certain other consultants offered more elaborate systems, which Taylor endorsed with varying approval. The two most important of these were the flamboyant self-publicist F. B. Gilbreth, who went on to add motion-study to Taylorian time-study (alpha-minus); and Harrington Emerson, founder of an *Efficiency Society* (beta-plus or delta-minus: Taylor was never quite sure).

It is hard to disentangle orthodox scientific management from these other strands. The confusion was equally great at the time. Gradually the 'radical' element in Taylorism – the need to reform managerial authority – became less evident, especially to trade unionists, and particularly after a legal battle in 1910 (the Eastern Rate Case) which transformed Taylor into a national figure and linked all efficiency systems together as 'scientific management'.

The Eastern Rate Case was fought to prove that certain railways could absorb a hefty wage claim through greater operating efficiency.[8] It aroused enormous publicity thanks largely to the flair of L. D. Brandeis, a demagogue, who led the case against the railway companies (and thus, indirectly, against the railway unions). Following it, a deluge of popular expositions of 'scientific management' flooded the press, in which Taylor's own *Principles of Scientific Management* (1911), with its bold assertions that management was a science based on natural laws, was virtually drowned.[9] In the atmosphere of this 'efficiency fever' unionism was inevitably portrayed as a menacing storm-cloud, and two strikes in 1911 roused public opinion – or at least the American right-wing press – to paroxysms of hatred for organized labour. The first of these was by bricklayers against Gilbreth's methods. The second, and more important for present purposes, was by government munitions workers against a genuinely Taylorian rationalization scheme.

This Watertown Arsenal strike was crucial for Taylorism in several respects.[10] Firstly, it forced Taylor to define his attitude towards unions more clearly. Secondly, it forced him into dialogue with them, which his direct 'heirs' continued along a path which would have horrified him. Thirdly, he was constrained to abandon the claim that 'genuine' scientific management had never produced a strike – a statement that, though unfounded, had often appeared in his propaganda. Fourthly, it made Taylorism a political issue in the American Congress and led to two public investigations of it.

General Crozier, the Controller of Ordnance, had shown interest in Taylor's system as early as 1906, and Taylor was eager for the prestige of a government contract for his followers. But Crozier dithered for several years. Surely time-studies would lead to strikes? And why was it necessary to pay bonuses if the new methods reduced job-times? (Significantly Taylor replied to this: 'I can assure you that you will meet with absolutely no success if you leave out [the system's] most essential feature'.)[11] But eventually Crozier gave way. The strike (by moulders) was an almost immediate consequence.

Taylor advised the General to fight the moulders directly. However, a leading unionist, J. P. Frey, who had already attacked Taylorism in another context, and who had friends in Congress, succeeded in promoting a call in the House of Representatives for an official investigation of the system. American Labour had in fact been counter-attacking the efficiency craze for some time. Even Samuel Gompers, the father of 'business unionism', had strongly criticized the 'intellectuals' (work-study men) who were trying to 'mechanize' the worker. And what precisely did Taylor mean in asserting that the 'natural laws' of management could operate only in an 'improved environment'?

A Special House Committee was called in early 1912, and Taylor was naturally its leading witness. He turned in an impressive performance, which produced almost 300 pages of evidence. (It is also extremely clever propaganda.)

In tone it is vigorous and self-assured, and clotted with autobiographical references. Nearly all his substantive remarks about his system and its rationale were, however, largely reiterations, sometimes almost word for word, of what he had written already. After repudiating the term 'Taylor System', he launched into a set-piece tirade against 'soldiering'. It is the result of the denigration of labour by the 'literary classes', of a mistaken belief in the 'wages fund' theory of labour (despite massive historical evidence for its falsity), but above all of the 'faulty system of management in general use'.[12] Senior managers were horrified at the notion of high pay for high productivity and, often collusively, resorted to systematic rate-cutting. Only scientific management could break the resulting vicious circle of bad faith.

Under the new order management must assume heavy burdens. Systematic study of the production process would reveal its 'laws': was this not 'science'? Workmen should be selected, trained and paid strictly in line with their ability to perform the new task-structures: was this not 'science' too? Thus, workers and the principles of scientific management would be 'brought together'. But Taylor noted: 'It is unfortunate, however, that this word "bringing" has a rather disagreeable sound, a rather forceful sound; and, in a way, when it is first heard it puts one out of touch with what we have come to look on as the modern tendency.'[13] But most trouble could be expected in 'bringing' management to accept their own subordination to 'science'.

None the less, it should be clear enough to all that these changes would introduce a precisely equal division of effort between work-man and manager. Workers should not be asked to use initiative; and this demanded great effort from the scientific manager in designing watertight work-measurement and control systems. Workers must, however, be allowed to retain full rights to exert themselves physically in the new systems, thereby earning high wages. One could hardly imagine a more equitable, more harmon-ious, more reciprocally beneficial relationship, except perhaps in the case of the team spirit of a baseball side and their coach.

Illustrations of scientific management in action were proudly retailed. Gilbreth's successful reduction of the basic operations in bricklaying from eighteen to five was given almost as much applause as his own work at Midvale and Bethlehem. But he seems to have misjudged the feeling of the committee, whose members insisted that rationalization was concerned merely with speeding work up, with discovering how fast it *could* rather than *should* be done. Taylor would have none of this. Firstly, if work-study resulted in excessive demands then it simply was not scientific. Secondly, workers thus exploited had a very powerful weapon to redress the balance – they could always quit. Such statements, and the insistence on the real possibility of the 'mental revolution' when the very fact of his being called up to testify marked its failure to materialize in practice, show Taylor's sometimes weak grasp of industrial realities.

Yet when the committee reported in the spring of 1912, he and his followers claimed they were, broadly, happy with its findings. These were that scientific management offered valuable organiza-tional suggestions but could give the production manager a dangerous measure of uncontrolled power. Controversy had abated a little. The studies at Watertown were resumed. Thanks to the immense publicity of the two previous years numerous attempts were being set in hand to introduce the full system, even in non-industrial fields such as banking.

But the underlying hostility of the unions remained. The last few years of Taylor's life were devoted to preventing the *rapproche-ment* with Labour that many of his followers now believed was essential to ensure the acceptance of the system. One indicator of this growing 'revisionism' was a rejoinder written by a 'disciple', C. B. Thompson, in reply to an academic appraisal of Taylorism.[14] Agreeing with the author's assertion that scientific management might expose the worker to excessive pressure, Thompson proposed that unions should collaborate in the determination of a 'fair day's work' and a 'fair day's pay'. Almost gratuitously, he remarked that Taylor's 'autocratic' background made him involuntarily hostile to collective bargaining.[15]

Taylor himself had now been pressed into dealings with unionists, but they were devious and unhappy. In 1914 he consented to appear at a meeting of the Wisconsin Federation of Labor. It was an embarrassing event. The representative of the state's federal employees read out the more explicitly anti-syndicalist passages of *Shop Management* and dilated on the Taylorite obsession with speed and rationalization (i.e. de-skilling). Then Taylor persuaded A. J. Portenar, a leading veteran of the International Typographical Union who had uttered mildly approving noises about the system, to visit fully Taylorized plants. Taylor was probably hoping to groom him for a propagandist role. Suspecting as much, Portenar made haste after his tour to announce that what he had seen, and what he had read in *Shop Management*, 'depressed him terribly': the system degraded everyone concerned in its installation and working.

The Watertown workers were once more proving restive, though to greater purpose. In 1914 they commissioned Miner Chipman, a former 'efficiency engineering' associate of Harrington Emerson, to prepare a report on the operation of the system at the arsenal. Chipman undertook an attitude survey as part of his appraisal. Over 90 per cent of the respondents expressed broad hostility to the system, and more than half of these were non-unionists. The report, which painted a picture of a work-force resentful of the failure to consult it and determined to sabotage the new methods, was sent to the Secretary for War. A bill forbidding time-study in federal establishments was introduced in the House of Representatives, and passed by the Senate almost simultaneously with Taylor's death in 1915.

An even more decisive political reverse in Taylor's last few months of life, however, was the government's decision to establish a Commission on Industrial Relations. Its terms of reference included 'efficiency systems and labour'. Worse still, it was to be chaired by R. F. Hoxie, Professor of Political Economy at Chicago and an exponent of a pluralist conception of industrial relations. Nor was this all. R. G. Valentine, after much discussion in the 'movement', was chosen to represent the scientific management viewpoint.

Valentine regarded democracy as an ultimate good, and trade unionism as a natural expression of it. At a conference of the Society for the Promotion of the Science of Management in December 1914, when the commission had already commenced work, he insisted that system-building in industry must be a 'group action'. Even the installation of closed shops might be necessary to further this. None of the management delegates supported such a novelty. But Hoxie, himself present, spoke up strongly in Valentine's favour.

Hoxie and his fellow commissioners surveyed thirty-five plants which claimed to employ Taylorian methods between January and April 1915. Their report stressed the lack of uniformity in the application of 'the' system. The widest variations in practice were over methods of time-study and task-design – matters at the core of Taylorism. Though psychological and sociological awareness would appear to be an essential qualification for time-study work, they noted, few time-study 'experts' possessed them and were habitually regarded as low-grade technicians.

As to the wider socio-economic consequences of the system the report affirmed that craft knowledge was indeed confiscated from the worker, that the union's regulatory effect on managerial power was dangerously reduced, and that, as a result, new problems were created which in itself, despite its technical value, the Taylor system was powerless to solve. Thus, although only four of the commission's nine members would put their names to the full report, there was a general feeling that 'classical' Taylorism had received official condemnation.

4

THE ROOTS
OF
TAYLORISM

Taylor's death and the Hoxie Report in 1915 were a watershed in the history of scientific management. In the next fifteen years the 'revisionist' Taylorites were able to come to a close understanding with the 'revisionist' leaders of American Labour. We shall consider briefly how this became possible in a moment, since its explanation reinforces that for the original appearance, the basic content and the course of Taylorism before the main actor left the scene.

It is an inversion of sound historical method to interpret Taylorism as the product of a solitary neurotic struggling against the current of the times.[1] The temptation to do so is certainly strong, thanks to the opposition Taylor attracted from both labour and management, and not least to the curiosity of his personal psychological make-up. Though Taylor's own crippled and obsessional psyche is not irrelevant to a full explanation of the *content* of his system, we shall disregard it here. The fact is that Taylor was essentially a man very much of and for his times. No one would have paid him the slightest attention if his message had not seemed a plausible solution to pressing problems confronting economically powerful groups in turn-of-the-century America, and to some extent elsewhere.[2]

Taylorian 'science', in other words, can be viewed as an unconscious politics: a set of policies to deal with specific topical problems, which were taken up because they appealed to the interests of influential groups but could none the less be presented to the less influential as also being in the interests of the vast majority. We must relate them, then, to a contemporary socio-economic situation; and, to a lesser extent, to a prevailing moral climate.

Since my main purpose has been to characterize Taylorism as a mode of understanding industrial behaviour, this necessary excursion into the landscape in which it is situated must be rather summary.

The main fact, so elementary that one can easily ignore it, is that Taylor's life coincided with the emergence of the United States as an industrialized economy and a major industrial power – in competition with industrialized European powers first for its own domestic market and then for international markets. Three facts which underline this transformation are, firstly, the fall from 53.5 per cent to 31.6 per cent between 1870 and 1910 of the proportion of the employed population in agriculture and other primary production;[3] secondly, the doubling of American exports in the ten years following the protectionist McKinley tariffs of 1890;[4] and thirdly, the acquisition of colonial territories and seizure of the Panama Canal Zone after a deliberately engineered war against Spain at the turn of the century. In less than fifty years an isolationist agrarian society transformed itself into an internationally aggressive, economically imperialist, industrial nation.

This pattern, similar, though on a more spectacular scale, to the experience of European powers such as Germany and Italy, obscures one difference which for a time delayed the appearance of certain social consequences of the change. This was the gradual completion of the settlement of the West. The disappearance of the Frontier was of more psychological than material importance, but none the less decisive. On the whole, probably few 'young men' (or new immigrants) had ever had an inclination to 'go west' if urban work was available in the East. But the vision of liberation from the ardours of life in the growing industrial cities had been an important safety-valve. After 1890, however, it became obvious to everyone that very little West remained to go to. This change is not altogether unconnected with the growth of American trade union membership by almost 500 per cent between 1897 and 1904.[5]

Immigration had also helped to postpone this development, in two ways. Firstly, the flow of new arrivals desperate for work sustained a buyer's market for labour (particularly unskilled labour). Secondly, since each new ethnic wave tended to enter the labour force at the lowest levels, native Americans and earlier arrivals were given better jobs. This collective upward mobility helped to confirm social philosophies of personal opportunity, particularly for those who were somehow more 'American' in their attitudes, as those who had been citizens for a considerable time felt themselves to be and to some extent were.

But the formation of large urban concentrations and the settlement of the West counteracted these divisive tendencies. So too did the very expansion of American industry itself, again in two ways. Firstly, of course, it abated the buyer's power in the labour market. Secondly, and rather more importantly, it stimulated the growth of individual organizations and industrial concentration – classic vertical and horizontal integration. The backyard workshop became a factory, and the family firm a public company. The trusts emerged. Work-forces were now masses of labour power to be shaped or bullied into becoming human machines that somehow worked. The harsh supervision adopted to solve this problem, the remoteness of the big bosses and their increasing preoccupation with financial manoeuvre and the mechanization and rationalization of work dramatized the separateness of capital and labour.

These processes, necessarily simplified here, stimulated the growth of unionism. But the obedience of the labour force was not management's only control problem. Indeed, it could be viewed as an aspect of the more technical problem of co-ordinating the work-process itself.

The growth of mechanization and mechanical complexity, coupled with the growth in the size of the typical factory, went hand in hand with the rise of the mechanical engineering profession. As the managing proprietor disappeared into the boardroom, the mechanical engineer naturally stepped into his place in the workshop. Accountants, the only other significant professional group in industry, could not adopt these directly co-ordinative functions for the obvious reason that they lacked technological knowledge. (Significantly, however, they too were soon to be faced with comparable problems of co-ordination as white-collar work-forces grew. When management began to assert its claims to professional identity it drew predominantly from these two occupations.)

Here, then, are the key features of the industrial situation which a plausible management science would necessarily reflect: the growth and concentration of industrial production; the intensification of problems of control; the growing power of labour; the withdrawal of the owner–manager; and the professional self-consciousness of engineers. As a solution to these problems it would have to supply a technical answer to each one. Moreover, it would have to convince the main parties involved that there was something in it for them; and this appeal would be all the more successful if it could draw on popular intellectual wisdom.

Nineteenth-century thought as a whole is generally optimistic. Again and again, one encounters the notion that 'Progress', conceived as both material and moral advance, is, somehow, a fortunate natural force guiding the destiny of mankind. 'Progress' had been given a particularly powerful boost by the industrial revolution and the rise of science, but this had merely accelerated a process that could be traced back to pre-history. However, there were more pessimistic undercurrents.

Economics, the 'gloomy science', had recurrently injected stern reminders that if material advance could in fact be sustained in the long run then it must be at the expense of hard toil for the many. The Malthusian doctrine of apocalyptic breakdown always lurked in the background. Individuals, of course, might win personal security or even make their fortunes, and it was morally desirable for everyone to set himself such goals – the puritan notion of work as self-dedication lived on in a variety of guises – but it was unrealistic to expect a general, rapid advance. Bodies such as trade unions which sought to secure this were spitting against the wind, or selfishly demanding a greater share from a more or less fixed 'wages fund' at the expense of other sectors.

Darwinian evolutionism, transposed to the social level, powerfully reinforced these sinister provisos. The 'struggle for existence' and the 'survival of the fittest' powerfully underwrote the institutions of the high-capitalist economy, particularly the labour market. Nothing must be allowed to meddle with this social manifestation of natural selection. That would be tampering with nature. Could trade unions be found in nature? Certainly not. Therefore they were a barrier to Progress. (Later, it was pointed out that nothing in the sacred texts of evolutionism denied that groups might well become the vehicles for survival no less than individuals.) A further logical extension of social Darwinism was that the industrially powerful had manifested their fitness for survival by their success, and they became champion adherents of the doctrine.[6]

This kind of attitude may not seem quite consistent with a reverence for the other venerated manifestations of Progress – political democracy and freedom. None the less, these could be accommodated fairly plausibly. 'Freedom' really meant not living in an absolutist monarchy, and the right not to be restricted by government legislation except for the protection of life and, *a fortiori*, private property. And democracy obviously meant parliamentary democracy, the right to cast a vote for someone who would see to it that the government would not restrict rugged individualism – someone who as like as not had more than adequately proved his own capacity for survival.

In one form or another, and in combinations suited to time and circumstances, these tenets of dominant class ideology – progress, individualism, the sanctity of markets and property, 'democracy' – were accepted in some measure by the population as a whole.

It is Taylor's distinction to have adumbrated a body of thought which seemed to meet the material needs of the American capitalist economy as it entered a new period: the technical needs for co-ordination and high productivity; the moral need for an ideology which would consecrate the new forms of authority and property relationships. As the day-to-day difficulties of managers in running the large plants and the growing restiveness of labour demonstrated, these needs were pressing. And Taylor's proposals, based on popular wisdom, constituted an almost perfect solution.

If he had been a conscious fabricater of social myths Taylor could hardly have done better than to christen his programme 'science'. This instantly appealed to the new middle-men of industry, the engineers; and more widely, to the less influential, the ordinary workmen, who were sometimes dubious about the beneficence of markets and strongly resented the autocracy of current managerial practice. Science was neutral. Science was progressive. Science might even overcome the iron laws of economics. Science would solve problems of co-ordination. Science would create high wages. Science would also generate high profits.

Taylor – unlike some of his successors – by no means deprecated the latter: he was fond of lecturing workers that a factory existed 'first, last and foremost' to make profits for its owners. Yet his greatest mistake was not to realize better, or sooner, that his gospel of scientific rationality would appeal least to the big capitalist proprietors. The logical extension of his doctrine is the centralized planning and control of the economy, i.e. state capitalism or bureaucratic socialism. The last thing the emergent finance capitalists of his day wanted – or could conceive – was such an order. Even the rationalization of the plant, as he discovered at Bethlehem, could interfere with their financial game.

This assertion may seem to overlook Taylor's difficulties with labour. Of course, his faith in the Mental Revolution was misplaced. But, better than he realized, the potential hospitality of American Labour to his philosophy was immense. He failed to recognize that the labour leaders would be ready to accept scientific management if only they were offered a position of honour in imposing it. The experience of his 'revisionist' heirs, aided somewhat by new industrial conditions, shows plainly the scope for collaboration.[7]

This collaboration was largely engineered by R. G. Valentine. His position as the leading Taylorian 'revisionist' was consolidated in late 1915 when he once more advocated full union participation in rationalization schemes to the Taylor Society. His audience still received his call cautiously. But the power of Labour became evident the next year. A bill was presented in Congress to forbid time-studies in Federal plants. Certain prominent Taylorians joined the National Association of Manufacturers in condemning this step. Nevertheless, the committee appointed by Congress to examine the bill was favourable towards it despite the opinion of most 'expert' witnesses. In the lobbies most Senators and Representatives tactfully abstained and it was passed.

The American Federation of Labor had been encouraged by the Hoxie Report. The arrival of the Wilson administration in 1917 produced a government sympathetic to collective bargaining. This became evident on American entry to the war: an Ordnance Department General Order decreed that war supplies should be purchased only from manufacturers who maintained working conditions which included opportunities for joint consultation. These and other acts heightened the public status of unionists, and prominent leaders were drawn into the war machine as propagandists.

The Federal authorities also made wide use of Taylorians as management consultants during the war. This taste of power, and the explosive growth of union membership to 5,000,000 by 1920, encouraged some Taylorians to anticipate an imminent new social order in which they would play leading parts. A short-lived propaganda movement, the 'New Machine', foretold the approaching collapse of American capitalism unless it could substitute 'service' (a favourite term of Ford's) for profit. Only the scientific manager could handle the problems of this transformation.[8]

For its part the A.F.L. was even beginning to demand government-sponsored research into methods of increasing productivity by limited rationalization. The developing accord was marked by the joint editorship of a Taylorian (Cooke) and Gompers of an issue of *The Annals* on 'Labour, Management and Productivity' which reiterated these themes.[9] Gompers began appearing as star speaker at management meetings where he stressed the humanizing effects of union objections to the contributions of scientific management, which were otherwise necessary and useful. The climax to this phase of *entente* was the establishment of President Hoover's 'Waste in Industry' inquiry, sponsored by the management societies and backed by the unions.[10] Five of its six reports were prepared by Taylorites. They showed that American industry was in many respects spectacularly inefficient, but that whereas only a quarter of the waste stemmed from labour at least half was the responsibility of management.

However, while understanding between unions and Taylorites continued to flourish during the 1920s, labour was on the defensive. The *patronat* made great use of a rising anti-Communist fervour amongst the American public by reviving the Open Shop campaign. Paradoxically, the Wilson government's sponsorship of joint consultation in the plant had paved the way for 'company unionism'.[11] Company welfare schemes, aping the model developed by Ford, removed certain grievances upon which the unions could play. Such developments, aided first by the severe economic recession of 1920–21 and then by the rising prosperity of the following years, reduced total union membership by a third.

Despite these setbacks the official union leadership seems by now to have become genuinely converted to the 'positive' elements in Taylorism. William Green, Gompers's successor at the A.F.L., enthusiastically preached co-operation with management – to apply the principles of scientific management, reduce waste and provide bigger pickings for all. American industry was gripped with 'co-operation fever'.[12] On retiring from the presidency of the Taylor Society in 1928 Cooke reaffirmed his own approval of collective bargaining and even suggested that Taylorites should urge workers to unionize. And the writer of a Taylor Society publication of this time called on the unions to employ Taylorites in their research departments. In 1930, the *American Federationist* issued 'Labour's Principles of Scientific Management'. Nadworny comments that these differ little from Taylor's own except for the demand that unions should be recognized and consulted in rationalization schemes.[13]

The slump put an end to all this. But this account shows that the unions could be reconciled to a reformed Taylorism, at least at national level. Management as a whole never was. Why? The Taylorians invested an almost equal effort in gaining its acceptance amongst the *patronat*, and largely failed. The answer has already been given; namely, full acceptance of the system would have implied a severe dilution of the rights of proprietorship.

I have digressed further into the origins and consequences of Taylorism than will be possible with any of the other approaches I shall consider. This has been occasioned by its particular importance as a practical movement which left lasting traces in the consciousness of working people and managers. As a workable managing system it was refuted by the opposition it generated. I have underlined its logical and other inconsistencies. Before leaving it, a recapitulation of its main assumptions about workers' behaviour would be useful, for these formed the reference-point for the scientific attack on Taylor which was carried out by various critics for long after he died.

The most striking element in Taylor's thought is his tendency to equate men with machines. This is brought out powerfully in his method of work-study and his notion of the 'quickest and best way'. In these specifications there is no recognition of individual psychological differences, nor any reliable notion of fatigue. The properly trained 'first-class man' is supposed to function as predictably as a piece of clockwork. He must be rested at appropriate moments. But to say this amounts to little more than conceding that a machine needs regular servicing.

Of course, the speed at which a machine will run depends upon the strength of the current or the octane of the fuel poured into it. Similarly, the worker can be encouraged to work harder by appeals to his materialism. The higher the money incentive, the greater his response.

Every other influence upon his behaviour, social or psychological – the workgroup, a trade union, managerial 'autocracy' or whatever – is an unnatural interference that must be removed to allow optimal functioning. It is a bizarre conception. Taylor's worker is a monstrosity: a greedy machine indifferent to its own pain and loneliness once given the opportunity to maim and isolate itself. It was against the psychological emptiness of this mechanistic conception that fire was first to be directed. Later its sociological barrenness, and the crudity of its economism, came under attack. Let us now turn to the work of the British human factor psychologists, in their attempt to rectify the first set of misconceptions.

PART II

HUMAN FACTOR
INDUSTRIAL PSYCHOLOGY

INTRODUCTION

Though the American public had instinctively recoiled from the Taylorian image of the worker, scientific rebuttal of its psychological assumptions was led by investigators in Britain. The importance of British human factor industrial psychology has been underestimated. By substituting an image of the worker as a complex organism for Taylor's greedy robot it opened the way to study of the less tangible influences on worker behaviour. Human relations theory depended considerably on its achievements. Later still, theories which explained work behaviour as a response to technology took up numerous problems it had first raised.

Despite its historical importance (and considerable intrinsic interest as a scientific orientation) human factor psychology is neglected. To some extent this neglect is understandable. Its literature is inaccessible; and it must be admitted that much of it makes somewhat heavy reading. The typical human factor research monograph has something of the air of an unwanted museum piece, which makes it rather depressing simply to look at the faded cover of a vintage report from, say, the Industrial Fatigue Research Board.

Fatigue itself is quickly induced by the sight of the list of obscure dignitaries inside the cover, the closely argued text, the meticulously drawn graphs and the ample reference to instruments such as Kata thermometers, Edney sling hygrometers and vane anemometers. These first impressions soon change; and at the very least the faith of the writer in the virtues of empiricism arouses a certain admiration.

'Such non-significant results are to be expected in all biological experimentation, but particularly in the psychological sphere, where the overlapping of mental and physical qualities present such baffling problems,' writes one of these dogged investigators in a discussion of his research methodology.[1] 'The negative results however,' he adds, 'are of real value in future researches and save others from traversing the same ground again.' Moreover, such painstaking thoroughness 'offers practically the only satisfactory way of dealing with some of our greatest social evils'.[2] These remarks summarize the whole philosophy of the British human factor psychologists.

Industrial psychology (of a kind) had emerged before the First World War in America and continental Europe, particularly Germany, and much work in this field continued in these countries during the 1920s. Why should British work at this period be singled out for special notice? In the first place, it was largely isolated from American developments, and this worked to its benefit. It was highly organized and the bulk of its effort was concentrated on the full exploration of a limited range of problems: by establishing the parameters of physical influences on work-behaviour it permitted others (notably Mayo) to proceed to other types of problem and theory. Committed initially to one type of explanation, the issues raised by its own findings forced it to widen its horizons. And lastly, it supplied irrefutable evidence of the scientific crudity of Taylorism.

It would be incorrect to imply that the thinking of early British industrial psychologists was monolithically solid or was determined uniquely by C. S. Myers. None the less, it retained remarkable coherence for a decade and Myers was its most vocal exponent. As founder and Director of the National Institute of Industrial Psychology and a member of the Committee on Industrial Psychology of the Industrial Fatigue Research Board, his official influence spanned the two agencies through which by far the greater part of research and consultancy in industrial psychology, and to a lesser extent teaching, were channelled. As publicist, fund-raiser and fixer he played the key role. For these reasons, as well as the convenience of not having constantly to write 'early British industrial psychologists', I shall refer to this group as the 'Myersians' – provided it is understood that this term does not imply a 'school' in the sense of a master of a theory and his disciples.

The National Institute of Industrial Psychology (N.I.I.P.) was founded in February 1921.[3] Myers, as a Cambridge teacher of psychology with an interest in applied fields, had been invited to give a short course of lectures at the Royal Institution in 1918, in which he advocated the establishment of centres of applied psychology in all major British industrial towns. This proposal caught the eye of the business community. It was well supported by several leading academic psychologists (this is one mark of Myers's wide contacts and personal charm – academics were generally suspicious of applications) and by certain big names in physiology. Psychology and biology were still intimately related; we shall return to some of the implications of this link below. Philanthropic Quaker firms were at the head of those promising support, but basic financial assistance was at first secured from the Carnegie and Rockefeller trusts. Myers left his university post to run the organization.

The institute grew rapidly in the 1920s. By the 1930s it had a technical and research staff approaching fifty, had attracted up-and-coming psychologists such as Cyril Burt and Eric Farmer, and counted such scientific celebrities as Sherrington and Rutherford amongst its supporters. It had provided consultancy services for 250 firms. It was also rapidly becoming insolvent. In its fifth general report its financially critical state was well advertised and potential benefactors were reminded, hardly with tact, that bequests would not be detrimental to their current incomes.[4]

The basic trouble was that the N.I.I.P. was intended to support itself on its consultancy work. Thus its problems were dictated by the needs of clients. This resulted in a wide spread of interests and an under-investment in basic research. It was forced to live largely from hand to mouth, and many of its findings on behalf of clients could not be published. Its most consistent set of studies in fact deal with vocational selection and guidance. None the less, a few other types of study were carried out, some in association with the Fatigue Board. And Myers was to claim that the confidence of workers was soon secured because 'the National Institute has endeavoured to base its ideals on sound psychology rather than on the superficial analogy with a piece of engineering mechanism'.[5] Persuading the boss was sometimes more difficult: 'He may already have suffered at the hands of some efficiency expert who, after spending a few hours in the works, has written a verbose, relatively useless report and has charged a correspondingly high fee.'[6]

Pure research was conducted elsewhere. The Industrial Fatigue Research Board (I.F.R.B.) was founded in 1918 as a direct successor to the Health of Munitions Workers Committee of 1915–17. It subsequently changed its title to Industrial Health Research Board in 1929; this change was related to changes in approach, but the choice of both the words 'Fatigue' and 'Health' reflect the kind of influence with which its workers had to contend both within its directorate and among themselves. From 1921 it fell directly under the Medical Research Council, and an examination of its board membership in the 1920s shows a heavy bias towards medicine and academic physiology, although a prominent trade unionist and an industrialist were judiciously co-opted, and Myers came to be given full board membership. But before it was disbanded in 1947 it was to produce ninety reports, and to move far from its early 'physiologism'. Moreover, its existence was relatively secure and it could explore problems in depth. Its main crisis occurred early, in 1921, when the government of the day attempted to axe it as an economy measure. This move was blocked by the protest of a group of Labour M.P.s.

The relations of the I.F.R.B. and N.I.I.P. were 'intimate and harmonious' according to Myers. There was some interchange of personnel, the I.F.R.B. funded some of the N.I.I.P.'s pure research, and their main thrusts of inquiry were largely complementary.

THE STUDY OF
FATIGUE

There are excellent reasons why men who called themselves psychologists should have devoted themselves to a study of fatigue in the first years of the I.F.R.B. The Myersians had been trained in a psychology which was regarded as part of physiology and biology, and as such at least a 'semi-hard' science. Fatigue appeared to be a relatively easily conceived and measured physiological condition. (This notion was soon abandoned.) Both scientific management and the First World War had made it a live issue, and there seemed some prospect of a practical reward. If techniques for reducing fatigue could be discovered support for other problems might be easier to come by: in this sense, one can almost view the heavy investment of the Myersians in fatigue research as a kind of scientific 'loss-leader'.

Thinking on fatigue in the early twentieth century today seems quaint, and some of the inferences drawn from it were macabre. When an individual engages in heavy exercise or labour his fatigue is manifested behaviourally in a rapid pulse-rate and heavy breathing. It was established that these signs of exhaustion are paralleled by chemical changes in the bloodstream. The concentration of lactic acid increases and that of certain bicarbonate compounds is lowered. Hence a 'hard' scientific test of whether an individual is really fatigued apparently would be to measure the toxins in his blood (since stimuli other than physical effort could produce heavy breathing or a rapid pulse). Certain enthusiasts went so far as to suggest that reagents might be discovered which, injected into the exhausted labourer, would neutralize the toxins which 'caused' fatigue. He would then presumably be available for work during the hours otherwise wasted in recovery through sleep!

Such an elixir was never discovered. The toxin theory of fatigue rests on a simple, mechanistic conception of fatigue, and an easily applicable test for it. It was one of the first achievements of the Myersians to show the inadequacy of the concept and the elusiveness of a simple test for it, certainly outside the laboratory. By 1924 Myers was to write:

If we continue to use the term fatigue in industrial conditions, let us remember how complex is its character, how ignorant we are of its full nature, and how impossible it is in the intact organism to distinguish lower from higher fatigue and fatigue from inhibition, to separate the fatigue of explosive 'acts' from the fatigue of maintaining 'attitudes', or to eliminate the effects of varying interest, of excitement, suggestion and the like.[1]

Cathcart reiterated these doubts even more forcefully a few years later. Even in the laboratory, 'It is questionable . . . if it will be ever possible to measure fatigue.'[2] And when we are considering fatigue in the actual work-place, 'Probably the best definition, which does not commit us to any explanation of its nature, is that it is a reduced capacity for doing work.'[3]

The first indications of the complexity of fatigue and the falsity of the toxin theory appeared in the emergency studies conducted by the Health of Munitions Workers Committee in the First World War. (The British Association also promoted studies and the dispersal of information.) The growing manpower shortage and increased demand for armaments had resulted in very long working hours. These led to rapidly diminishing returns, for labour productivity declined and absenteeism and accidents rose sharply. Nineteenth-century philanthropic employers had already shown that excessive hours were self-defeating. Robert Owen, for example, had reduced hours in his New Lanark factories to ten and a half hours a day, when fifteen or sixteen were common elsewhere, with no loss of output. At the opposite end of the century the Salford Quaker magnate Mather had reduced weekly hours from fifty-three to forty-eight in his engineering factories. This had actually resulted in increased production. Inquiries from the American Bureau of Labor in 1904 showed that the benefits had been retained for eleven years.

Although some limitation of hours in British government factories had been introduced before 1914, the prevailing belief was that extra hours obviously increased production. Yet this was untrue even where the workers' speed was determined by machinery: beyond a certain point accidents, absenteeism, scrap and sabotage resulted in a net reduction over the day or week. This was rapidly established by the war-time studies. Any reduction in hours cut the incidence of accidents, absenteeism and scrap. A drop in daily hours from twelve to ten increased net daily output. A further reduction from ten to eight hours (on a six-day week) continued this trend except for certain tasks which were machine-paced. Days below eight hours brought a small rise in hourly output but lower net daily output.

Reducing the length of the working day can be viewed as lengthening of the major rest-pause between working spells. Taylor had of course shown that rest-pauses could help increase total output, and in so far as he held any kind of systematic view of fatigue it was a physiological one. It might at first appear that physiology could explain the H.M.W.C. results. However, this was precluded by two further crucial findings. Firstly, the productivity gain did not appear immediately after the reduction in hours, but in a period up to several months later. Secondly, a reduction of twelve hours to ten (17 per cent) brought a widely disproportionate decrease in accidents (50 per cent). It is, of course, impossible to screen a large work-force daily for the presence of toxins, but these results show that such measures were unnecessary in any case.

The Myersians supplanted the notion of physiological fatigue with that of industrial fatigue, but with some misgivings. As we have seen from Myers's and Cathcart's remarks it was regarded as a provisional concept embracing several orders of phenomena, whose utility was to be judged solely by its results. Two distinctions were, however, pressed home.

The first was conceptual. Myers continually emphasized the difference between *clonic* and *tonus* activities. The former comprise sudden intense contractions of muscles leading rapidly to evident signs of physical distress: this is his 'fatigue of explosive acts'. The latter are concerned with maintaining posture and rhythmical, co-ordinated work. With the advance of mechanization, fatigue of the first kind becomes less widespread. That from the second increases and 'fatigue certainly exists in the central nervous system, in the sense of diminished excitability consequent on previous excitement'.[4] It is this kind of exhaustion, which is slow and cumulative, and can to some extent be fought off voluntarily – for example in pursuit of incentives – which lies at the core of industrial fatigue. Once it has reached pathological proportions co-ordination and work-rhythm deteriorate. The worker will seize rest-pauses, become ill, or with loss of concentration become prone to accidents. This condition must be warded off by adjusting the length of the working day and instituting official rest-pauses. Their timing depends partly upon the work being done, but also on the individual worker: individual psychological differences are even more important in many types of work than physical variations. Hence the Myersians' interest in vocational selection.

The second distinction which the Myersians soon emphasized was the essential difference between laboratory and factory studies. Laboratory studies were viewed as artificial and mainly concerned with clonic activities. Discussing the interpretation of individual work-curves, which had emerged as the classic method of studying human fatigue, Farmer stated:

A fatigue curve proper is obtained by getting subjects to perform a test calculated to produce fatigue fairly rapidly. Such a test is not the ordinary occupation of the subjects, but is the invention of a psychologist who has very different ends in view from those who invent industrial processes. Such tests cannot possibly have the same meaning for the subjects who perform them as an industrial process has for operatives who have been performing it many hours a day for many years.[5]

In fact, laboratory studies on the continent reached a similar conclusion at this period, and were approved by the Myersians. For example, in Germany, Atzler's work on the rationalization of effort was to be importantly modified by Ulbricht.[6] Investigating in depth the operation of cranking to determine the minimum effort for maximum outputs, Atzler proceeded to propound a basic set of rules to guide the design of all work-tasks. This recalls Taylor's work. However, although some of Atzler's prescriptions are reminiscent of Taylorism, for example that muscle must correlate positively with the physical effort demanded, others directly modify it. A minimum use of energy should aways be sought, 'useless' intermediate movements should not be completely eradicated, and the energy needed for body support should be minimized. And, with repetitive work, moments of variety, such as to fetch materials, should be deliberately introduced.

Ulbricht was able to show that subjective psychological perceptions in fact intervene. For example, in cranking, the length of the spoke used for winding which is subjectively perceived as optimum is actually longer than the physiological optimum as defined by calorie usage. This introduction of the human factor parallels Myersian thinking about fatigue, which posited a distinction between peripheral (biological) and central (or mental) fatigue – exhaustion produced by continuous excitement of the narrow range of muscles activated by a badly designed task. The latter type, it was becoming evident, was partly mediated by individual perception. This realization led naturally towards a study of monotony.

Friedmann describes the whole search for a test of fatigue as a 'utopian enterprise'.[7] The complexity of the state of fatigue and the impossibility of its direct measurement forced the Myersians to adopt indirect indicators which were themselves unsatisfactory. Lost time, labour turnover, sickness and mortality rates were all potential indicators, but poor record-keeping by firms and the intervention of other factors limited their utility. Attempts to use them did, however, sometimes lead to other worthwhile findings – for example, that some individuals are more liable than others to cause accidents. Output was chosen as the most reliable guide. Even the explanation for the regularities discovered there could only be hypothetical however. And as attention turned to lighter industrial tasks, improvements in output often accompanying the experimental introduction of rest-pauses could not be explained solely in terms of either peripheral or central fatigue. Why, for example, should output rise just *before* a pause as well as just after?

Their early physiological bias led the Myersians in a second direction. It had long been recognized that adverse environmental conditions could rápidly produce all the behavioural consequences of physical exhaustion. Consequently, a very considerable part of the Myersian effort was devoted to establishing the ideal environment for varying kinds of work. Up to 1930 about 25 per cent of their reports were devoted to this branch of inquiry.[8] Some of these findings have proved a lasting contribution to the ecological study of work, and to what might be called the 'Colt Ventilation' approach to industrial behaviour.

The atmosphere of the factory should be cool and dry rather than hot and humid; the air should waft gently rather than cling stagnantly or eddy in sudden gusts. Temperature should vary between different sectors of the workshop, and in any one sector at different periods during a work shift. Failure to observe these canons – which were given quantitative optima for different occupations – may result in loss of production and loss of tempers. (In Britain the Colt Ventilation Company is noted for its advertisements in the Sunday supplements which, with little understatement, drive home a similar message.)

Lighting must be carefully adapted to the work in hand, leaving no deep shadows or vivid contrasts, and sited to reduce dazzle and reflections. Noise and vibration were likewise shown to have some effect on the worker's output and emotional condition. Continuous, rhythmic noise is preferable to abrupt clattering, and 'meaningful' noise to a cacophony.

It is worth noting that these environmental factors range from those which are readily measured to those which are perceived largely subjectively. Individual differences become significant in response to noise: the heat felt before an open-hearth furnace gives less room for subjective perception. This is not to say that the realistic measurement even of temperature did not generate substantial problems. The seriousness with which they were tackled is often mind-boggling. In one report H. M. Vernon ventures to suggest that 'common experience shows that what is true for the kata-thermometer is not necessarily true for the human body' and explains how he has attempted to 'clothe' it, 'but in vain'.[9]

Even so, in studies of this type we see a broadening of the factors considered by the late 1920s. In a study by Vernon and Bedford of absenteeism in coal-mining in 1928, absenteeism was correlated not only with sickness and accidents, which were viewed primarily as the result of environmental factors, but also with 'voluntary causes'.[10] While the approach here remained essentially 'positivist' (for example, absenteeism was linked to variables such as 'distance of workings from pit bottom' and 'distance of homes from colliery'), the investigators came close to proposing sociological explanations for some of their findings. Voluntary absenteeism was more common among workers who lived near large towns. The investigators toyed with the idea that this might reflect a greater availability of jobs for wives in towns, but decided: 'Another and more likely explanation is that in the larger towns there is more distraction to be found in the way of sporting events, excursions and other amusements.'[11] This explanation is unimportant; what is interesting is that it should be conjectured at all. It is one indicator of a subtle shift in Myersian thinking towards a 'softer' methodology. This important change is much more evident in studies of monotony in industrial work undertaken throughout the 1920s, a review of which follows in the next chapter.

7

THE DISCOVERY
OF
MONOTONY

The Myersians' interest in monotony sprang from their concern with fatigue, and at first the two phenomena were not fully differentiated. This extension of study was significant. Monotony is a subjective psychological condition, though its appearance is related to objective conditions. Individual psychology and individual differences mediate between these conditions and any behavioural consequences. Such consequences are themselves less measurable than those which result from fatigue, whether the investigator relies on direct or indirect methods. The effects of monotony may be estimated by measuring the worker's rate of output, but this gives little indication of the extent of his boredom as a subjectively experienced condition. Only the subject's own reports can establish its degree. At first the Myersians shied away from the loss of 'rigour' involved. But they were eventually obliged to adopt this course.

The notion that monotony is not simply an aspect of fatigue occurs first in I.F.R.B. studies in 1924.[1] In a study of light industrial work Vernon and Bedford found that rest-pauses were most effective when the worker controlled his own work-pace; and they stimulated the output of low producers more than high producers. The investigators also remarked that workers snatched unofficial rest-pauses and fetched materials themselves whenever they could. Both of these were put down partly to a desire to escape monotony. In an experimental study of rest-pauses Wyatt concluded that the drop in work-rate in the middle of a work-spell was primarily due to monotony. After the introduction of an official break, the work-rate rose just before as well as just after it.

In a more extensive report published the same year Vernon examined the amount of variety present in a large number of repetitive industrial jobs (the cycle-times of the operations studied were as little as one to four seconds).[2] It became evident that workers did attempt to introduce variety whenever they could. Comparing the effect of changes of activity in a factory setting and a laboratory study, Wyatt and Ogden arrived at somewhat inconsistent results. In the laboratory, unvaried spells of work on a single activity resulted in lower output and quality. In the industrial experiment, a large number of changes in work operation throughout the day seriously cut daily output. Reducing changes to every half hour increased production by up to 20 per cent. Maintaining work on the same task all day increased output even further. However, the operators complained about the monotony of this arrangement.

More ambitious studies were set in hand to explore the effects of boredom further.[3] The results of the first of these were fairly predictable. Uniformity of task was generally less productive, activities were best changed every one and a half hours (though more frequently when the work was physically tiring), and workers preferred some resemblance between two consecutive tasks.

The second is much more interesting.[4] Very little previous I.F.R.B. work is similar to this study. Not only was 'introspective evidence' (i.e. the remarks of workers in interview) introduced, but the design of the research and presentation of the findings took into account previous research and wider psychological theory. Monotony and fatigue were at last decisively separated as concepts: 'Boredom . . . is a psychical state which may exist quite apart from fatigue, and must be separately considered in any industrial inquiry . . .'[5] Referring to the work of Münsterberg and more recent laboratory studies the writers pointed to the possible effects of individual differences and the precise nature of the task performed, since monotonous work varied significantly in its propensity to induce boredom. This might be related to the nature of the mental 'set' which was engaged and its compatibility with intruding desires.

Six different kinds of repetitive work were examined – two types of filament-winding, inserting (an operation in making electric-lamps), wrapping soap, packing chocolate and weighing tobacco. Each group was observed for a minimum of six weeks. Aware of the 'Hawthorne Effect' which was to cause excitement on its rediscovery in Chicago several years later, the investigators were careful to compare 'before' and 'after' production records 'to eliminate any disturbing effects which the presence of an observer might be thought to produce'.[6] Conversation and behaviour, as well as the rate of working, were carefully recorded. Each worker was also given an intelligence test.

Nearly 75 per cent of the workers reported that they felt moderate or considerable boredom, and this was at its most intense at certain periods of the day, particularly in the middle of the spell of work. Its onset was registered by variations in the rate of working and a measurable drop in output when it was felt most severely. The estimation of the passage of time was seriously impaired during phases of intense monotony (and this seemed partly to explain variations in work-rate).

All this is more or less what one might expect. More interesting was the investigators' attempt to relate boredom to individual characteristics and the work situation. It was established that the sense of boredom was more likely in the more intelligent operatives, though, contrary to the findings of some previous laboratory studies, they also tended to be more efficient workers. Again, operatives varied in their ability to perform work automatically, and 'temperamental tendencies are important determinants of boredom, and need special investigation'.[7] The technical features of the work seemed to operate as follows: where the task was highly automatic, or where it demanded complete concentration, boredom was reduced. The latter was easily explained. In the former, the worker's mind could wander freely or he could engage in distracting conversations with his mates. The most boring tasks were those demanding partial or intermittent attention.

Once again, the evidence indicated that suitably introduced rest-pauses or changes of activity could reduce monotony, and that some individual adaptation to an initially uninteresting task might be achieved. Payment by results might also ward off boredom. But the most intriguing claim of all, totally unsuspected from previous work of this kind, and seized on later by the Mayoites, was that work in 'compact social groups' kept boredom at bay:

The amount of boredom seems also to bear some relation to number and proximity of operatives employed. An isolated operative ... is much more susceptible to monotonous conditions than the individuals composing a large group of operatives doing the same kind of work, when mass suggestion has a greater play, conversation can be freely indulged and full expression given to 'intruding thoughts and desires'.[8]

Myersian psychology, publicly at least, embodied an essentially behaviourist model of man and a radically empiricist method. Most of its practitioners viewed clinical methods with extreme caution and were much concerned to demonstrate the 'scientific' nature of their work to academic critics. Yet even workers like Vernon and Wyatt were gradually forced towards a more clinical (and even sociological) viewpoint. At least one Myersian, May Smith, seems to have been basically sympathetic to this approach from an early stage.

In an early paper for the I.F.R.B. she remarked that most observers' descriptions of the factory 'are like skeleton outlines, or those wire reproductions of the correct movements of motion study; they are quite true, but they lack humanity'.[9] The 'mechanical point of view' (i.e. behaviourism) in psychology and scientific management was to be deplored, especially since it appeared 'even in discussions of intelligence'. Industrial students, she insisted, should recognize the human complexity of industrial milieux, particularly the variety of human personalities present.

Her attempt at a typology of industrial 'personalities' was no more than a first step. On the managerial side she identified 'explosive', 'over-anxious', 'obsessive' and 'self-controlled' types; on that of labour, 'truculent', 'ultra-weak', 'fantacist', and the type who 'seeks a position in other fields'. These types were not portrayed merely as accidental products of individual differences, but as resulting also from the clash between the 'instinct of self-assertion' and the authority relations of industry. (One can dismiss this typology as simple-minded, but the worker 'types' correspond to the conventional sociological patterns of rebellion, retreatism, ritualism and innovation in response to a situation of stress.) Smith was evidently trying to challenge the notion that a given mixture of workshop conditions will produce a unitary, universal response. Considering her connections, this was a bold and novel step.

Smith's clinical–sociological proclivities reappeared in her study, carried out with Culpin and Farmer, of telegraphists' cramp.[10] This ailment had long been a recognized occupational hazard, with complex symptoms, ranging from generalized muscular weakness to mental blocks about punching a particular character, and an obscure pathology. As early as 1911 a British government investigation had concluded it must be a disease of the central nervous system. No single objective cause had been determined, though it was related in a few cases to length of service, the hours worked, the 'style' of the operative or the type of keyboard worked on. Loss of muscular control could be rapid or protracted but in no case could any anatomical correlate be isolated.

The investigators examined and tested large groups of sufferers, non-sufferers and apprentice telegraphists, employing all the standard apparatus or ergographs and similar instruments, and carefully controlled such factors as age and experience. But they added a medical study which included clinical interviews. These showed fairly clearly that cramp was a psycho-neurotic complaint. Respondents emphasized the strain of the work and the need to remain calm. Officious supervision sometimes prevented this, and the work was generally subject to social and psychological pressure. Messages had to be encoded rapidly and accurately to 'a rigid objective standard of behaviour' with a potential critic at the other end of the line whose complaints would immediately become public because the work was done in the presence of others. 'Nervy' telegraphists found this upset the delicacy of their touch.

Sufferers were typically fearful of others and excessively self-critical. They might be social isolates, obsessively concerned with the physical surroundings of their work, and express phobias about the dark, traffic and meeting strangers. But despite a vast array of individually expressed neurotic symptoms, Smith and her co-authors were able to posit an 'ideal typical' cramp-prone subject: he was anxious, solitary, fearful, dependent and worried about his career progress.

Study of a control group from allied occupations (typing and clerical work) disclosed equal proportions of cramp-prone subjects. Since the complaint did not derive from the muscular demands of telegraphy, why were analogous symptoms absent in this group? The investigators concluded that the social aspects of the work situation in telegraphy encouraged the onset of cramp in those liable to suffer, in two ways. First, the immediate social pressures of the job raised the emotional temperature. Second, worries about promotion added to the sufferer's general anxiety. Most perceptively, they noted that cramp was rare in the United States. But there, telegraphy did not offer a career, and cramp-prone subjects presumably selected themselves out of the occupation. In Britain, fear that a career might be terminated could bring on the very disability which increased that risk.

A rigidly bio-psychological perspective was, then, discarded in this study, though tight research design was maintained. However, it offered pointers to a less salutary future. In her analysis, Smith briefly referred to the work of Janet on individual neurosis; and in later work with her associate Culpin she pursued this clinical line further.[11] Unfortunately, although she managed to avoid Elton Mayo's excesses, this was to reinforce the preoccupation of Mayo and his followers with individual maladjustment in industry to the detriment of more worthwhile investigation.

8

THE MYERSIANS
IN
RETROSPECT

The developments I have sketched help to explain the change of title of the I.F.R.B. (to the Industrial Health Research Board) in 1929, and that of the *Journal of the National Institute of Industrial Psychology* to *The Human Factor* in 1932 (*Occupational Psychology* from 1938 onwards). The physiological bias of the early work, and its accompanying behaviouristic image of the worker, were gradually corrected. This does not mean that the I.F.R.B. 'style' immediately disappeared. In 1938, for example, Wyatt and Langdon replicated and extended their earlier studies of fatigue and monotony,[1] but in doing so they anticipated the important work of Baldamus in the 1950s on the phenomenon of 'traction'.[2] And the influence of American developments, as well as that of their own earlier studies, was manifested in their discovery that workers pick 'pleasant working companions' as the most important attribute of a job.[3]

Again, as late as 1941, the H.M.W.C. studies of hours of work were repeated under war-time conditions. This, however, was necessary to demonstrate to the Minister of Labour, Ernest Bevin, who 'knew' that output 'obviously' increased with hours, that he was dangerously mistaken.

But from about 1930 an open concern with less quantifiable

82

aspects of behaviour and the forces operating on it became more 'respectable'. In Myers's collection of readings, *Industrial Psychology* of 1929,[4] although the bulk of articles deal with the kind of topics in which the N.I.I.P. and I.F.R.B. respectively specialized, there are discussions of the social and economic environment of industry. Admittedly, the conceptual frameworks adopted lack sophistication. For example, in his contribution on 'The Human Factor in Industrial Relations',[5] Drever accepted instincts as the essential motivating forces of behaviour. But, he asserted, they express themselves in the form of the pursuit by subjects of perceived interests, probably as a member of a group; and 'a social group is not a mere aggregation of individuals' because 'when an individual is a member of a social group his impulses, feelings and behaviour may be modified in various ways and degrees, dependent on the group in question'.[6]

Membership of several groups with competing claims on loyalty, Drever continued, is a fact of industrial life: 'The worker is compelled by the necessity of earning a living to face daily the situations presented in the factory' with no escape because 'he is so enmeshed in the net of circumstance – a family to support, no other employment available, and the like'.[7] Because of the uncertainties of a market economy the organization could not become the primary focus of his industrial group life. If he were given more say in its affairs, and perhaps a share in its profits, such integration might occur for the benefit of all.

Cathcart had expressed similar views in a book on industrial psychology a year earlier.[8] As an academic physiologist, Cathcart was clearly more at home in assessing findings on fatigue and environmental factors. But he clearly acknowledged: 'When man must be one of the determining factors in every fact and hypothesis, economic or other, in connection with industry, no firmly established laws can be deduced';[9] and 'I have dealt with what may be called the strictly workshop conditions which play a part in the great questions of optimum conditions of labour',[10] (though out-plant factors exert a powerful, if obscure, influence. And when, in an early section, he claimed that 'Man is indeed an irrational being', and briefly referred to McDougall's concept of the 'group mind', he linked this with the emergence of 'huge soulless organizations'. Noting that these factors complicate the study of work behaviour, he avoided any kind of Mayoite conclusion that work behaviour is basically an attempt to combat the soullessness of modern life.[11]

The recognition of such factors implied no fundamental change of course but was the extension of a basic viewpoint which had been present (though largely suppressed) all along. Appraising the approach of the Myersians as a whole Friedmann remarks: 'Man, with the whole of his personality, is again introduced ... The abstract worker conceived by the Taylorians – a crude composite of laziness and desire for gain – yields to a complex being, both body and mind, in whom an all-important act such as work involves the whole personality.'[12]

The human factor school, it should be emphasized, deliberately confronted Taylorism. From 1920 Myers consistently attacked the notion of the 'one best way'. An early article developing this theme brought a rumbustious reply from the Gilbreths.[13] While agreeing that two workers never perform a task in exactly the same manner, the dynamic couple proudly maintained: 'We shall continue to specialize on the best demonstrator of the best method', because 'the best results can come only when the worker learns first the One Best Way and practises it to the point of automaticity'.[14] (They appended a castigation of 'the wasteful methods of even the most intelligent of workers, namely, the surgeons, whose time and motion wastes are so great today that more than 10 per cent of the ether minutes of the patients can be eliminated in any operation'.[15]) Myers's objection that the Gilbreths's 'therbligs' (a measurement of work) had 'no psychological or physiological interest or basis whatever' was met with sarcastic fury. To clinch the argument that they themselves were qualified psychologists they recalled that 'we have written the first book on the Psychology of Management, and we use it daily in our work'.[16]

Myers renewed the attack in his book of 1924[17] (which was originally delivered as a series of lectures at Columbia University), noting that Taylor's procedure of basing time-studies on an expert worker 'would now be regarded as unsound – scientifically, sociologically and psychologically'.[18] ('Sociologically', because 'class loyalty and fear of unemployment are potent causes of restriction of output even when the workers are paid by results'.[19]) The N.I.I.P. had at first been suspected by workers of being an agency of scientific management, and:

They could quote passages from Taylor's *Principles of Scientific Management* or from his *Shop Management* such as his remark ... 'You know just as well as I do that a high-priced man has to do exactly as he's told from morning to night' ... that the worker must 'bear in mind that each shop exists, first, last and for all time, for the purpose of paying dividends to its owners'.[20]

He praised the 'intuitive opposition', which has a 'sound psychological basis', of British workmen to The One Best Way. Such notions, he pointed out, only survive where immigrant labour is cheap and unions weak.

An example of a less direct kind of attack on the underlying articles of Taylorism is Eric Farmer's discussion of incentives.[21] This recalled that rewards have both economic and non-economic aspects; that workers seek both; that the acceptable level of each varies with time and place; and that no hard-and-fast rule can be given as to whether the material rewards should be paid as a piece-rate or as an hourly rate, given that one merely wishes to maximize output.

There is little question that the Myersians' assault on scientific management was largely the product of *scientific* disagreement with the psychological assumptions of Taylorism. But part of its vigour derived from genuine humanitarian concern on the one hand and, at least in Myers's own case, tactical concerns on the other. If industrial psychology was to prosper, the workers' doubts that it might merely be Taylorism in a new guise had to be laid to rest. Similarly, managers had to be shown that it produced better results than they could expect from the Taylorian techniques.

To reconcile these needs and to maintain the respect of academic circles for the new field demanded tactful compromise. The Myersians set out to show that they could go one better than the scientific managers; that they could simultaneously make work easier for the operative and lower its costs for the manager, on the basis of carefully accumulated empirical knowledge. This attempt was, granted its limited objectives, highly successful. Yet a compromise is a compromise, and the Myersians paid two severe penalties. The first was that a large proportion of their problems had to be taken over from the scientific managers. The second was a certain fragmentation of effort. Both are reflected most obviously in the work of the N.I.I.P. It had to live by its consultancies. A good number of these were concerned with the organization and design of work. When these studies aided theoretical generalization they did so in the least economical way.

Again, the preoccupation of the I.F.R.B. with fatigue and the N.I.I.P. with selection techniques, although obviously valuable in demonstrating the complexity of the human factor besides the crude mechanical man of the Taylorians, postponed consideration of other variables influencing behaviour, and thus subtly reinforced a 'harmonic' ideology of industrial relations. As Friedmann has remarked: 'Always present is the postulate of an individualistic psychology which can be better understood and judged only by the study of other aspects of the "human factor" ';[22] further:

The question is not raised here of knowing whether this same man works in the same way in the different workshops through which he passes, depending on the relations with his comrades, his foreman, his employers, his union organizations – in a word, whether the methods and output of his work are not related to considerations broader than the organism's own psycho-physiological characteristics.[23]

This latter assertion is not entirely true, but it comes close to the mark.

This is not to denigrate the very substantial and important discoveries of the Myersians, or to question their good faith. Neither can be doubted. Rather it is a reminder that the products of scientific effort and the direction of inquiry depend on more than gaps in knowledge and available brain-power. The problems an investigator chooses, and his method of investigating them, are always influenced by the ideas of the scientific community with which he identifies, by the perspectives of the broad social class to which he belongs, and by the needs of the people who fund his work. It is extremely difficult for the investigator to detect and acknowledge these forces, and even more so to neutralize them. In industrial studies, with their obvious practical and ideological potential, the need for such vigilance is additionally pressing. Yet it is precisely here that the most upright investigators have been caught off guard.

9

THE
HUMAN FACTOR
IN
AMERICA

It is common to remark nowadays that the 'failure' of the Western Electric researchers was due to their having adopted the perspectives of human factor industrial psychology. By 'failure' is meant their neglect of institutional and historical factors in designing and interpreting the studies, which is the natural accompaniment of the essentially behaviourist orientation of the Myersians. All this is true, but incomplete. Equally, the investigators ran into trouble because they came late to the Myersian approach, did not fully understand it, and therefore failed to take full advantage of its achievements, particularly in designing field studies. They were also overimpressed with Mayo's clinical enthusiasms, and with Warner's anthropological insights.

They thus fell between several stools. I shall analyse this failure in more detail in the next part. Here I shall try to indicate some reasons why they failed to profit fully from the Myersian achievement. For, if they had, the Western Electric studies might now be much less controversial; and, though less well known, the object of more general respect.

What evidence do we have that the Hawthorne workers were not fully acquainted with the Myersian *opus*? Fairly lavish reference to their work is made in the early sections of *Management and the Worker*. But this book was not published till 1939. Later I shall raise the possibility that this familiarity was largely retrospective.* A more generous suggestion is that they knew of this work but did not appreciate its relevance, especially as a guide to research procedure.[1]

However, we have a more direct piece of evidence. In *Human Problems of an Industrial Civilization* Mayo sets his early review of the Western Electric work partly in the context of selected Myersian studies. In discussing them (and incidentally showing most enthusiasm for the 'clinical' work of May Smith), he plainly states that 'industrial inquiries undertaken in the United States have been driven, step by step, to similar methods and assumptions. This is of some interest, because *there was at no time during the early development of the inquiries any relation between the investigators here and in England.*'[2]

What explains this lack of contact? Mayo had reported some of his early work to a conference of the British Association Psychology Section; he had published in the J.N.I.I.P. in the 1920s; and Myers had lectured and published extensively in the United States.[3]

There seems to be no direct explanation for this lag in communication – if it was that, and not a lack of interest. But an indirect answer may be found by considering the origins and organization of industrial psychology in America, its characteristic mode of finance, and its research preoccupations. Examination of these factors, which are closely related, present a contrast with the situation in Britain.

A full account of the development of industrial psychology in America has been provided by Baritz.[4] I shall concentrate on its most salient features. The essential differences with Britain are as follows: (i) interest in industrial psychology was aroused earlier; (ii) its growth and organization had pronounced 'free market' characteristics; (iii) it was obliged, consequently, to live almost entirely on its ability to produce rapid results (and sometimes on its wits); (iv) its problems were largely dictated by demand; and (v) it none the less achieved considerable influence. The latter achievement may also have made it somewhat complacent.

* See below, Chapter 13.

Applied psychology in the United States drew its inspiration from two sources: the work of Sir Francis Galton on individual differences, and the painstaking investigative techniques pioneered by Wilhelm Wundt from the opening of his Leipzig laboratory in 1879. It was promoted by two important enthusiasts, James McKeen Cattell and Hugo Münsterberg. The relevance of differences in individuals to industrial problems is evident. If different individuals possess varying aptitudes (thanks to heredity and/or environment) they will perform better in some occupations or tasks than others. The rationality of industry, and the contentment and abilities of its personnel, can be developed by careful pre-selection. But the divination of these variations should proceed by means of careful measurement. Wundt's techniques pointed the way, and both Münsterberg, who arrived at Harvard in the late 1890s, and Cattell had studied under him. Cattell had also sat at the feet of Galton, and became Professor of Psychology at the University of Pennsylvania earlier in the decade.

Although Cattell's was the first chair in psychology to be established in the United States, the subject had by no means been ignored in academic circles. But it was tied closely to philosophy, especially the philosophy of William James. Until well into the twentieth century, in fact, many philosophers claiming an interest in psychology looked askance at the kind of work Cattell and Münsterberg were doing. For a time real 'respectability' lay with instinctualism, building on the ideas James had put forward. Popular enthusiasm for the instinctualist approach, too, was lively if we go by such indicators as the sales of William McDougall's *Principles of Social Psychology*.[5] And through writers such as Tead instinctualism was to make its own kind of contribution to the psychological discussion of industrial problems.[6]

Instinctualism rejected the rational man of economics, and, in that sense, was indirectly useful for confronting the technicism of the scientific managers. But it faced three increasingly urgent criticisms. First, how many instincts were there? James had identified twenty-eight, McDougall telescoped them to eleven, other theorists offered their own taxonomies. The problem of classification led to much inconclusive argument. Second, the instinctualists proved consistently better as coroners than prophets: they could point wisely to the instincts which had provoked an accomplished act, but could not specify what kind of acts a subject might perform in the future. Third, and encompassing the previous complaints, their approach was not 'hard' enough, i.e. they could not make measurements. In these respects the academic establishment with which the applied psychologists had at first to contend was profoundly different from that which the Myersians faced.

Wundt himself was displeased with the direction his former pupils took. He was not interested in applications. His programme was to determine universal mental structures and processes through measurement and computation. He was searching for the enduring 'psychological man' behind individual differences, and deplored the appropriation of his laboratory methods for a study whose aim was to map and underline the variety of human mental factors.

Until the First World War progress towards the acceptance of aptitude testing was not rapid, nor did the students of individual differences come out as strongly against Taylorism as one might have expected. In the early 1900s Münsterberg had polled employers on the traits they looked for in different classes of worker, and his results were to lead him later to condemn the psychological dilettantism of scientific management and advocate the thoroughgoing participation of psychologists in industry. But a full study of the relationship between individual differences and actual performance would have required greater resources than were available at this time, and neither Cattell nor Münsterberg were eager to become consultants to business at the risk of their own intellectual integrity. Taylorism anyway was no more than a fringe movement in industry until the publicity following the Eastern Rate Case in 1910. As Baritz reminds us: 'The engineers raised most of the problems with which the later psychologists grappled.'[7] But those problems were not yet clearly formulated.

Moreover, managerial enthusiasm for applied psychology before the 1914 war derived from its imputed potential as a tool for manipulating consumers rather than producers. A growing number of articles on the use of psychology in advertising appeared in the trade press at this period. Less reserved in his concern to meet the immediate requirements of industry than Münsterberg or Cattell, Dill Scott, a professor at Northwestern University, published his *Psychology of Advertising* in 1908.[8] It was quite successful. Scott was also offering a testing service to industry before the outbreak of war (a client of 1915 was the Western Electric Company). Another academic psychologist Walter V. Bingham, by now also believed that the science of the mind was sufficiently developed for legitimate application and formed a consultancy at the Carnegie Institute of Technology. It was soon successful.

The ground had therefore been well prepared for the widespread acceptance of applied psychology in American industry before the war. American involvement in hostilities rapidly completed the process. The American army quickly established a Committee for Psychology in 1917 to speed up the placing of recruits. Scott, Bingham and J. B. Watson were set to devise tests. Eventually, they were administered to almost 2,000,000 men, and were believed to identify successfully both subnormals and officer material. In fact, most of these tests sought to measure intelligence rather than aptitudes. Scott, incidentally, believed not only that ability could be reduced to a simple scale-score but that the scores could legitimately be computed from interviewer judgements. But criticism of such misconceptions appeared only later. At the time it was believed the army programme had been a signal achievement; and its discovery that a large proportion of recruits were mentally unfit was thought a great public service.

Applied psychology thus achieved much favourable publicity, massive development funds and full respectability. The stress on individual differences also coincided with a period in which unreconstructed Taylorism was coming under attack on other grounds. Aware of the need to gain the confidence of labour, Cattell himself went out of his way to convince Gompers that psychology could be a genuinely impartial servant of both parties in industry, as scientific management had unsuccessfully claimed to be, and Gompers readily concurred.

The market for psychological expertise in industry expanded explosively immediately after the war. The academics soon put their consultancy activities on a regular business basis. Scott founded a Scott Company in 1919 and Cattell followed with his Psychological Corporation (a kind of psychologists' co-partnership) in 1921. Another body through which academic expertise was channelled was the Personnel Research Foundation (1920), though it had broader aims than the application of tests.

Two developments, however, marred this general picture of acceptance and success. Firstly, as they had with scientific management, the 'fakirs and charlatans' cashed in. Fringe operators were soon offering off-the-peg tests to companies, at cut prices, and even by mail-order. 'Character-analysts' (who could detect promise or uselessness from a subject's physical build or racial background, if necessary from a photograph), phrenologists, palmists, graphologists and other self-appointed specialists in the science of the mind and its mysterious powers were all able to exploit the businessman's unclear distinction between real and phoney occupational psychology.

Secondly, many companies who had employed respectable agencies began to complain that the results were less remarkable than they had been led to expect. The suspicion that the tests were not valid predictive instruments began to spread. It was increased by the outbreak of controversy amongst academic psychologists about the merits of various testing instruments and methods of applying them. Criticism of the war-time programme also arose, suggesting that its supposed measurement of intelligence had really been the assessment of educational attainment. These embarrassments were, however, fought off. After all, few of the critics were prepared to state that there was nothing in testing. Most argument was about technique and inference, not about more fundamental issues of method (or ethics).

From this brief account the climate into which Myersian human factor psychology was imported should be clear. Applied psychology in America possessed an intellectual establishment, a fairly clear accepted problematic, a substantial degree of self-confidence and a consultancy tradition which often favoured the short cut to rapid results in a highly competitive market. In the light of this one can understand better the reason for any lack of interest in the British work. Its plodding caution in research and institutionalized scepticism in interpreting findings must have made it seem quite comically old-fashioned.

In a way, then, it is not surprising that the first main effort to work outside the prevailing fashion was made by a foreigner. Mayo, whose contribution we shall review in more detail in the next part, had arrived in the United States in 1922. His first industrial assignment was in a textile mill in Philadelphia. Mayo's various publications about this study are somewhat muddled.[9] They do not make his approach, or even his main conclusions, entirely clear. (This, of course, made it much easier for him to reinterpret his findings after the Hawthorne studies.)

There is some superficial resemblance to the research style of the Myersians. The 'enlightened and humane' management of the factory had asked Mayo to solve the problem of a 250 per cent labour turnover in their mule-spinning department (in other workshops it stood around 6 per cent). At ten hours per day over a five-day week, with forty-five minutes for lunch, the hours were by no means excessive; they were even generous, by the standards of the day. Mayo none the less conjectured that the physical demands of the work created severe postural fatigue and awarded a group of experimental subjects two or three ten-minute rest-pauses spread throughout the day, during which operatives were required to lie down and relax. This is reminiscent of I.F.R.B. work. Less so, however, was Mayo's failure to obtain prior output records or to compare the performance of experimental and non-experimental subjects. It was merely known that the shop as a whole had never produced enough to earn a group bonus.

He noted that the experimental subjects were 'pleased' with the change, and the spirit of the shop as a whole was better. Management awarded the rest-pauses to everyone, and output records, which were subsequently kept more carefully, rose above the threshold required to earn the bonus. When the rests were abolished by junior managers, following a rush order, output declined. Mayo intervened with the company president, who ordered their reinstitution. Output returned to its high level. Moreover, turnover declined to virtually nil and remained at this low level for at least five years. Mayo interpreted these results in his first report of the study in primarily physiological terms. Output supposedly rose mainly due to relief from postural strain.[10] But there is a psychological hedge. Informal interviews had shown the workers' thoughts to be dominated by pessimistic themes. Rest-pauses allegedly permitted a temporary respite from these 'reveries'.

The early lighting experiments at Hawthorne began shortly after this, in the winter of 1924–5. Mayo had nothing to do with them, and the precise source of their scientific rationale, if there was one, is unclear. The first set compared changes in artificial lighting with output in three departments. No results could be deduced. In the next, workers were split into two groups matched for previous output and located in separate buildings. The lighting of the experimental group was varied, but output for both groups showed a more or less identical increase. The tests were repeated excluding all natural light. Again both groups increased their output, the experimental one even when lighting was reduced to a very low intensity. Further 'informal experimentation' demonstrated that subjective interpretations of the change was an intervening variable.

Thus the stage was set for the two Relay Assembly Test Room and the Mica Splitting Test Room studies. The aim of these was never to test for social influences on output behaviour, but to relate output to physical and physiological variables, and to test the effect of incentives. The experimental design and control of these studies was inadequate and will be discussed in the next part.[11] Two points should be made at this stage, however: the approach adopted in both these and the lighting studies was squarely in the 'human factor' style; and the investigators were quite clearly either totally unfamiliar with the work of the Myersians at this point or had totally misunderstood it. We shall probably never know which. But it is hard to believe that if the British work had been well known to them the investigators would have made so many obvious slips in their research design.

When he came to write *Human Problems* Mayo had read some of the I.H.R.B. studies (and through his contacts with Henderson absorbed some basic facts about the physiology of work). He seized on the work of May Smith on telegraphists' cramp and on Wyatt's and Fraser's study of monotony. Armed with this ammunition he reinterpreted his own Philadelphia Study in a manner consistent with Myersian findings and his own convictions about industrial neurosis. These were extended to the Hawthorne data with profound consequences.

Clearly the human factor approach had its own very pronounced limitations. Equally, Mayo was capable of gifted insight into the wider forces which impinge on workers' attitudes and behaviour. It therefore seems regrettable that his introduction to the British approach was not more thorough, prolonged or at first hand; and further, that the Hawthorne studies had to be conducted in a climate where sponsors often lacked patience. It is true that Western Electric were more tolerant than most American firms, but it is plain that the company always expected a big payoff. This, they mistakenly believed, they eventually found in the shape of the Counselling Programme. It was necessary to revise the image of the industrial worker projected by the Myersians. It was disastrous – at that time, and granted the purposes of these studies – to ignore their lessons in research procedure.*

* If only their warnings about 'Hawthorne Effects': 'Indeed, sometimes the mere presence of the Institute's investigators and the interest they have shown in the employees' work has served to send up output before any changes have been introduced' (C. S. Myers, *Industrial Psychology in Great Britain*, p. 28). Well into the 1940s, American applied social scientists continued to 'discover' the human factor school: see C. F. Harding, 'Uniformities in Human Relations Tentatively Established', *Applied Anthropology*, January–March 1944, 37–44. Harding concludes that 'the British studies reviewed demonstrate the extreme importance of social behaviour in determining output'; this seems based on a very hasty reading – an amusing sign of which is Harding's supposition that May Smith was a man.

10

IN CONCLUSION

Rigorous industrial psychology emerged in Britain when it did because the British war effort was threatened in the middle of the First World War. That, anyway, was the immediate reason; but it is hardly a full explanation.

In theory, it should have been pioneered in the United States. There, the popular reaction against Taylorism anticipated many of the conclusions which the Myersians were to establish scientifically. Moreover, America was far better supplied with academic psychologists; and, as we have seen, industry was more prepared to try out their ideas. But American psychology had prematurely broken its links with biology, and the applied psychologists looked on their theories as a commodity, a packaged product, for sale in a highly competitive market. Aptitude tests sold best, so individual psychological differences became the major scientific problem. Industry, too, looked for rapid results, and this prevented the lengthy study and cautious generalization which the Myersians later showed to be necessary.

The British context was even less hospitable to a Myersian approach before the war.* Taylorism had never gained more than a

* Though one or two studies were undertaken before it, notably by H. M.

toehold, and academic psychology was a minute force more concerned with justifying its presence in universities than with searching for pickings in the corridors of industrial power.

Both of these facts reflect Britain's more general situation as a parasitic economy, a centre of international finance dependent upon returns from foreign investment whose increasingly archaic industry supplied captive imperial markets.* There was no economic motive to innovate through the rational exploitation of scientific knowledge. Psychology and scientific management were neglected for the same underlying reason that chemicals and electrical goods were. The industrialist had no need for them.

But the country did need them, as the war soon made plain. And now, paradoxically, the academic seclusion of psychology became an advantage. When it was called to the industrial front it was scientifically uncompromised, and, having government backing, did not need to compromise.

For two years Britain had tried simultaneously to fight a major war and maintain *laissez-faire* economic practices. Faced with growing signs of collapse in 1916 the government had to create a centrally co-ordinated economy. The Health of Munitions Workers Committee was one rather small but significant outcome of this rationalization of the war-machine.

It tackled a set of problems which could remain unrecognized, or could be ignored, in the peace-time economy. Taylorism and applied individual psychology – and later, human relations – were essentially concerned with problems of motivation and compliance. Though such problems certainly did exist in Britain during the 1914 war, they were secondary to objective bio-psychological constraints on worker productivity. These hidden limits on production could only become apparent in the entirely novel circumstance of the total disappearance of unemployment. In peace-time, the elasticity of the general supply of labour could hide the inelasticity (beyond a critical point) of individual effort. War conditions drama-

---

Vernon. See Cathcart, *TheHuman Factor in Industry*, Oxford University Press, 1928, ch. 3.

* For a short discussion of the socio-economic context, see E. Hobsbawm, *Industry and Empire*, Penguin Books, Harmondsworth, 1969, ch. 9.

tized this fundamental biological – and fundamental economic – truth.

But if war conditions made the biologically grounded psychology of the human factor relevant, peace soon made it seem redundant (except as a humanitarian exercise) to those with power to employ it or to agitate for its use in the factories. Once stagnation and unemployment returned, and the government retreated from its economic responsibilities, businessmen could see little use for Myersian expertise, and the trade unions became preoccupied with a fight to find, not to humanize, work.

In view of this situation it is perhaps remarkable that the Myersians survived at all. As we saw earlier they indeed led a precarious existence, propped up by very slight and grudging official support, the contributions of Quaker firms, the donations of individual philanthropists and their earnings from the more commercially oriented work of the N.I.I.P. Without the diplomacy of Myers they might never have survived.

What is most interesting about Myers is his insistence upon maintaining scientific rigour. One could argue of course that even if he had personally been prepared to lower his standards his scientific associates would have preferred to go out of business rather than follow his lead, and that he knew this. But I believe his faith in science, not only for its own sake and as a material force but as an humanitarian enterprise, was entirely authentic. He seems to have believed that it was shared by a small but increasingly important group. Winning acceptance would be a long-term effort, but was likely to succeed eventually – provided he demonstrated the efficacy and independence of industrial psychology – as the target audience grew in influence. This strategy was the most rational he could have adopted.

Myers's propaganda was not aimed so much at business or government leaders as at progressive managers and social democratic politicians. The managerial stratum in Britain was just beginning to acquire self-consciousness in the 1920s. Many of its spokesmen, much more explicitly than their American counterparts, espoused a socialist version of the technocratic credo: the industry of the future would be operated by scientifically literate professional managers sympathetic to organized labour with highly efficient production.[1]

This movement did not grow so rapidly as some, including Myers himself, expected; and the industrial unrest of the mid 1920s reduced the new managers' enthusiasm for an alliance with organized labour. The leftist technocrats never became a decisive third force in industry. Yet many of their ideas did gain a vague general acceptance. Amongst them was the notion that scientific study of work was valuable. Myersian psychology was thus assured of a small but growing clientele which had no use, or respect, for the scientific prostitute.

But it is noteworthy that this branch of industrial studies had to wait till 1939 for full security, when another war brought to the fore many of the problems it had already dealt with, and government intervention ensured that they were confronted on a wide scale in a rational way. Unlike Taylorism or human relations, human factor psychology lacked glamour. It was intrinsically much more valuable than either.

PART III

HUMAN RELATIONS

11

REASSESSING
HUMAN RELATIONS

Introduction. Some readers are likely to begin this book here, while others may leave it till last or even omit it. They will do so because they already know a good deal about human relations in industry. No other branch of industrial studies has raised so great and lasting an interest outside academic circles. Massively popularized and violently attacked, it has been the centre of a semi-public controversy for almost forty years.

Those even slightly acquainted with this debate will know that human relations is nowadays very much in disgrace.* Old-fashioned economists have ridiculed its rejection of money as the central motivator of work behaviour; political liberals have attacked its denial of individualism; radicals have raged over its assertions of workers' irrationalism and moral dependence on management; industrial managers have discarded its unworkable manipulatory techniques; sociological researchers and theorists of all colours have documented its methodological, theoretical and ideological lapses.†

* At least, in Western countries. Soviet industrial theoreticians have for a number of years shown some enthusiasm for Mayoite ideas.

† See H. A. Landsberger, *Hawthorne Revisited*, Cornell University Press,

Just about everything seems to have been said, and many times. Naturally some readers will feel that there is no point in reminding themselves of what they know already; others with more sadistic tastes may be looking forward to a novel staging of the ritual slaughter.

But is the prevailing understanding of human relations definitive? Probably not. The present sweeping hostility to the movement prevents, in particular, an appreciation of the internal diversity of the approach as an intellectual fabric. For example, human relations is still too often equated with the work and thought of Elton Mayo. But any reasoned rejection of the approach as a whole must hit more targets than this – perhaps rather easy – one.

I aim, then, to bring out the variety of human relations. I hope that this procedure will also throw some light on the more general issue of how theoretical ideas come to diversify and change in social investigation.

The disadvantage of this emphasis is that it will not leave much space to discuss human relations as a practical movement amongst managers, or as a managerial ideology. Luckily, though, both of these themes have been treated fully by others.[1]

Despite its internal diversity human relations did possess strong unifying features as an approach to industrial behaviour. According to its spokesmen, whose word has been accepted somewhat uncritically, its originality lay in its sociological conception of industrial events. In fact, for many years 'human relations' and 'industrial sociology' were virtually interchangeable terms.

This sociological approach manifested itself at two main levels, though differently at each one. The first is usually that of a work group in an organization. Here, behaviour (particularly productivity or co-operativeness with management) is thought to be shaped and constrained by the worker's role and status in a group. Other informal sets of relationships spring up within the formal organization as a whole, modifying or overriding the official social structure

---

Ithaca, N.Y., 1958; C. Kerr and L. Fisher, 'Plant Sociology: The Élite and the Aborigines', in M. Komarovsky, ed., *Common Frontiers of the Social Sciences*, Free Press, Glencoe, Ill., 1957; W. H. Whyte, *The Organization Man*, Penguin Books, Harmondsworth, 1960, ch. 3–5. More specialized criticisms will be noted below.

of the factory, which is based upon purely technical criteria such as the division of labour.

The second level is society as a whole. Sometimes explicitly, but more usually as a set of ritual assumptions, industrialized society is viewed as a shaky fabric. Its scale, diversity and constant change is thought to frustrate a basic human desire for intimacy, consistency and predictability in social living. Lacking this wider social certainty, workers purportedly seek to manufacture it at the workplace by means of informal organization.

The foregoing is necessarily oversimplified but it should indicate that the sociological credentials of human relations are questionable. The study of informal organization advocated might better be termed anthropological – or even ethnographic – since it promotes a view of factories as unique societies in miniature. A genuinely sociological approach would not ignore a factory's group-life (supposing it has one) but would seek from it generalizations about industrial relationships as a whole, relating it to the wider social attachments and experiences of the different categories of personnel.

This naturally requires the conscious adoption of some empirically justified image or model of the social formation as a whole. Successful analysis of particular industrial situations cannot proceed without an explicit framework of this kind. Typically, the model employed by human relationists was adopted implicity. Moreover, it was inaccurate and value-laden.

Their image of the worker derives automatically from it. He is compulsively social – obsessed, in W. H. Whyte's terminology, with 'belongingness' and 'togetherness'.[2] And it is presumed that he wishes to belong above all to a work group and experience the 'togetherness' of collaborative work. Nor need he be conscious of these innate impulses, which supposedly underlie all his actions at work and may be channelled for constructive purposes by socially literate managers.

These preliminary remarks about the status of human relations as sociology must be expanded and qualified in due course. But they provide a reference-point for assessing the contributions which will be examined.

Inevitably, this discussion will be critical. It would, however, be wrong to suppose that the human relationists made no important contributions to organized knowledge. No one denies that the face-to-face relationships of the work-place – its micro-politics – are interesting objects of study in themselves or relevant to a full understanding of industrial events. In drawing attention to them the human relationists served a useful function.

Unfortunately, they did more than draw attention to them. They made them the hub of their analysis. Further, by abstracting face-to-face relations on the factory floor from their wider – and objective-social context, they encouraged the misconception that they could be altered ('improved') by purely local intervention.

Mayo and the Western Electric studies. There are two major obstacles to understanding human relations. They are the Western Electric studies (the 'Hawthorne experiment') and Elton Mayo. Critics and enthusiasts of human relations both take the studies as their main empirical source. Mayo is likewise regarded as the prime sociological theorist of human relations.

Distortion results from this emphasis.* The studies are one group among many, some of which were better executed, more interesting and in some ways more influential. Responsibility for their prominence lies largely with Mayo, whose popularizations of them reached a mass audience. (Unfortunately, too, the two definitive reports of the studies are lengthy and sometimes unclear; synopses of them are biased by the mechanics of compression as well as by partisanship.) Again, Mayo's celebrity as a *sociologist* reflects his talent for publicity and is quite unwarranted.

But the prominence (and identification) of the studies and Mayo cannot be ignored. Before assessing fairly the neglected strands in human relations we must try to reduce it. I shall deal with Mayo first. This, however, cannot be done without a brief account of the studies. The synopsis that follows will also be essential in evaluating the work of Roethlisberger and Dickson later, and as background

* Landsberger (op. cit.) was the first to point out the important differences between Mayo's, and Roethlisberger's and Dickson's, treatment of the Hawthorne data. See F. J. Roethlisberger and W. J. Dickson, *Management and the Worker*, Wiley, New York, 1964.

to this whole part. But readers should bear in mind my comments above about condensation and bias: unclear or apparently tendentious statements should be checked against *Management and the Worker*.

From the mid 1920s to the early 1940s the Western Electric Company undertook a complex programme of experiments, investigations and action research into industrial attitudes and behaviour at its Hawthorne Works in an industrial suburb of Chicago. Various outside bodies, the Harvard Business School being one, advised the company on research strategy, the interpretation of results and practical implementations. Western Electric was a large, bureaucratized, technically progressive firm, employing over 40,000 workers at Hawthorne, with a reputation for good company welfare policies.

Four phases are distinguishable in the research. The first lasted from November 1924 to roughly the end of 1928 and utilized an approach comparable to British human factor industrial psychology. This phase overlaps with the second, or clinical phase, which concentrated on interviewing; between late 1928 and mid 1931 a quarter of the Hawthorne work-force were processed. From November 1931 to mid 1932 the researchers adopted an anthropological method. The anthropological phase was terminated by the slump, but in 1936 interviewing was resumed in the form of personnel counselling. This final manipulatory phase continued into the 1940s, and aimed to increase company control over neurotics and trouble-makers by giving them therapeutic depth interviews.

1. *The human factor phase.* This consisted of a series of experiments on the relation between output and illumination; and three investigations of a range of mainly bio-psychological influences on the output of three small assortments of workers. The lighting experiments have been mentioned already.* They showed no conclusive link between the quality of illumination and output, and were too poorly designed to demonstrate anything but the need for careful controls in scientific research. The second series aimed to be more systematic and are described below.

(i) First Relay Assembly Group. This experiment began in April

* See Chapter 9 above.

1927 and was halted by the slump in August 1932; but only the results obtained to June 1929, when thirteen experimental periods had been completed, really interested the researchers or are mentioned by commentators on the studies.[3]

Six women operatives were taken from their normal department and placed in a separate test room. Before segregation their output of relays (switchboard components) had been secretly measured and they continued with this work in the test room. At the first of a regular series of briefing meetings with the research staff they were allowed to comment on the test room arrangements and told to work naturally throughout the experiments. They also received an initial, and periodic, medical check. An observer was located in the test room, with rather unclear duties, but he was supposed to ensure that the girls' attitude to the test remained constant. How he was to gauge constancy, or maintain it, was not clearly specified.

Over the first two years the girls' conditions of work were progressively changed. Early on they were placed on a group-bonus incentive scheme; this was followed by experimental exposures to rest-pauses of varying length and duration, free snacks, shorter hours and a shorter working week. Usually, but not always, old privileges were retained when a new one was added. In the twelfth period all privileges were temporarily removed. In the next, they were restored.

During all but one of these periods the hourly output-rate of the girls rose, even during the deprived twelfth one. By June 1929 it was 30 per cent higher than base. The observer noted increased friendliness amongst the girls. They liked the test room. Their former workmates in the department expressed envy for their conditions and the girls were aware of this. At an early stage two operators (1A and 2A) were replaced for uncooperativeness.

In time, the observer became more friendly with the subjects, assumed more supervisory duties, and shielded the girls from their nominal supervisors. However, from July 1929 onwards, the situation began slowly to deteriorate. The girls expressed less interest in the experiment, new replacements had to be made, and from the summer of 1930 they showed anxiety over their security (the slump was beginning) and output began to fall. The last two years were marked by bitterness and hostility.[4] By August 1932 all had been transferred or laid off except operator 2, who was made a temporary clerk.

(ii) Second Relay Assembly Group. Before the first Relay Assembly Group study had reached half-way, the investigators began to assess its results.* They seem to have been coming to the conclusion that the rise in output was not due entirely either to better materials and methods, lower fatigue, less monotony or the small-group incentive; but they decided to re-test some of these factors on other groups.

To test incentives, five experienced relay assemblers were selected (by a foreman). They remained in the normal department but were paid by the same group bonus incentive method as the first group. They received this for a nine-week period, during which their average individual output rose nearly 13 per cent. Before this experiment, these operatives had shared the envy of the regular department for the first relay group, and they expressed rivalry with it during the test – which was discontinued because their higher earnings spread discord in the department.

(iii) The Mica Splitting Group.† With the Second Relay Assembly Group *no* change in the conditions of work had been made. Only the incentive matched the situation of the first relay group. A second test room was therefore established and another group of five girls exposed to changes in working conditions. But their method of payment was not changed (they were already receiving an individual piece-rate bonus). Five changes in working conditions were made over two years. These were not identical to those of the first relay group, but were all deemed to be increases in privileges. However, at times they were required by management to work overtime; and in September 1930 the experiment was stopped through shortage of work.

Average hourly output in this group rose 15 per cent in the first year and fell again in the second (as business declined), but

* Or so it appears. *Management and the Worker* gives a very incomplete picture of the research process at this stage.

† This experiment actually began three months *before* the Second Relay Group study, but continued for some time after its termination.

individual variations were more marked than in the other groups. The group never cohered properly and the girls were temperamentally and socially very dissimilar.

2. *The clinical phase*. Before the foregoing experiments were concluded – indeed before the second relay group was established – the company began a programme of interviews which became progressively more extensive and sophisticated. Prompted in part by criticisms of management, overheard in the first relay group, it began 'essentially as a plan for improving supervision'.[5]

At first, the interviews were rather formal, relatively structured, and excessively to the point. (A standard inquiry was: 'Is your boss a slave-driver?') Replies were analysed for the nature and strength of the respondent's attitude towards eighty topics (ranging from advancement and payment to dirt, the restaurant and of course supervision). Male workers emerged as more economically oriented than women, who stressed desirable working conditions.

Gradually, however, a more open-ended approach to interviewing emerged. Respondents were allowed to talk about those issues which preoccupied them. It was realized that an individual's replies cohered in a subjectively rational way, that criticism of an object like washrooms might symbolize the company as a whole, and that systematic variations in attitudes related to function and status in the plant.

Finally, an interviewing technique close to therapeutic counselling was devised to explore these 'social sentiments' in depth. It demonstrated a relationship between attitude to work and the subject's wider social attachments and responsibilities, but this link was not thought as important as that between his work situation and attitude.

Some of the last interviews to be conducted were amongst supervisors. These brought out the connections between the fears and tensions felt in this stratum and its marginal position between the workers and 'real' management. They showed the pervasiveness of 'sentiments' amongst non-manual groups, and, as Landsberger has pointed out, that these supervisors were anticipating human relations in their view and handling of workers.[6]

3. *The anthropological phase*. Depth interviewing had shown the complexity of the factors influencing attitudes and behaviour in the work situation. In November 1932 the investigators adopted a new research strategy, based on observation, which they hoped would illuminate the dynamic relations between these factors. Advised by the anthropologist Lloyd Warner, they established an Observation Room to study the on-going social relations of a group of fourteen male workers.

Engaged on wiring, soldering and inspecting banks of telephone switchgear, these men were segregated in the Observation Room and set to work on their normal jobs. An observer sat in the room, as inconspicuously as he could, noting the men's interactions. (Periodically, the subjects were also called away for interview.)

The workers rapidly accustomed themselves to the observer's presence. It was soon discovered that although few of the men properly understood their group incentive payment method all of them held a precise notion of what constituted a fair day's output. Practically all were capable of exceeding this, and on frequent occasions did so. However, they would then report a false output figure close to the norm and work more slowly the next day. Individuals who persistently overproduced were castigated by their fellows as 'rate-busters'; consistent underproducers who falsely reported achievement of the norm were dismissed as 'chisellers'.

Technically, it would have been possible for supervisors to check each individual's daily output report. But this would have been a nuisance; and anyway over the week reported and actual production moved into balance. Moreover, it soon became clear that first-line supervision connived at this and at more sophisticated breaches of company rules which gave the men a measure of control over their work situation and optimized their economic returns and ease of work.

But the men's economic shrewdness, exercised to its limits as the depression worsened, interested the investigators less than the social mechanisms surrounding their restriction of output. Various rough measures of interaction established the existence of two cliques within the group as a whole. Members of one tended to adhere more closely to the output norm and were ascribed high prestige.

Conformity to informal rules in general was carefully policed. Even physical sanctions ('binging') and social isolation (an inspector who 'squealed' to management about some malpractices was ostracized) backed up the more common checks of abuse and ridicule.

Besides his general status each member was found to have what might be called a group identity (often conveyed in a nickname – 'jumbo', 'cyclone' etc.). Certain individuals assumed roles of leader, diplomat or morale-booster. The skills of the latter were in especially high demand as, increasingly towards the end of the seven-month experiment, unemployment loomed.

4. *The manipulatory phase*. In 1936, after the depression (and a spread of unions amongst Western Electric workers), research was restored in the institutionalized form of personnel counselling. Theoretically the counsellor was an uncommitted independent who applied the findings of the Interview Programme that troubled individuals could 'talk off' their obsessions. At the same time he embodied management's need to 'commit itself to the *continuous* process of studying human situations'.[7]

There is considerable reason to believe that any serious research purpose which may have motivated this scheme initially soon evaporated. Counsellors took on a manipulatory and intelligence role which all found socially demanding and the sensitive ethically unacceptable.[8]

In the next chapter Elton Mayo's connection with these studies and their position in his thought as a whole will be examined.

THE THOUGHT
OF
ELTON MAYO

Human relations, as we noted earlier, is persistently equated with the work and thought of Elton Mayo. In its simplest form this misconception goes along the following lines. 'Social man' was discovered by accident during the Western Electric studies at the Hawthorne plant in Chicago some time around 1930; these studies were conducted by Elton Mayo; subsequently the human relations movement was formed under his leadership to propagate and apply the findings; Mayo thus became the mid-century industrial counterpart of Taylor.

This is a grotesque distortion of the facts, but an excellent myth. 'Social man' had actually been discovered – or perhaps, fabricated – by the great nineteenth-century sociologists Pareto and Durkheim. He was rediscovered in modern industry thanks largely to the biochemist Henderson and the anthropologist Lloyd Warner. Admittedly, the evidence was obtained at Hawthorne, but Mayo never conducted these studies. As a movement human relations was diffuse, and Mayo never led it except in a symbolic sense – and largely from the grave. Only the comparison between Mayo and Taylor, in part at least, stands up; but its relevance is uncertain.

Human relations essentially reflect practical problems occurring in the stage of industrialization reached by American industry in the late 1920s, aggravated by the militancy of labour in the 1930s. Equally, it is one aspect of the wider response of the American social scientific élite to the moral shock of the depression and the underlying social conflicts which it dramatized.

Mayo's ability to recognize these emerging social problems, and to popularize attractive explanations and solutions for them, turned him into a kind of human relations superstar. We would probably understand the movement much better if we could simply switch off the limelight. The potency of the myth prevents this, and it is certainly true that some of Mayo's personal experiences and preoccupations shaped human relations theory and practice. But in this chapter I shall try to dim the light and draw preliminary attention to the star's strong supporting cast.

A constant theme in all Mayo's work is the rootlessness of individual existence in industrialized society, ascribed variously to childhood trauma, obsessive reverie, the suppression of a natural human tendency towards spontaneous collaboration, or to anomie. His eventual solution for this was to demand that the work-groups of large organizations should be made the focus of social living, responsibility for this integration being entrusted to an élite of socially skilled managers.

We shall examine this palliative in more detail later. For the present, however, it is worth noticing that Mayo's own early life seems at times to have shown signs of rootlessness. The same goes for his thought. Quite unlike Taylor, he lacked any definite purpose until early middle age, and virtually until his death his practical proposals were subject to modification.

Mayo's youth, culminating in 1919 in a book (*Democracy and Freedom*)[1] which portrayed democratic politics as symptomatic of social ill-health and explained left-wing radicalism in sub-Freudian terms, was certainly not quite what one would expect from an advocate of social conformism.[2]

Mayo was born in 1880 in Adelaide into a large Victorian middle-class family. His school and university progress was of the enigmatic kind which nowadays is often a prelude to departure on the hippie trail. Family tradition, and his businesslike mother, pushed him towards medicine. But, unlike two of his six brothers and sisters, he never stayed a course. After dropping out at Edinburgh, where his worried parents had sent him following poor progress at Adelaide, he actually did drift around in England and West Africa for a number of months.

His unquestionable intellectual energy only found some direction after he returned to Australia in 1905. He met a professor of philosophy who advised him to study psychology. Mayo took to it immediately, and was appointed a lecturer at the University of Queensland soon after qualifying. During the First World War a number of shell-shocked soldiers were referred to him for treatment. He threw himself into his work, and his success earned him a professorship in 1919.

These clinical achievements and his attraction to the ideas of Janet, which tended to represent social conflict as the product of individual maladjustment, are an important pointer to his distinctive contribution to human relations technique, i.e. personnel counselling. *Democracy and Freedom* introduces his lifelong obsession with social harmony, and more than hints at the messianic and apocalyptic tone of his later theoretical writings. But it contains none of their 'sociology'.

Mayo had virtually no knowledge of sociology until 1926 when the biochemist Lawrence J. Henderson introduced him to Pareto's theories. In 1922 he had left Australia for the United States, disenchanted with its excessively vocational university system. Future leaders, he argued, should also be trained in the social sciences.[3] America was more progressive in this respect. Almost immediately after arrival he was offered a research post at the Wharton Business School of the University of Pennsylvania, thanks to a public lecture in Philadelphia which impressed one of its administrators.

This led directly to his work in a local textile-mill, which was discussed in an earlier chapter. Mayo's contemporary reports of these studies show that he was then unaware of the work being done by the British industrial psychologists. They lean heavily on psychiatry, stressing the individual basis of industrial conflict ('pessimistic reveries' about childhood and other traumas). A few informal sociological remarks do creep in, but these almost directly *contradict* the later sociological assumptions of human relations.[4]

At the time, this application of psychiatric perspectives to industrial problems must have seemed strikingly original. Moreover, the research had benefited the company handsomely. When the Graduate School of Business at Harvard University decided to establish an industrial research programme in 1926 its dean, Wallace Donham, recruited Mayo, who immediately struck up a lasting friendship with Henderson.

Henderson, who had a solid reputation for his biochemical studies of the blood, was to examine the physiological aspects of work through a Fatigue Laboratory which was set up within the new Department of Industrial Research. He probably drew Mayo's attention to the British human factor studies, and he certainly introduced him to classical sociology and current social anthropology.

Periodically, the social sciences are deeply influenced by scholars trained in a hard discipline. As a biologist Henderson was struck by the organic analogy – the superficial parallels between society and a living organism. In social thought this has recurred since Plato, but it had been applied with originality by Durkheim at the turn of the century as a method of distinguishing between the moral frameworks of industrialized and preliterate societies. The British anthropologists Malinowski and Radcliffe-Brown were currently developing Durkheim's ideas to fashion a systematic functionalist theory of society.

Functionalism tells us that a society is structured as a system of institutions and social roles. Each of these 'organs' has a distinctive function which contributes in its own way to the maintenance of the system, as do the brain, heart, lungs, limbs, etc. in biological adaptation and survival. Clearly, though, the analogy is faulty. It suggests, in particular, that it is as dangerous to tamper with a social institution as it is with (say) the human brain. This has led some anthropologists to defend head-hunting amongst primitives simply because its abolition changes the society. Its conservative value-content likewise biases the analysis of modern societies.

By throwing his biochemical prestige behind the organic analogy Henderson was to encourage functionalist theory in general sociology (pre-eminently through Talcott Parsons, another of his Harvard intimates). Its suggestion that conflict is a necessary sign of social pathology supported conclusions Mayo had already reached by another route.

Henderson's overriding passion, however, was for the theories of Vifredo Pareto (himself a nineteenth-century engineer turned social theorist).[5] Pareto's ideas are complex, but what most impressed Mayo was his notion of non-logical action. This allegedly predominates in social life and springs from 'sentiments' (a largely unconscious predisposition or state of mind). People impelled to act in a certain way by a 'sentiment' can only offer a *rationalization* for their behaviour, not a genuine scientific explanation or theory. Pareto also believed élite rule was inevitable. This part of his thought is rather elaborate, but Mayo concluded that pervasive 'sentiments' disqualify the majority from rule because they function mainly to sustain stability in face-to-face relations.

It took Mayo several years to absorb these new influences. This is apparent in a report of the department's first assignment. Mayo's account of it is brief and anecdotal. Work in a factory in a small Mid-Western town had been disrupted by ethnic tensions. The company solved the problem by ousting the trade union (which represented only the native Americans and had links with the Ku-Klux-Klan) and substituting a company union. According to Mayo this simultaneously reduced the racism of the workers and their former obsession with pay-levels.[6]

Paradoxically, Mayo's description of these events is probably his most sociologically sensitive account of any concrete industrial situation. His recognition of specific links between the developing in-plant situation and the social structure of the community is especially striking.

But this theoretical commentary is appallingly confused. The practical study of labour relations, he declares, requires the integration of several approaches: 'These approaches must be physiological and biochemical . . . psychological and social.' He demonstrates this with a blockbusting series of references to Henderson's physiological discoveries, the work of the Myersians, Mayo's old psychiatric mentors, the functionalist anthropologists and Durkheim.

If his capacity to relate these contributions coherently was less than impressive, his readiness to preach was otherwise. Passages attacking class-consciousness as a psychopathological obsession which lowers production are heavily italicized. Industrial managers have a duty to themselves and society at large by redesigning work to prevent the 'reverie' which causes it, etc.[7]

When Mayo wrote his first book dealing with the Hawthorne studies (*The Human Problems of an Industrial Civilization*) his ability to amalgamate plausibly the ideas that aroused him had developed.

Two points should be stressed again here. First, Mayo did not conduct the Hawthorne studies. Second, we shall never know exactly what happened at Western Electric. The books which give the most factual detail (Roethlisberger's and Dickson's *Management and the Worker*, and Whitehead's *The Industrial Worker*) appeared long after the main experiments finished.* Meanwhile, *Human Problems* had appeared. It may be that Mayo's treatment of the studies, which made them and him celebrated, completed a process of cross-fertilization inhospitable to exhaustive and accurate reportage.

The studies themselves were from the beginning a company-based operation controlled by G. A. Pennock, a Western Electric engineer interested in personnel work. Aided by W. J. Dickson (another company man) he established a Division of Industrial Research in February 1929. The Business School provided it with advice from 1927, when Pennock approached Mayo about the puzzling illumination experiments – *after* the first relay assembly experiment had started.† There is no evidence that even Roethlisberger or Whitehead, let alone Mayo, did any leg-work in the factory.

With Donham and Henderson, Mayo certainly liaised with Western Electric's highest managers (C. G. Stoll and W. F. Hosford)

* Approximately seven and six years respectively. Such delays are sometimes inevitable because of the mass of data to be handled or desirable to protect the anonymity of informants. If so, the authors should recognize the dangers of writing in the 'anthropological present tense', i.e. as if conditions observed several years previously still pertain.

† Significantly too, Mayo's help is not acknowledged in *Management and the Worker* until the Interview Programme is discussed.

– in the company's offices in New York, not in Chicago.* Doubtless he showed interest in the progress of work and suggested new lines of inquiry. But it was the anthropologist W. L. Warner who influenced the design of the bank-wiring room experiment.[8] Even in the Interview Programme the degree to which Mayo was involved is uncertain.

As noted already, the researchers eventually adopted non-directive depth interviewing techniques reminiscent of those favoured by the psychopathologists Mayo had admired for fifteen years. But this substitution was made only after the extraordinarily crude directive methods had failed. One can scarcely believe that Mayo would have sanctioned these primitive techniques if he had been fully consulted before the programme began.

At no time in his life did Mayo show either the patience or scepticism which social research demands. He was a natural propagandist and at this time he was especially busy. In 1930, for example, he produced six publications, including one of the first brief accounts of the early work at Hawthorne. (It appeared, interestingly enough, in *The Human Factor*.[9]) His real role in the Western Electric research is clear: he was its self-appointed publicity officer.

His *Human Problems* (1932) confirmed this position. By any standards this book is unscientific, though clearly Mayo believed its policy recommendations were scientifically grounded. But his choice of evidence was thoroughly selective.

Its least tendentious section is a review of the human factor approach, where he concludes, quite correctly, that biological influences on work behaviour are important only in extreme situations. His treatment of the Hawthorne material, however, is thoroughly uncritical. (I shall give only a few instances of this credulousness in what follows.)

The output improvement of the first relay assembly group is attributed not to financial incentives but to a complete reconstruction of the group's industrial situation, by which Mayo means that its supervision became more friendly and understanding. This ignores the facts that: (i) members were deliberately selected for

* Later, overall company responsibility passed to M. L. Putnam.

their co-operativeness; (ii) two uncooperative members were soon replaced;[10] (iii) one of their replacements urged her associates to make high bonuses because she had unusual family responsibilities;[11] and (iv) the second relay assembly group responded to financial incentives.[12]

This 'conclusion' produced the Interview Programme, which aimed to improve supervision. A crucial finding was that while 'statements critical of material conditions were fairly reliable ... statements critical of persons were not'.[13] Mayo is reluctant to believe that many supervisors can be harsh or dictatorial in 'an industry of the highest standing'. Worker reports to the contrary betray 'obsession'.

Roethlisberger and Dickson were later to provide evidence, however, that many Hawthorne supervisors were autocratic.[14] Moreover, Mayo himself cites only two cases of workers who were obsessively 'overthinking' their situation (and one possible victim of a 'clash of cultures') amongst the first several hundred workers interviewed.[15] None the less, he is convinced that these findings are firm evidence of a wider societal breakdown.

Citing the work of the Chicago ecological school of sociologists, he argues that the Hawthorne factory is situated in a particularly anomic community, and contrasts it with the traditionalism and stability of 'Yankee City' (Newburyport). His Harvard colleague Warner's investigations of this small industrial town in New England certainly seemed at that time to support Mayo's view of the link between community and industrial harmony. A year later, however, this tranquillity was shattered by a massive strike.*

Mayo could not have foreseen this, but it underlines the bias of his distinction between irrational and non-logical behaviour. The former supposedly derives from social maladjustment and manifests itself in, for example, the Hawthorne workers' criticism of supervisors; the latter characterizes the apparently unselfconscious co-operativeness and personal contentment attributed to work-groups like those in 'Yankee City'.

Unlike Pareto, then, Mayo uses non-logical behaviour as an evaluative concept. Once an individual begins to reflect on his social

* See Chapter 13 below.

relationships he courts personal unhappiness and threatens 'human collaboration in work, which, in primitive and developed societies, has always depended for its perpetuation upon the evolution of a non-logical social code . . .'[16]

Because he (quite inappropriately) equates such reflectiveness with individualism and economic acquisitiveness, Mayo feels able to relate social disintegration to the *ideas* of liberal pluralism – not, it should be stressed, to the capitalist relations of production which underlie these ideas. Mayo was quite insensitive to any such linkage. Consequently, the political observations of *Human Problems* degenerate into radically right-wing ideology: in effect, a plea for corporate Fascism, albeit with a human face.

According to Mayo, liberalism has fostered anomie by stressing individualism; and liberal political institutions cannot cope with the resulting social disorder and industrial strife. Indeed, they only aggravate it. Salvation lies in discovering a socially skilled administrative élite who will treat the problem at source, i.e. by nurturing vital non-logical impulses amongst industrial work-groups.

In these passages Mayo gyrates between slick superficiality ('the problem is not that of the sickness of an acquisitive society; it is the acquisitiveness of a sick society')[17] and grotesque naïveté: Socialism, Communism and Marxism 'seem to be irrelevant to the industrial events of the twentieth century', except that they 'probably express the workers' desire to recapture something of the lost human solidarity'.[18]

At times his absurdity verges on unconscious comic genius, as when he quotes from one Brooks Adams to seal his case for a new caste of industrial manipulators: 'I take it to be an axiom,' Adams assures us, 'that perfection of administration must be commensurate to the bulk and the momentum of the mass to be administered, otherwise the centrifugal will overcome the centripetal force, and the mass will disintegrate. In other words, civilization would dissolve.'[19]

His disregard for economics is astonishing. Militant British trade unionism is portrayed as an attempt to perpetuate stable social relations. Could Mayo have been totally unaware of the British unemployment rate between the wars?

The British case also allows him to drive home his rather

simplified version of Pareto's theory of the circulation of élites. British management's failure to recognize that its workers strike not for pay or work but social incorporation proves its obsolescence. But he believes all countries (including the U.S.S.R., which of recent years has shown much enthusiasm for Mayo's thought) need the new Guardians of social health: 'Better methods for the discovery of an administrative élite, better methods for maintaining working morale. The country that first solves these problems will infallibly outstrip the others in the race for stability, security and development.'[20]

It can be argued that the countries which were to apply a logic of non-logic and élitism most sweepingly were the Fascist powers who precipitated the Second World War, towards the end of which Mayo wrote his *Social Problems of an Industrial Civilization.*[21] Mayo believed, however, that the war overwhelmingly proved his case.

'*If our social skills had advanced step by step with our technical skills, there would not have been another European war :* this is my recurrent theme,' he pleads.[22] At least *Social Problems* is more specific about the nature of these skills. The crucial arts are leadership and counselling. In the 1920s Mayo had reserved clinical interviewing for experts and hedged on its efficacy.[23] Now he declares, 'This is a very simple skill, but it can have the most astonishing effects in industrial situations.'[24]

Mayo is so impressed with the idea that 'after a few such interviews' uncooperative workers 'return to work with the declaration that they have "talked it off" ', that a report of his old Philadelphia study now emphasizes the role of the nurse as a counselling interviewer and that of the company president as a leader. His chapter on Hawthorne concentrates almost exclusively on the Interview Programme.

Counselling and leadership are indivisible, and both are aspects of communicating. Through skilful communications the manager builds teamwork by expanding the worker's 'desire and capacity to work better with management'. Higher education should be redesigned to develop communications skills, especially therapeutic interviewing, amongst recruits to the élite.[25]

Teamwork had not been mentioned in *Human Problems*; not

even the teamwork of the bank wiring group in maintaining an output norm was discussed. But two studies of labour absenteeism in America in which Mayo was involved during the war convinced him of its potentialities, and *Social Problems* represents their slender and ambiguous findings as proof.[26]

The type of team that most excites him is one which 'comes into being only when someone in authority, or conceived by the workers as representing authority, definitely works to create it'.[27] Detailed study of *one* such group had shown that the supervisor and leading hand devoted the bulk of their time to communications. The size of the sample here is, of course, small; and though Mayo notes that the team leaders protected their followers from the interference of middle managers and time-study men he thinks this vital fact is something 'I need not discuss'.

Scientific caution was never Mayo's strong point and all this 'evidence' is subsidiary to the social philosophy it purportedly establishes. This is more or less a reiteration of what he had written a dozen years previously. The 'rabble hypothesis' of economics and scientific management, which pictures men as lonely self-seekers, must be inverted: money means less to man than the gratification of his non-logical sociality. (Critics dismiss this as a tribal hypothesis.) The managerial élite must fashion an 'adaptive society' based on these premises. To give Mayo his due, this pervasive manipulation is represented as an historic categorical imperative; but he hardly plays down its supposedly tonic effects on productivity.

Mayo died soon after *Social Problems* appeared but his ideas enjoyed a great vogue amongst managers for twenty years after his death.[28] His academic associates within the human relations orbit acknowledged his primacy and all of them shared, and some of them developed, some but not all these ideas. To understand human relations it is vital to separate his work from theirs. Several points to emerge from this sketch of his work and thought may clarify this separation.

To begin with, Mayo was primarily a psychiatrist. His basic concern was with individual neurosis and maladjustment. Once Henderson had introduced him to sociology he picked from it only those theories which seemed most relevant to individual stress and to the social medicine on the grand scale which he believed could relieve 'obsession'.

Next, as a psychiatrist Mayo's impatience to help people made him a very poor scientist. Several examples of his own shaky command of research technique and willingness to accept the poorly researched conclusions of others have been given. They could be multiplied many times. Even his willingness to reinterpret his own work and revise his explanations, an otherwise praiseworthy ability, reflects a growing dogmatism rather than healthy self-criticism.

Again, Mayo's personal charm and gifts as a publicist seem to have protected him from the discipline and criticism which might have made his work more thorough and his pronouncements more cautious. Once *Human Problems* had suggested answers to managers faced with difficult workers, and offered them membership of an élite of paternally benevolent administrators, Mayo's scientific fate was sealed. To adapt Voltaire, Mayo fashioned the manager in his own image and the manager returned the compliment.

Mayoism emerged rapidly as the twentieth century's most seductive managerial ideology. What, after all, could be more appealing than to be told that one's subordinates are non-logical; that their uncooperativeness is a frustrated urge to collaborate; that their demands for cash mask a need for your approval; and that you have a historic destiny as a broker of social harmony?

And the man who had 'proved' this was an unusually sincere 'scientist' with thoroughly sound views on political radicals, trade unions and government intervention in industry. Taylor's promises of greater worker output had not been entirely warranted. Mayo promised this, the worker's devotion, and social prestige. And somehow his proposals for securing them rang true.

No wonder industrial sociology, so closely identified with this sincere but dangerous psychiatrist, experienced a boom in the late 1930s onwards from which it is still recovering. Luckily, however, though compromised by Mayo's jeremiads and often enough ready to countenance manipulation, other human relations theorists possessed greater respect for the complexity of industrial situations and scientific inference. In the next chapter the work of Mayo's colleagues at Harvard University Business School will be examined.

THE
'HARVARD GROUP'

Introduction. In this chapter I shall examine the work of writers whom I regard as representative of what is sometimes called the 'Harvard Group'. In fact, there never was a fully established Harvard Group; and although there were a number of colleagues who could be so described, these writers do not adequately represent it. If we are looking for a complete consistency in method, theory and values then there is perhaps only one serious candidate – Mayo.

But it is true that Harvard in the 1930s did contain a collection of industrial students whose mutual assistance and, in lesser degree, influence, was extensive (Henderson, Mayo, Whitehead, Roethlisberger, Warner, Homans, Chapple and Arensberg, for example).

These individuals were attached either to the Business School or the Department of Anthropology, and contributed mainly to one of two major research projects; the Hawthorne studies (Business School) or the 'Yankee City' studies (Anthropology Department). Although the latter project was not primarily industrial it was to yield a major industrial monograph (*The Social System of the Modern Factory*).[1] Furthermore, most of its personnel were later to form the nucleus of the Chicago, or 'interactionist', branch of human relations. And its leader, Warner, provided expertise for the anthropological phase of Hawthorne.

To simplify matters, the writers I shall deal with are those who contributed to the Hawthorne project. By concentrating on them I hope to show that the 'Harvard Group' was a relatively heterogeneous assemblage, and that some of its members' work deserves revaluation.

Roethlisberger and Dickson. Previously I suggested that Mayo's selective use of the Hawthorne data distorted understanding of the studies. What, then, is their true value? Because they remain an important source of ideas and inspiration this is a live question. But it must be taken jointly with another: what is the value of *Management and the Worker*?

Roethlisberger's and Dickson's monograph was the definitive report of the studies. Earlier, though, we wondered whether it was affected by Mayo's advance publicity. Though we cannot determine exactly how much, there are certainly signs in the book that ideas which supposedly guided the design and interpretation of the research were fully applied to data only some time after their collection. Accounts of the painstaking elimination of unproductive methods and hypotheses, which form so much of the text, therefore have at times a decidedly enigmatic flavour.

Forty years after the studies were undertaken, and over thirty since *Management and the Worker* was published, there is no way of finally establishing the book's completeness and reliability as a record. For assessment purposes the most sensible procedure is to accept it initially as it stands. This certainly permits a useful evaluation of the studies as a research programme. Subsequently, this can be modified by an examination of the book as a document and theoretical essay.

The studies have certainly been overpraised as a 'classic' research programme, but much about them is thoroughly creditable. The sheer doggedness of the investigators, eagerly collecting masses of data over several years, is impressive: the administration of so many thousands of interviews has rarely been matched. Likewise, the willingness to accept advice and attempt novel methods compares well with the rigidity of many investigators.

This relative open-mindedness and caution must at times have annoyed the company's higher management, who obviously never viewed the programme as a purely scientific enterprise. There must have been times when justifying the sheer cost of the growing Pennock–Dickson research 'empire' required diplomacy and conviction. Again, it appears that the investigators developed a sympathy for their subjects different in kind from the rather strict paternalism of the company towards its employees. A capacity for imaginative identification with subjects, albeit limited and variable, is more often than not an asset to sound research.*

True enough, handling of subjects – those of the first relay assembly group in particular – was sometimes patronizing, even heavy-handed. But this reflected inexperience rather than a fixed image of workers as irrational tribesmen who needed firm treatment. No image of the worker, or of the organization, seems to have crystallized until a fairly late stage. One result of this, as Landsberger has stressed, is that data which support a variety of such images were generated and reported.†

However questionable the interpretations finally favoured, the rejection of the radical behaviourism marking the earliest experiments – paralleling the advance of British human factor studies – constituted a breakthrough. Again, whatever the defects of the final images imposed on the data, they do not rely upon a Mayoite contrast between an anomic wider society and blissful social harmony in the plant.

During the central investigations, in fact, human relations skills were considered feeble, even rather pathetic, *ad hoc* measures adopted by hard-pressed supervisors caught, like other categories of employee, between inescapable structural pressures. The manipulative phase itself did not consist of experiments to test leadership skills.

---

* The investigators seem to have been most sympathetic towards junior supervisors, rather less so towards manual workers, and (diplomatically?) evasive about their views on more senior managers.

† This question will be raised again below: such ambiguity is itself something of an ambiguous virtue.

If the team had concluded that such skills *were* potent and legitimate they certainly could have tested them systematically.

Finally – though I would not press this point – the investigators were somewhat unlucky that the depression occurred when it did. Furthermore, they did try to assess its effects on the studies – incompetently by all means: but the drastic effects of the change hopelessly complicated their already daunting problems of analysis.

In all, then, the studies embodied a decidedly diligent, relatively open-minded and generally ethical search for valid knowledge about industrial behaviour and (in the event) the organization as a structured entity. In view of the intra-company control, these achievements are remarkable.

But these properties are ambiguous. Each virtue has a corresponding vice. Open-mindedness as to method and interpretation, for example, can lead to a lack of focus and direction, and there is a danger of accepting poor advice. To resist only partially pressure from a sponsor is to fall short of genuine independence.

In method, the Hawthorne team were too plastic. In research technique they were often slapdash even by the standards of the day. It seems fairest to concentrate criticism of the programme on these grounds. Failures in judgement on the theoretical, practical and ideological dimensions are admittedly related to them. The development of the team's theories did proceed alongside the investigations; but in *Management and the Worker* they are naturally reported in a finalized form. The execution of the investigations, however, involved a series of concrete events less amenable to reflective revision.

A fair review of Hawthorne as a research project is impossible because subsequent refinements in research technology, to which it contributed substantially, are difficult to ignore, nor should they be. None the less, even by standards then pertaining the researchers committed a surprising number of blunders.

The human factor phase adopted the experimental method. This demands the controlled exposure of subjects to experimental stimuli and the careful measurement of any ensuing effects. Achieving satisfactory control and measuring effects with human subjects remains extraordinarily difficult. Several elementary precautions do, however, reduce the likelihood of spurious or inconclusive results.

For example, individual experimental subjects or groups, and a matching control group, should be selected by identical (preferably statistically random) sampling methods from the overall population; if the experiment demands isolation, both groups should be isolated under identical conditions; the experimental stimuli should then be imposed singly on the experimental subjects; and the results of any one exposure should be assessed before introducing a further one.

Such elementary precautions were not observed in the two Relay Assembly and the Mica Splitting experiments. The failure to establish control groups is especially surprising, because controls had been used in the previous illumination studies. The investigators did regard the second relay and the Mica groups as controls. But neither were matched satisfactorily to the first relay group; nor were their exposures (to the small-group incentive and improved conditions respectively, but not to both) managed identically.

Moreover – and this is crucial with social experimentation – all these experiments occurred at different times: in the case of the Mica group the onset of the depression demonstrated the importance of this time factor – or should have done. A logical mind (assuming it did not need to contend with an impatient sponsor) might have foreseen such problems. But, apart from that, they had all been amply discussed and ingeniously handled by the Myersians in Britain.* Were the investigators ignorant of this literature? Was there wilful disregard for it? Did the sponsor refuse to foot the bill? We shall never know what explains this curious failure to exploit Myersian expertise, though I suspect the first possibility.

Alex Carey, in his devastating critique of these experiments, has exposed many further eccentricities of design and concluded that the results equally plausibly suggest the finding that the investigators rejected, i.e. the force of incentives.[2] This prompts a final remark about the celebrated 'Hawthorne Effect'.

Actually, there are at least two 'Hawthorne Effects'. The first is that supposedly discovered accidentally in the lighting experiments, i.e. that the mere knowledge that he is an experimental subject

---

* The work of Myersians is mentioned in *Management and the Worker*, but – significantly – only with regard to problems of *interpretation*.

modifies the subject's behaviour. (The Myersians had also dealt with this in the 1920s.) In designing the first Relay experiment the Hawthorne investigators, contrary to widespread belief, took careful account of it. The observer was in fact placed in the test room to neutralize it by ensuring that the girls' attitude to the experiment remained constant.[3]

Eventually, however, he became a kind of friendly supervisor. When the investigators claimed later that production rose because the experiment transformed the subjects' total industrial situation they had his change of role very much in mind. But this second 'Hawthorne Effect', which was to inspire a generation of managerial theorists about the potency of democratic supervision, also demonstrates a gross lapse in experimental control.

Whitehead's account of the first relay group makes it abundantly plain that, at least initially, the observer's democratic credentials were less than convincing.[4] After the two uncooperative subjects were replaced, one of their substitutes assumed a leadership style more reminiscent of the driving, production-oriented variety than any other. The observer seems to have done little to check this rather different upset of constancy – including the constancy of his role as disciplinarian. If the experiment were not subject to so many other contaminating influences one might even conclude that the real 'Hawthorne Effect' centres round driving leadership.

Before these investigations ceased, interviewing superseded experimentation as the main research method. This apparently accidental change of course was actually to yield the most sociologically interesting (and probably most reliable) data. At the time of the switch this could hardly have been predicted. Logically, the investigators should have refined their experimental techniques. Quite possibly this would have led to valuable results. They had done no more than *flirt* with the experimental method. Later they flirted with anthropological method. At first, they merely flirted with interviewing. Subsequently, however, apparently under Mayo's clinical spell, it became their consuming passion.

Rightly, the semi-clinical depth interviewing techniques finally evolved are still held in high esteem amongst teachers of research methods.[5] This is no place to debate the finer methodological problems of the interview method as a whole.[6] Likewise, any ethical objections to the interviewing in this *clinical* phase seem to me poorly grounded: as Landsberger has noted, the company did use some of the material to improve conditions; and the programme may have benefited employees indirectly through relaxation of some harsher supervisory practices.

What remains bewildering is the saturation coverage of the programme. A substantial minority of employees were polled. Why some sampling scheme was not adopted remains mysterious. Even a crudely structured sample would have maintained acceptable representativeness. (It might also have increased the reliability of data through reducing exhaustion in the interviewers and concentrating the programme in a shorter time-period.)

The anthropological phase grew more naturally from the clinical phase than the latter did from human factor experimentation. The Bank Wiring group study, however, hardly deserves its perplexingly widespread and durable reputation as a model of industrial ethnography. Certainly the investigators exercised ingenuity in its design and execution.[7] Commentators likewise point out that the investigators seem to have realized that rich behavioural data could only be obtained by researching less actively.[8]

But even this commendation would be challenged by many research theorists. Except in very superficial ways the observer was not a participant. Thus, while his descriptions of personnel, practices and relationships is kindly in tone it is also patronizing. If he had truly shared the life of his 'people', or had been capable of a truly sympathetic identification with them, perhaps the bank wiring men would have entered sociological folklore less as a kind of industrial Keystone Cops and more as they objectively were – a group of worried men faced increasingly with the deprivation and stigma of unemployment.*

For the Hawthorne team to have planted a secret participant observer in a shop-floor group would have been ethically outrageous. But even disregarding this moral barrier, operational and

---

* It takes no great psychological perceptiveness to recognize the growing horseplay in the observation room as simple tension release, or even as a propitiatory ritual.

methodological complexities would have undermined such a manoeuvre. There was, in fact, no way in which the company itself could have undertaken research of this kind acceptably. The whole status of the bank-wiring study as actually undertaken is therefore problematic.

It is noteworthy, too, that the strategy of segregating the group in a special area derived from a revived interest in factors affecting output.[9] Data gathering was linked to this aim. The researchers' judgement seems to have been that in-plant factors overwhelmingly determined work attitudes and behaviour (i.e. output behaviour).

Yet interviewing had indicated the potential influence of out-plant social factors on in-plant phenomena. The whole thrust of the bank-wiring study systematically suppressed these discoveries. Examination of the group members' external attachments was thoroughly superficial.

In fact, superficiality and selectivity devalue *all* those data which were collected. The observer kept a daily record of 'significant happenings', which eventually amounted to 400 typed pages. A 'significant happening' was presumably one which, in the observer's judgement, related to social control of production. Can a record which averages just over one page of 'significant' observations per day convey anything like a full account of developing interpersonal relationships? Anyone who has attempted observation of social situations would find the idea ludicrous. (This criticism applies equally to the observation data on the first relay group.)

As a research programme, then, Hawthorne displays a methodological and technical incompetence remarkable even by the standards of the day. All social investigators must adapt standard methods, and improvise on occasion. But there is little evidence that the investigators fully familiarized themselves with contemporary research technology. Even their use of the Harvard Business School's expertise seems to have been either casual or belated. Mayo's advice on interviewing illustrates the latter; Warner's on the bank-wiring study the former.

I can offer no sound explanation for these failures. To be charitable to the investigators, it is worth remembering that the sheer administrative burdens of a major investigation conflict with methodological self-discipline. Again, though Western Electric was a uniquely patient sponsor for those days, one may presume that there were pressures on the investigators, or that they felt some obligation, to earn their keep.* If little direct evidence supports this, experience does.

Maybe an additional explanation lies in the theoretical proclivities of the researchers themselves. Were they, from a quite early date, trying to prove some point: specifically, the weakness of economic influences on workers' behaviour? If *Management and the Worker* is at all reliable as a report of the evolution of the investigators' thought it supports this hypothesis strongly.

Commentators have noted that Roethlisberger and Dickson protest far too much their perplexity over surprise findings and their diligence in checking them. The variability of this scepticism is demonstrated most strikingly in the denial that the first relay group's output-increase could be attributed to its incentive alone, or that the bank-wiring group's restriction of output mainly reflected fear of unemployment. Quite against their own evidence, they single out changed supervision and fear of technical change respectively as the key variables.[10]

An underlying predisposition to devalue (though not to dismiss) monetary and economic influences goes far to explain the form and course of the studies. Subsidiary to this is an inclination to locate the crucial variables within the plant. To recapitulate: though the interview programme amply demonstrated the vital importance of workers' out-plant affiliations it was followed by a study presuming the primacy of the in-plant situation.

However much such biases affected the running of the studies themselves they certainly stamp themselves on *Management and the Worker* as an interpretative essay. Fifteen years ago H. A. Landsberger's *Hawthorne Revisited* provided the first and, as far as I know, the only reasonably balanced assessment of Roethlisberger's and Dickson's work.[11] It is strongly recommended to

---

* Compare Mayo's somewhat fatuous prefatory remarks with the authors' statement that 'Management regarded these experiments primarily as attempts to build up a sound body of knowledge upon which to base executive policy and action'; Roethlisberger and Dickson, op. cit., pp. xiii, 184.

readers who wish to pursue this question in greater depth. Here I shall merely summarize Landsberger's main points, before adding one or two of my own and briefly commenting upon Landsberger's own critique.

The very least to be said for *Management and the Worker*, Landsberger argues, is that its plodding documentation compares well with Mayo's excited tracts. Readers are provided with enough information to challenge its conclusions. It acknowledges some force in economic incentives and conditions. It describes the design of investigations in some detail. 'Hawthorne Effects' are discussed. Supervisors and managers are often portrayed unflatteringly, both in their treatment of workers and of the research team. Little faith is expressed in standard human relations techniques.

Again, the authors eschew any image of workers as entirely irrational or non-logical tribesmen in overalls. 'Sentiments' may govern *some* of their actions (and those of managers too), including the formation of informal groups. But much of their action embodies a subjectively (and even objectively) rational component – their response to incentives and resistance to technical change, for example.

Nor is it true that out-plant affiliations are ignored. Certainly, the effects of union membership on work behaviour are omitted. But during the main investigations Hawthorne was a non-union plant. Actually, Landsberger seems to have overlooked the fact that some interviews suggest that union officials were trying to recruit members in Hawthorne: the company's known anti-union policy could have affected the attitudes to their work of potential (or secret) recruits. But he is correct in claiming the authors express no hostility to unions as such.

Managers and supervisors, too, typically cut a poor figure. The first relay group experiment is reported largely as a tale of escape from arbitrary supervision. The interviewing programme aimed to improve supervision. Interviews with junior supervisors showed that they had been considerably bullied by higher managers. Invariably harassed, frequently petty, and sometimes ineffectual, the Hawthorne managers seem poor candidates for the Mayoite élite.*

---

* In this respect, Roethlisberger and Dickson differ importantly from Whitehead.

Implicitly at least, the book suggests that the structural requirements of efficient production impede the formation of such an élite.

Finally, Roethlisberger and Dickson have very little to say about the effects of some supposed anomie in the wider society on the deportment of workers. Stressful familial situations are often referred to in discussing the attitudes and behaviour of individual workers, particularly when these impose heavy financial responsibilities or check the 'Americanizing' influence of plant experiences on social activities. But Hawthorne is not conceived, or proposed, as an actual or potential community for uprooted obsessives.

Against this some very serious faults must be recognized. (Curiously, Landsberger does not include the eclectic methodology and blundering research technique.) One of the gravest faults is a highly selective conception of industrial conflict and its sources. While several varieties of intra-plant conflict are examined, their causes are located within the organization. Output restriction supposedly stems from resistance to technological change, not from any wider hostility to management, from the experience of being managed or – here they are least perceptive – from economic self-protection.

Because the book was published in the late 1930s, after the slump and substantial unionization of Hawthorne workers, Landsberger rightly stresses that the authors 'committed a well-nigh incredible sin of omission' in failing to notice that the conditions they had observed a decade before might have some bearing on this surfacing of open conflict.[12]

In their later theoretical chapters the authors also introduce a concept (the human organization of the plant) which apparently embodies 'the collective purpose of the whole organization'. Thus while the social system of the factory is not naturally harmonious, its human organization is – or presumably, should be.[13] Further, the collaboration of the first relay group is regarded as of a higher order than that of the bank-wiring group. (Because the former did not split into cliques; or because it was more *manageable*?)

Moreover, in the two final chapters which briefly outline the 'counselling programme', the authors endorse managerial manipulation. Landsberger emphasizes that these 'how-to-do-it' chapters are vague and contradictory. The first relay group's co-operativeness allegedly arose from a distinct battery of supervisory practices. Yet co-operativeness was a chief criterion of selection into it, two operators were dismissed for uncooperativeness, and a replacement, as we noted earlier, became an informal production-centred supervisor.

Finally, the authors do not mention that the Hawthorne counsellors were expected to adopt an active role. Subsequently the Wilenskys were able to report from first-hand experience that a counsellor did not need to be contacted by a troubled worker before adjustment services were applied.[14]

Unfortunately, Landsberger also makes several extravagant claims for the studies and the book which require comment. He suggests, for example, that the studies were impeded by the 'radically behaviourist direction' of industrial research when they began.[15] He is presumably referring to the British human factor work. Yet by 1927 the Myersians were modifying their approach. Despite the frequent reference to the work of the Myersians in *Management and the Worker* there is no sign that the studies benefited at the design stage from the British work.

He claims also that delayed publication promoted misunderstanding of the book. It was misinterpreted even by human relations enthusiasts. If they had examined it more carefully they would have modified their theories and practical proposals. There is something in this. But if the authors themselves believed their colleagues were making such misinterpretations why did they not disabuse them? They had ample opportunity for doing so, both informally and in print.

Landsberger's re-assessment dissolves into an apologetic based on the 'Biblical authority' techniques. Two examples of this are worth citing.

Management and the Worker presents a very sensitive picture of the forces which today draw classes together and pull them apart. Differences in levels of income; the worker's economic status and security; his subordination in a large impersonal organization; differences in past background and present interests; new barriers to social mobility in the form of educational requirements for promotion – they all tend to produce a clearer differentiation between workers and management, and they are all described in greater or lesser extent in *Management and the Worker*.[16]

This is quite true. But it is one thing to touch on such matters, or even to describe them at length, and quite another to locate them in an adequate theoretical scheme. In fact they are located in an interpretative framework which tends (at times quite arbitrarily) to reverse their significance. The book is, after all, more than a piece of reportage. Landsberger's faith in the critical powers of some readers is excessive, as this second extract also demonstrates. 'Whatever the author's personal deficiency in interpretation, however, the mere presentation of data which allows others to judge the contribution of any discipline or variable, illustrates the merits of the comprehensive approach.'[17]

This presumes that sufficient data *are* presented in the book to permit such reappraisals, and that none of any significance were 'washed out' by the authors' theoretical and value preferences.* I find this difficult to believe. Again, data which may *permit* plausible or more accurate interpretations are not the same as data which *encourage* them. In fact the data as a whole do precisely what they were meant to do, i.e. encourage acceptance of Roethlisberger's and Dickson's deficient interpretations.

What are these deficiencies? Particular lapses have been repeatedly noted. Here I shall concentrate upon the authors' overall view of their material, presented mainly in their chapter 24 ('The Industrial Organization as a Social System').

It is widely held that they offer here a Mayoite image of the firm, relying upon a contrast between on the one hand a formal organization structured by rational managers in line with the logics of cost and efficiency and, on the other, an informal organization erected by workers to procure the social certainty their non-logical 'sentiments' demand. All these terms certainly occur, and the only scholarly references are to Henderson's book on Pareto. But this is a crude reading.

---

* Or by other constraints. The investigators themselves habitually admit gaps in their data and then proceed as if they did not exist. See Roethlisberger and Dickson, ibid., p. 538, for example.

My own is as follows. The organization is a social system performing two functions, the production of goods and the supply of individual satisfactions. This social system possesses two chief aspects, which interact: the technical organization and the human organization. The former consists of 'all those physical items related to the task of technical production', i.e. technology in its hardware sense. The latter *includes* what might be called technology as software, i.e. the division of labour into work-roles. But it also comprises a social organization, which, when analysed, itself splits into formal organization and informal organization (this might be termed 'liveware').

The formal aspect of the social organization is constituted by hierarchical and functional categories of personnel (the authors distinguish between managers, technologists, supervisors, office workers and manual workers). It operates to secure both economic objectives and *formal* co-operation between personnel. By itself, however, it does not necessarily secure sufficient co-operation. Informal organization arises more or less spontaneously to satisfy individual social needs. In so doing, it may supplement formal organization beneficially (from the point of view of output especially): this occurred in the first relay group. Or it may conflict with formal organization, to the detriment of both the informal group and the organization: this occurred with the bank-wiring group.

Clearly the authors regard informal organization as inevitable, but not necessarily dysfunctional – indeed, potentially the reverse. Further, all company personnel are involved in it to some extent. Likewise, all personnel are motivated by the logics of cost (values for judging organizational profitability), of efficiency (values about organized co-operation) and of 'sentiments' (values about gratifying face-to-face relationships).

However, managers and workers espouse these logics in varying degrees. This results from varying familial and professional socialization and from experiences at work. The balance between the forcefulness of the logics can vary in any individual or group. Rapid technical change in particular may increase the force of sentiments, thus reinforcing dysfunctional informal structures. The equilibrium necessary for organizational effectiveness demands managerial intervention, because 'the limits of human collaboration are determined far more by the informal than by the formal organization of the plant'.[18]

Evidently, a Mayoite manager could read into this a Mayoite message. But, as already noted, the implied trust in human relations conflicts with the authors' other statements; and in fact it appears almost as an afterthought – is this a shred of comfort to the sponsor? Such an interpretation is by no means preposterous if one takes this chapter, which is often unclear, as a whole. In my view a thoroughly plausible interpretation of this passage would characterize it less as an essay in human relations theory than as an advance contribution to the technological implications approach. Consider this statement:

> The two aspects into which an industrial plant can be roughly divided – the technical organization and the human organization – are interrelated and interdependent. The human organization is constantly moulding and re-creating the technical organization either to achieve more effectively the common economic purpose or to secure more satisfaction for its members. Likewise, changes in the technical organization require an adaptation on the part of the human organization.[19]

Without anticipating the fuller examination of the technological implications approach in the next part of this book, several properties of it may be noted now. One, the organization tends to be viewed as a system embodying a reified common purpose. Two, a technology (both as equipment and as a set of work-roles – hardware and software) realizes this common purpose. Three, technology is thought to mould worker behaviour and relationships (liveware).

All of these assumptions underlie the quoted passage. Roethlisberger's and Dickson's theory, then, possesses the chief virtues and vices of the later approach. In its favour is a recognition that the technical apparatus severely limits human-relations manipulation of liveware (informal organization). Against this, it underplays the influence of out-plant factors, and is strongly behaviourist.

Nothing could be more ironic than that Roethlisberger and Dickson, the chief empirical authorities of the human relations movement, apparently ascribed to the structural properties of the organization a non-human power to determine human action. The behaviourism of the human factor school, whose perspectives they supposedly rejected, was unconsciously resurrected in a new guise.

T. N. Whitehead. Establishing the distinction between Mayo and his main Harvard associates will be furthered by brief reference to Whitehead. Here the division is most tenuous. Whitehead might be termed 'Mayo's Mayo'.

He is known as the author of a strongly worded tract (*Leadership in a Free Society*) published in the mid-1930s and similar in tone to Mayo's *Problems* books.[20] It is full of breast-beating over social breakdown and, in effect, invites industrial managers to step in to restore order. But his real claim for attention rests on his *The Industrial Worker: A Statistical Study of Human Relations in a Group of Manual Workers.*[21]

Whitehead was British with a background in hard science, and had worked for the Admiralty. His father was the celebrated A. N. Whitehead. He was an associate professor at the Harvard Business School when he published *The Industrial Worker* in 1938.

The first thing to notice about this book is its title. For a competent statistician it is a daring one indeed: generalization is to be based on *one* case (the first relay assembly group at Hawthorne). Secondly, it is an analysis of the statistical and observation material (for the whole five years of this experiment) collected by the company researchers: these data were handed over to Whitehead as an independent expert. His main task was to seek out any correlation between output and objective factors – fatigue, health, the weather, etc.

No such correlations of any significance were discovered, whereupon Whitehead proceeded to analyse the group as a small society undergoing continuous change. One volume of the study presents the tabulated statistics as a whole and, as such, is a *tour de force*. The sociological volume is less impressive. For these reasons the book made much less impact than *Management and the Worker.**

Of course, it covers only a fraction of the studies, but Whitehead's treatment of the relay group attempts to replicate Roethlis-

* A further possible reason is that it is long, opinionated and boring even for specialists.

berger's and Dickson's approach to the bank-wiring group, i.e. to examine its developing social relations. Its two main virtues are its revelation, sometimes unconscious, of facts about the first relay group which Roethlisberger and Dickson play down or omit, and its highly confused recognition of the changing or 'processual' element in social life.

These virtues are often combined. The example I shall mention here is Whitehead's examination of the leadership role assumed by operator 2 (who replaced the uncooperative operator 2A) when she joined the group in January 1928. As he notes, 'from now on the history of the Test Room revolves around the personality of Operator 2'.[22] A typical illustration of her leadership style is her reaction to a poor set of output figures: 'Oh! What's the matter with those other girls? I'll kill them.'[23]

Whitehead also reveals plainly that supervision in the main department was dictatorial, that the group were – in effect – deceived when the investigators told them to work normally, and that the depression seriously undermined morale – amongst much other intriguing information. (For instance, when the original group was disbanded in 1932 they were briefly replaced by a team of substitutes. This was thought to be broadly sound from the methodological point of view!)

But his image of the group as a 'small society' whose members' behaviour was governed by radically Paretian 'sentiments' reaches a pitch of absurdity unequalled even by Mayo. 'Obviously,' he assures us of Operator 2, 'the instinct for combination was strong compared with the persistence of her aggregates.'[24] The anomie of Chicago is heavily stressed. Hawthorne, with its immense workforce and national connections, is a stabilizing social focus. (Compare Roethlisberger's observations about 'large, impersonal organizations.') And Hawthorne managers *already* constitute the Mayoite élite, for its executives 'acquire an attitude towards their work which is most easily compared with that of civil servants in a few European countries'.[25] (From a former Admiralty bureaucrat this was no mean compliment.)

There is no point in expanding upon Whitehead's misinterpretation of the situation or his flagrantly pro-management biases. What should be clear enough is his poor showing besides Roethlisberger and Dickson as an analyst. *The Industrial Worker* is nowadays of little more than antiquarian interest as a theoretical essay. As an illustration of élitist propaganda masquerading as science, however, it is a document of the utmost value. That said, I am happy to leave it to specialists and move on to something of far greater importance.

W. L. Warner. It is tempting to promote Lloyd Warner as a sort of tragic hero of human relations. *The Social System of the Modern Factory* which he co-authored with J. O. Low, for my money is the most intelligent and sensitive monograph the school produced.[26] Its sociological observations are often dazzling; but, better still, they are linked to historical and economic analysis of considerable insight. Regrettably – infuriatingly – these achievements are devalued by a persistent, almost wilful bias. But if the book had appeared ten years earlier human relations might have had a much briefer vogue and influence.

Since its field material was collected nearly fifteen years before the book's publication in 1947, the delay in its appearance is striking. Administrative overload and theoretical disagreements with associates probably account partly for this procrastination. (This statement will be explained later.) The main reason, however, revolves around priorities. The book was the fourth volume of the 'Yankee City' series, which reports the mammoth investigation Warner led in Newburyport, Massachusetts, in the early 1930s. Warner was primarily interested in 'Yankee City' as a community, especially in its class, status and ethnic ranking systems. These topics were covered in the first three reports.[27] The industrial report had to wait its turn.

This decision demonstrates more than a methodological choice, for although the community reports emphasize the many lines of cleavage in the town they leave an overall impression of relatively harmonious integration. Yet the focal point of *The Social System of the Modern Factory* is a strike which split the community down the middle in early 1933. The reported data, and indeed, much of the analysis, make it apparent that (to adopt Marxist terminology) the 'uneven development' of the 'Yankee City' workers' class-consciousness was suddenly redressed: the local proletariat was transformed by the trauma of the depression and the strike from a 'class-in-itself' into a 'class-for-itself'.

Even Warner had to recognize that the community had lost something of the harmony that apparently had previously characterized its surface social relations. In fact, his explanation of the strike relies partly on emphasizing that, beforehand, these relations had been becoming more brittle. Essentially, he finally claims, the strike reflected community breakdown; and, in embracing unionism, the workers displayed their quest for community.

This bias, I suggest, is reflected in the timing of the appearance of *The Social System of the Modern Factory*. In the book itself it reappears in a much more arbitrary form: arbitrary because we are repeatedly told that material which not only speaks for itself but is deliberately amplified by the authors *themselves* really means something quite different from what it is obviously saying.[28]

A brief examination of what the book actually says is worth setting beside what the authors intermittently protest it says. The immediate cause of the strike was unemployment in the shoe industry, 'Yankee City's' staple, which came to a peak in late 1932. In March 1933 the previously deferential, unorganizable shoe-workers struck spontaneously against further wage-cuts and redundancies. Solidarity was virtually total, crossing previous ethnic, religious, sex and skill divisions. Within a month the strikers had joined, and become the most active group in, an industrial union; and the employers had capitulated.

This explosive change must be viewed against a backcloth of long-run economic and technological change. Economically, shoe-making had progressed from a local cottage industry to a strand in the fabric of nationwide finance capitalism. Ownership and control of tools and products had gradually fallen from the hands of the immediate producer. Various stages of capitalist organization succeeded one another, until a period when 'full capitalism has been achieved; the manufacturer is now the owner of the tools, the machines, and the industrial plant; he controls the market'.[29] Under 'super-capitalism' the local economy is subject to global forces beyond its workers' control or comprehension.

In parallel, shoe-making was transformed from a skilled handi-craft to a mass-production process. Mechanization and rationaliza-tion slowly replaced a division of labour based on craft specialization and seniority to one of fragmentary, machine-paced job functions uniformly low in status. Opportunities for promotion decreased, and contacts with superiors were rendered increasingly distant and formal, as the scale of operations grew and employers recruited professional managers to plan and oversee production. All these changes were of course made because they increased efficiency and therefore profitability.

The concentration of workers in large units, subordinate to machines, performing broadly similar semi-skilled routine tasks, with broadly similar pay and conditions, with little chance of promotion, subject to the decisions of distant bosses in line with the uncontrollable fluctuations of a mysterious economy, produced an industrial proletariat in which the depression triggered a final awareness of a common situation and common interests.

One need hardly elaborate on this, though Warner's and Low's 'Marxism' is rather less vulgar than this compression suggests. But having provided a perfectly acceptable explanation of events, the authors then proceed to 'explain' it. The class-consciousness and class-action of the workers were certainly affected by objective socio-economic conditions, they agree; but these mask the workers' 'real' concerns, which are to do with their status in the plant and in the community, and with pursuit of the success ethic of the Ameri-can Dream.

The disappearance of a skill hierarchy in shoe-making robbed the worker of the opportunity for achievement in his occupation. He could no longer acquire prestige amongst his workmates, and sank into the anonymity of an undifferentiated mass.[30] Simultaneously, he lost status in the community, whose own coherence and identity was imperilled by the advance of mass society.

In their final chapter the authors foresee catastrophe unless better provision can be made for the individual's search for status (by which they partly mean rank) and community (a necessarily stratified, or ranked, entity).[31] One possibility lies in government promotion of greater social mobility, but they do not place much faith in this. For workers, an alternative – though a highly limited one – lies in trade unions. But the final solution is quite stunning:

Great international capitalistic enterprises, often monopolistic in character, have succeeded in crossing national boundaries and have developed methods of organizing some of the diverse economic units of the world. Opponents of such systems continue to fight what the authors believe to be no more than rearguard battles which only delay advance. Such capitalistic enterprises are the enemies of nationalism, and, as citadels of capitalistic power, they are the foes of labour and of the remnant forces of nineteenth-century liberalism. The cartel, one of the most powerful forms of international capitalism, must be recognized as a new social structure, developed by us in our desperate efforts to reorganize human behaviour to function on an international basis. At the present time such economic institutions may or may not be evil in their effect, but international institutions of some kind are absolutely necessary if the world is to evolve a reliable international order.[32]

Admittedly, these monoliths must be 'complemented by church, associational, and political hierarchies' in the 'new social order'.[33] But in it 'the social principles characteristic of hierarchies will be stressed more than at present, since the peoples who compose it will be more diverse and more difficult to organize, and the need for lines of authority and responsibility will be greater than in any other time in the history of man'.[34]

This outdoes Weber for 'metaphysical pathos' over inevitable bureaucratization; and Mayo himself was rarely so apocalyptic.

To be fair, however, this bizarre peroration, which contradicts so much of the foregoing analysis, is attached too artificially to the main text to take very seriously as a practical proposal, or even as an invitation to make the best of the inevitable. What it highlights is Warner's ambivalence towards his 'Yankee City' material, and, *a fortiori*, to contemporary America.[35]

Of all the 'Harvard Group' he seems to have possessed the most independent and critical mind. This is all the more remarkable in view of his background and training. As a functional anthropologist (he was a graduate pupil of the arch-Durkheimian Radcliffe-Brown) he joined Harvard determined to apply in an industrialized setting the anthropological techniques he had mastered in his study of Australian aborigines (the Murngin).[36] Certainly, his functionalist training caused him to overstate the similarities between the

Murngin and the citizens of Newburyport, especially the importance of kinship ties, social rank and general community attachment and cohesion to the latter.*

He shared, too, the alarm of his rather patrician Ivy League colleagues over the depression and labour unrest of the 1930s. Unlike them, however, he quite clearly perceived that these social problems had a crucial economic dimension which had very much to do with the ownership and control of productive wealth: 95 per cent of the text of *The Social System of the Modern Factory* is evidence enough of that.

Having made the inevitable inference, he rejected it. Nearly all his books deal with the contradictions in American life; but increasingly he portrays them in the safe, 'sociological' way as clashes between abstract social principles or values.[37] It may not quite be tragic, but it is certainly depressing, that he could not – or would not – accept the logic of his economic and historical insights.

The influence of *The Social System of the Modern Factory* was much less than it deserved. It did, after all, appear when human relations were about to come under serious attack. Maybe this critical reaction partly explains its extraordinary undervaluation. Warner was, too, an ex-Harvard man who had given advice on the Bank Wiring study at Hawthorne. In 1947 he was chairman of the Chicago University Committee on Human Relations in Industry. (The 'interactionist' branch of the movement he headed there is dealt with in the next chapter.) With a background like that critics scarcely needed to read the book before passing judgement.

Because I believe it deserves better recognition I have devoted more space to it than I shall to others that were more influential at the time. I also hope it has helped to establish the heterogeneity of the 'Harvard Group' (and 'group' is hardly the correct term), which was by no means composed entirely of rank ideologists and scientific incompetents. All showed these faults to some degree – and which social scientist does not? A limited and selective rehabilitation is now due and possible.

---

* At other times his comparisons are brilliant if extravagant, for example his parallel between Memorial Day and the Murngin Cult of the Dead.

THE
CHICAGO
SCHOOL

Introduction. By the mid 1930s, latent differences between the Business School coterie and the Anthropology Department at Harvard were coming into the open. These tensions partly account for the later migration of Warner and a large proportion of his research staff to Chicago. In spite of his personal charm, some of the 'Yankee City' workers were beginning to find Mayo's influence irksome. There was no serious complaint against his values. The source of disagreement was methodological.

We saw earlier that Mayo's clinical approach was grounded in psychiatry. This emphasis is anti-sociological since it focuses attention on persons as individuals rather than as social actors. Mayo's selections from sociological 'grand theory', too, were guided by this underlying methodological individualism. The resulting disinterest in social relationships and social processes worried the anthropologists. There was a further consideration. The Hawthorne research had moved from the hard human factor approach to the soft anthropological phase. It appeared that each had produced valuable results. What if the two methods could be combined to get the best of both worlds, a kind of 'anthropology with numbers'?

This renewed interest in measurement was stimulated by the

methodological doctrines of a Harvard physicist, P. Bridgman.[1] Central to Bridgman's thought was 'operationalism'. To simplify, operationalism insists that no branch of empirical study qualifies as true science unless its concepts translate into corresponding 'operations'. These operations consist of concrete, replicable measuring procedures. If this translation is impossible, the concept is vacuous. Conversely, if *some* measurement operations are feasible these *define* the concept. Consequently, a sociological concept like 'integration' possesses meaning only in so far as we can specify objective and measurable indicators of it. Subjective, unquantifiable impressions of the level of social integration in a group – including those of the group's members – are inadmissible.

The question whether in the social sciences operationalism is operable (or desirable in so far as it is) will be taken up later. Two members of the 'Yankee City' team in particular, Conrad Arensberg and Eliot Chapple, were convinced it was.

George Homans, who was appointed a junior fellow at Harvard in the same year (1934) as Arensberg, portrays him as a keen theoretician and lively debater who passed up few opportunities to share his ideas.[2] Warner had entrusted him with devising a general theory to explain the 'Yankee City' material, and Arensberg invented what came to be known as 'interactionism'. The 'Yankee City' series certainly shows its imprint; but it is most marked in the industrial studies undertaken after the group had arrived in Chicago. In the meantime Arensberg had conducted an anthropological study in rural Ireland.[3] Whether his absence impeded or expedited the write-up of the 'Yankee City' material I do not know.

Applied Anthropology. Arensberg issued the first systematic specification for his brand of interactionism in association with Eliot Chapple (Arensberg's Arensberg; he resisted his mentor's later modifications) in 1940.[4] Group life, they argued, is created by contacts, or interactions, between organisms ('including men'). Group life is amenable to rigorous scientific study because: (i) the participants are readily identifiable; (ii) the frequencies of different contacts can be computed; (iii) the sequence of interactions, and of the acts composing them, is evident (because time is unilinear).

Furthermore, the observer who adopts the technique is liberated from personal or scientific preconceptions about the forms of social life. The observations, which restrict themselves severely to the behaviour of the persons observed, will automatically detect any regularities in conduct which are 'really there'.

This may or may not be 'the method of natural science and the discovery of natural law',[5] but it is certainly operationalist. By implication, any subjective feelings or meanings a person associates with his interactions can only be treated as *dependent* variables. Consequently, as Homans remarked of the method: 'To put the matter crudely, whether a man liked another or not depended on the timing of the interactions between them, but the interaction did not depend on the liking.'[6]

The practical inferences are evident. To put the matter even more crudely – and why not, as we are dealing with preposterous assumptions – if a foreman wanted to become liked by a worker he had merely to adjust the timing of his encounters with him. Arensberg and Chapple, in fact, believed they had discovered the key to reliable social engineering, and its potential sales appeal did not escape them.

Soon they had founded a Society for Applied Anthropology, Inc., which published the first issue of its house magazine *Applied Anthropology* in late 1941. Chapple, as editor, could hardly have been franker about its objectives. It was to be 'devoted to the solution of practical problems of human relations', particularly 'how to increase our human adjustment and at the same time . . . increase our technological efficiency'; and it addressed itself to 'those concerned with putting plans into operation, administrators'.[7]

Administrators were left in no doubt that members of the Society for Applied Anthropology, Inc., claimed to be able to supply manipulatory expertise. Many early editorials read like material from a job–placement bureau. It is a sweeping understatement to say that the applied anthropologists had confidence in their product. One writer goes so far as to claim they could have averted the unrest of the depression period. Strikes and 'political unpopularity' were simply problems which could be solved in precisely the same way as any other engineering problem.[8]

But this aggressive self-confidence was relatively short-lived. From an early date a tension became obvious between the editorial sales-patter and the articles actually published in the periodical. Descriptions of changed eating habits on Pacific islands and similar esoterica outnumbered industrial reports in the first five years. Moreover, the latter show that strict operationalism was soon discarded in the field. Chapple and Arensberg were forced to climb down.

In the later 1940s a distinct shift in the approach to industrial situations occurred. As early as 1946 one article conceded that 'while the development of a code of restriction of output is in one sense an attempt at protection for the group, at the same time it expresses a feeling that workers are different from management – that their motivations are quite apart from those of management-oriented employees'.[9] The whole approach and tone of a celebrated piece ('The Industrial Rate-Buster', by M. Dalton) published in 1948 is poles apart from the original philosophy.[10] A year later the journal in fact changed its name to *Human Organization*.

The retreat was moral no less than methodological. The Mayoites justified managerial manipulation as a social mission. The applied anthropologists were more frankly technocratic: manipulation was industrial social engineering to boost industrial efficiency. This stress, aggravated by the hard-selling tone of the journal and Chapple's and Arensberg's combative self-confidence, rapidly brought them into worse odour than the Mayoites themselves.

It is amusing to note that Arensberg contended that this reaction resulted largely from a Mayoite failure of communications. 'We are often asked,' he wrote in assuming editorship of *Applied Anthropology* in 1947, 'and more often scrutinized, for our "values" ... It is possibly our interest in the concrete which is strange or repellent to many persons.' Purposes had been misconstrued merely by the 'historical accident' of the choice of title for the journal. The Society for Applied Anthropology, Inc. recognized that outsiders might mistake its consultants for manipulators. To banish such a risk it was preparing a professional code of ethics.[11]

But the revision of policy which followed was not caused by academic remorse so much as by intellectual defeat. Whatever its

wider methodological failings, radical interactionism proved mech-
anically inoperable. Even under laboratory conditions, with a
team of carefully trained observers, the obstacles to distinguishing
and recording interpersonal acts in full are well nigh insurmountable. The work of Bales is proof enough of that.[12] Distinguishing
the sequence of acts, which Arensberg believed was straightforward,
is actually one of the thorniest problems. To be fair to him, eventually he conceded this; Chapple did so more reluctantly and less
graciously.[13]

Yet the features and effects of 'operationalist' interactionism
were not altogether negative. Because it demanded meticulous
attention to interpersonal activities, and the inclusion of all relevant
interactions, it encouraged investigators to steep themselves in the
ongoing life of industrial plants as a whole. Observations had to
extend beyond 'the' work-group to workers' interactions with
managers, work-study men and union officials. Observation thus
became more inclusive than that undertaken amongst the bank
wiring men.

It could thus lead in two fruitful directions. A sensitive observer
could not long overlook the fact that interactions are influenced by
the ecology of the workplace, for example by the layout of machinery.
Further, he would perceive that their form is affected too by the
organization of tasks, whether productive or managerial. These
properties vary somewhat from one plant to another, since different
products require different manufacturing processes and control
systems. In sum, interactionist method facilitated the transition to
the technological implications approach.

The implicit theory of *Management and the Worker*, as noted
before, also pointed in this direction. But *en route* lay a serious
pitfall which *Management and the Worker*, with its stress on the
uniqueness of the human organization, and interactionism, with its
even stronger emphasis on the ramifications of relations throughout
the plant and their complex, interdependent development, heavily
camouflaged. This trap lay in viewing the plant as a *unique network*
of evolving personal contacts.

This particularizing risk was, paradoxically enough, amplified by
the evident need to rectify one of the glaring methodological

idiocies of operationalist interactionism, i.e. its deliberate neglect of personal feelings and motivations as possible determinants of patterns of association. By reintroducing personal meaning as a crucial analytical reference-point, the student of plant life might take a profoundly anti-sociological course. Like that of contemporary enthusiasts of subjective sociology, his analysis would deteriorate into a series of anecdotes about colourful personalities and their strange deeds.* The work of W. F. Whyte illustrates all these dangers and possibilities, and is the crucial link between this part and the next.

W. F. Whyte. Because I shall discuss only that part of his work which facilitated the transition between the human relations and technological implications approaches my treatment of Whyte will seem unfair to those who know his recent writings.[14] Whatever their defects, they certainly impress me more than those of his former interactionist colleague George Homans with his eccentric conviction that the bases of social life are psychological.[15] Space also demands a selective treatment of Whyte's work in the relevant period.

Whyte is the only major survivor of the human relations years. No doubt this is partly due to his celebrated charm and sincerity. Again, many people only know of him as the author of *Street Corner Society*, a classic community study and sourcebook on participant observer method.[16] It is hard to portray this former inhabitant of 'Cornerville' (and as such, an accessory to electoral malpractice) as any sinister 'servant of power'. But Whyte was undeniably a manipulationist during his Chicago years. If he survived it is partly because his brand of human relations accepted unions as partners in man-management. Even more, it is because he constantly revised his ideas.

Between the late 1930s and early 1950s Whyte revised Arensberg's interactionism, fell into the story-telling trap, struggled out again, and laid the ground for technological implications. In the

---

* See Chapter 27 below. Interestingly, like their precursors, recent subjectivists become pugnacious about the philosophical grounding of their style: unlike them, however, they champion an 'unscientific' sociology.

process, he rehabilitated economic incentives as important influences on worker behaviour.

Though Whyte concedes that academic opportunism played a part, his conversion from community to industrial studies was logical enough.[17] He graduated as an economist and embarked on his study of Cornerville in 1936 with an interest in racketeering. At Harvard, he encountered the 'Yankee City' anthropologists who were later to move, almost *en bloc*, to Chicago and concentrate largely on industrial research. Arensberg coached him in research methods. Whyte also seems to have had a certain rather woolly do-gooding streak. Industrial problems probably seemed to offer better opportunities to 'help'.

Whyte arrived in Chicago in the early 1940s and for a brief period collaborated with Burleigh B. Gardner. Gardner was a former 'Yankee City' investigator. Less creditably, he had connections with the counselling programme at Hawthorne. Not surprisingly, then, the flavour of their joint reports might be characterized as Mayoite interactionism. Reviewing the growth of unionism and strikes amongst American foremen in the war years, for example, they portray the foreman as a 'marginal man' caught between contacts with, and loyalties to, both managers and workers.[18]

They lavishly prescribe solutions. Managers must be nicer to foremen because 'the first-line supervisor may largely determine the extent of co-operation or friction between workers and management'; he secures co-operation by fostering teamwork through communications. All the contradictions of Mayoism and interactionism, in fact, combine in this piece. They are neatly summarized in the following: 'He [the foreman] does good turns for them [the workers], unobtrusively, as a natural part of his behaviour, and they reciprocate',[19] i.e. he manipulates without being a manipulator, and the manipulation is necessarily effective.

But strict operationalism had been abandoned in this analysis. Whyte's own brand is demonstrated in his reviews of two cases of industrial conflict resolution. In one, an entrepreneur (Buchsbaum) had refused to recognize his workers' union. Touched by the restraint of a strike-leader who prevented his enraged followers from attacking blacklegs, however, he suddenly invited a delegation to his office. Buchsbaum and the leader took to one another. As the relationship developed, the workers began to suggest economies in work-planning and Buchsbaum recognized the union.[20]

In the second, the story covers a longer period (twelve years), during which a factory's human relations passed through the phases of unorganized conflict, organized conflict and organized co-operation.[21] Again, the turning-point was the transformation of the relationship between a reactionary boss (Gossett) and a 'bolshy' union leader (Love). In both cases management and union learnt to trust one another and be 'good listeners'. But *rapprochement* occurred only after certain critical encounters which changed the whole course of communications.

But why were communications misdirected beforehand, and how could they run properly after these key events? Whyte's explanation is in terms of four central concepts: interactions, sentiments, symbols and activities. I do not propose to discuss these here. Suffice it to say that they are all mutually influential. Thus a sentiment could govern an activity, and an interaction generate a symbol – vice versa and *mutatis mutandis*. Whyte imposes them after the fact to explain why the story developed as it did.

For example, when Gossett first met Love he refused to shake his hand. This, understandably, intensified their dislike of one another. In Whyte's language, the initially hostile sentiments resulted in an interaction which symbolized this hostility and aggravated the hostile sentiments. The reader may wonder whether applying this conceptual apparatus is worthwhile or legitimate, and he is quite right to do so. Indeed, the jargon is shown to be even more inappropriate when we learn that Love, being a Negro, misconstrued the 'symbol' of Gossett's snub.

To go straight to the heart of the matter, Whyte's interactionist scheme (as used here) systematically eliminates any sociological or other generalizing explanation of events. Everything – even the power play between groups – is particularized. When we ask 'why did human relations change?' the only real answer is 'because the relations between *these* humans changed'. That this unsatisfactory reply is couched in a grotesquely scientistic jargon is all the more lamentable.

Finally, it is worth noting that it is not only the characters in the story who are stripped of any wider social identities or attachments. The plant is also sealed off from politico-economic events of some consequence, for example the war and the Taft–Hartley Act. Even a six-month industry-wide strike in 1946 is treated as a kind of interlude or close season after which the *dramatis personae* return to the important business of interacting in the plant.

Whyte is indeed an enigmatic figure, for the book reporting this second case appeared several years after he first remarked that he was 'interested in observing the impact of technology on the social system' of the factory.[22] He first followed up this interest in his book *Human Relations in the Restaurant Industry* (1948).[23] This, however, is a popularly written work, with much advice to restaurant managers on keeping employees happy, containing little systematic theorizing. In an accompanying scholarly paper, however, Whyte showed how an interactionist approach could be fortified by linking it with an examination of formal structure and layout and equipment.[24]

In a large restaurant the formal structure of work-roles such as manager, waitress, chef, dishwasher, etc. is complex and hierarchical. Role incumbents must communicate constantly. In most formal structures initiations – orders or instructions – flow from high to low status positions. But because customers' initiations in a large restaurant can be injected at several levels a low-status worker often initiates for a superior. Resenting this, a high-status worker can retaliate successfully by delaying response to the initiation. Demands for quick service for a hurried customer relayed by a waitress to a counterhand, for example, will result in his slowing down. This increases the pressure on the waitress.

Whyte suggests that while an acceptable or optimum pattern of initiations can be conceived abstractly, the business of measuring the requisite interactions is too complex. None the less, a reduction in interaction often improves attitudes, especially when the initiator is of low status. But how can interaction be pruned in restaurants, where constant communication is vital?

Whyte's reply is: exploiting layout and equipment or technology. He then discusses various devices which permit communication without contact. In restaurants, phones and public address systems may help; but personal symbolic contact, by means of the voice, remains. High counters, however, and impersonal spindles on which orders are spiked sever all face-to-face contact and therefore the presentation of inhibitory symbols.[25]

Shortly afterwards, Whyte developed these insights about technology as hardware, or layout and equipment, and software or formal structure.[26] Here he anticipated Joan Woodward's work on the link between technology and organization, threw doubt on the generality of classical principles of organization and even suggested that human relations skills were subordinate to organizational restructuring for improving co-operation and performance.

This was progress indeed. Only two crucial elements of human relations remained to be rejected: its neglect of out-plant influences on in-plant action; and its unconcern for financial incentives as motivators. In *Money and Motivation*[27] Whyte faced up to the task about as squarely as he could have. In many ways this book is still the best general treatment of the whole issue of incentives as they operate in factory situations. Unfortunately, however, there is still too much interactionist conceptual clutter, a certain management bias and a tendency to view factories as social and economic islands.

Incentives are pictured as symbolic stimuli. But the connection between stimulus and response is complex. Pavlovian psychology, for example, shows the conditioned reflex becomes less prompt with time, and confusion over the meaning of a stimulus produces individual disorientation and lethargy. In industry we find a similar phenomenon.

Rate-setting is usually haphazard:

As we examine the rate-setting process and the economic results of increased production we are forced to conclude that the connections between the symbols and the promised rewards are neither simple nor consistent. This does not mean that the piece-rate symbol will evoke no response. It does mean that the response will be importantly influenced by the context of human relations within which the symbol is offered.[28]

The context of human relations has many dimensions: the relations of individual workers to the work-group, the relations of the group to other groups and their relations with management. Acquisitiveness is a socially acquired trait and even in the United States varies between groups. Incentives therefore appeal strongly only to a small minority of 'rate-busters', are regarded with indifference by 'restricters' (who prize the social bonds of working life), and between them is a heterogeneous category of workers torn between group-loyalty and cash.[29]

The work-groups in a plant make up a social system which can reach equilibrium. Disturbances to this are created by group earnings that are discrepant with the status of its members, or by changes in the flow of work which affect group prestige. Once social and economic status becomes discrepant, the affronted groups will seek to resolve the dissonance. In terms of interactionist theory, the symbol of changed status provokes a change in sentiments (hostile attitudes), which in turn change activities, for instance a production slow-down in an adjacent department, and hence change interactions by producing hostile encounters, or dissociation.

Where a work-group is in conflict with management, a 'loose rate' will result in quota restriction, a 'borderline rate' will be defined as impossible but workers will perhaps make out, and a 'tight rate' will produce 'goldbricking'.* Where co-operation prevails, the loose rate still evokes a quota, but at a higher level, the borderline rate will be given a fair trial, and the tight rate will be submitted for re-negotiation. (Note that these activities largely *define* conflict or co-operation, and the continuance of quota restriction under co-operation deserves more comment.)

To maintain harmony between working groups, which is constantly threatened by the changes following in-built technological advance, the manager needs to plan with regard to social as well as technical and short-run financial criteria. Co-operation can be built by the manipulation of sentiments and activities.

How do we change sentiments and activities? How do we build sentiments of co-operation when conflict existed before? ... The general answer to these

* Quota restriction aims to avoid spoiling a loose rate by overproduction; goldbricking involves ignoring the incentive and falling back on the basic hourly rate. See D. Roy, 'Quota Restriction and Goldbricking in a Machine Shop', *American Journal of Sociology*, 57, 1952, 427–42.

questions is simple: *we change sentiments and activities through changing inter-action*. And we change interaction through changing the symbols that are presented to the people in question or through changing the work-flow or the organizational structure.[30]

Symbols such as the work-study man with his threatening aura cannot be changed by propaganda, by counselling or by any other form of communications. Experience proves that 'sentiments are not changed through such a direct approach'.[31] But the symbol can be changed by changing the man – too often the time-study man is a failed engineer unfitted for his key role – and by restricting his freedom of action. Changing the work flow and the structure are alternative lines of attack. The first is clearly a production engineering task, and the acquisition of greater social scientific knowledge by engineers is a matter of urgency. The second depends partly on liberating originations in the plant. Workers at the bottom of the organizational power-pyramid do not initiate for anyone. Their appetite for a share in control is thus diverted into production restriction. Legitimate originations from them can, however, be fostered by grievance procedures and by suggestion-schemes.

Studies of co-operative situations show that originations from management to union, and vice versa, from workers to union, and so on, are all highly developed. Later research, Whyte argues, may enable quantification of the optimum frequencies and content of all such origination channels. (This is a nostalgically Arensbergian touch.) Meanwhile, management must accept unions and forge the structures which facilitate collaboration. All this begs the questions whether multilateral originations can procure collaboration, or merely express it, and whether some originations, and some originators, are more important than others. What happens when workers' originations are deemed impermissible?

Whyte himself recognized that these prescriptions were too general. The last chapter promises to outline 'a practical programme of action'. His main suggestion is the Scanlon Plan.* The main feature of schemes like this is that workers obtain a bonus equivalent

* Named after Joseph Scanlon, a former leader of the United Steelworkers of America and notable business unionist of the 1940s.

to savings gained through implementing suggestions submitted by them on a *collective* basis. Normal suggestion-schemes are based on the brainwaves of individuals, which must be submitted in writing. They fail because the inventive fear the reprisals of their associates or foreman and that management will not reward them properly. Many suggestions, anyway, are hare-brained because the isolated worker cannot appreciate technical complexities or express his ideas in the correct jargon.

Under the Scanlon system suggestions are worked out in group sessions. This certainly can reduce resistance to change, promote teamwork and permit the refinement of ideas thanks to the pooling of expertise. Some have even called the scheme 'revolutionary', since management participates more fully and workers can demand that it should implement change.

But Whyte acknowledges that the Scanlon system sometimes fails badly. He ascribes this to 'semantic confusions' amongst managers, that is, ideological prejudices about the worker. These must be discarded. For their part unions must recognize that participatory schemes demand a change of their activities. Both sides must abandon their 'winner-takes-all' or 'zero-sum' notion of power. Power, according to Whyte, is just 'an ability to   things done'.[32] Management usually *appears* to be the dominai   istrial partner, but this is simply because it is able to get things done. Once the participative philosophy is embraced by accepting originations from the union and the workers, the relationship becomes reciprocal and the workers share power. This 'revolution' will oblige managers to become true leaders.

While all this shows Whyte's increase in sophistication since his early Chicago days, it still relies excessively on interactionism. Although out-plant influences are acknowledged, they are not very systematically explored; and those that are discussed (the social background of 'restricters' and 'rate-busters') rely heavily on the work of his students (who contributed chapters to the book).[33] None the less, the influence on in-plant behaviour of technology and formal organization are decisively thrown into the ring. Whyte also emerges as a champion of participation.

This was to be a key theme of the 'neo-human relations' theorists of organization discussed in the next part. Whyte's ideas here are partly derived from a final branch of 'classical' human relations which must be noted. These psychological Mayoites were a brief but powerful force, and their work will be summarily examined in the next chapter.

THE
PSYCHOLOGICAL
MAYOITES

Mayoite industrial psychology took as its chief problem the effect of leadership on work-behaviour. There were two major reasons for this. Firstly, psychologists generally had been more excited by *Management and the Worker* than sociologists. The Hawthorne studies had begun within a psychological framework, and had shown the limitations of the 'human factor' approach. 'Changed supervision' had purportedly overridden economic and physiological variables.

The second reason was due to the influence of Kurt Lewin. Lewin, a refugee from Nazi Germany, was a passionate believer in democracy. Clearly, the idea that less authoritarian supervision could simultaneously boost both the morale and productivity of workers was something to excite him. But Lewin was also a powerful theorist whose ideas spread rapidly in the late 1930s. His 'field theory' derived from his admiration for hard science, particularly physics. It viewed an individual's behaviour as the product of forces operating upon him; and, in a social situation, he himself was a force exerting reciprocal influences.

Although this kind of imagery has its uses it can easily lead to absurdity or mystification. Lewinians tend to take it over-seriously, talking of 'vectors' and 'force-fields' and other pseudo-physical – and totally hypothetical – phenomena. (A Lewinian subject does not move: he 'locomotes'.) Clearly it tends to suppress the idea that human action can be calculated and voluntary. Lewinians deny this; but voluntarism can only be fitted into their scheme with difficulty.

Field theory can be viewed as the psychological equivalent of Arensberg's interactionism. It has the same concern with operationalization (though the borrowing of concepts from physics prejudges the nature of human activities). Everyday terms like 'leadership' obviously carry numerous and often vague connotations. Lewinians overcome this problem by talking of 'initiations'. For example, if A is observed to issue suggestions or orders to B, C and D, and they respond to these 'initiations' more often than A responds to their initiations, A may be called their leader. Similarly, 'participation' may be operationalized and measured by noting how often A invites their comments or suggestions on a proposed course of joint action.

This precision must be matched by methodical examination of variables. Ideally, this demands laboratory conditions where all variables other than that being tested are rigorously controlled. If one were testing the relation between 'participation' and 'performance' (the Lewinian term for output), for example, one would recruit experimental and control groups carefully matched for age, sex, skill etc. The field theorists, however, were eager to work in real-life situations whenever they could, conducting experiments on actual work-groups. Unconsciously, the Hawthorne team had indulged in action research of this kind. The loss of control implied in abandoning laboratory conditions was regarded as adequately compensated by the verisimilitude of experiments with real work-groups.

Research by Feldman in the 1930s had shown that the productivity of industrial work-groups varied with their supervisors, but no attempt had been made then to specify what characteristics of the supervisor might account for this.[1] The first major experimental work to suggest some clear relationship between the nature of leadership and group performance was in fact a study of boys-club hobby groups by Lippitt and White, the first report of which appeared in 1940.[2] (It was enthusiastically received by some as scientific proof that Hitler was wrong.)

This study indicated that while autocratic leadership might sometimes ensure as high a productivity as democratic, the latter kind was generally superior in this respect; furthermore it produced much less tension and frustration in the group. (An extension of the studies to test the impact of *laissez-faire* leadership style was to give little comfort to anarchists: such groups were both tense and unproductive.) The latter study is important not just for the lead it gave but as an example of action research. Patterns of conduct appropriate to the various styles of leadership were calculated beforehand and acted out by trained assistants in a concrete field setting. The ethics of this may be controversial, but the artificiality of a laboratory setting was avoided. This increased confidence in the results.

A further set of experiments which prepared the way for the entry of Lewinian psychology into the human relations orbit were conducted in the war by Lewin himself. Although concerned with dietary habits – problems not immediately relevant to the dilemmas of the industrial manager – they seemed to show that producing a change in behaviour desired by an administrator is simplified if a group of persons can first be led to agree amongst themselves on the need for change, and are brought together afterwards to review adherence to the new pattern.[3] The Lewinians were beginning to realize the Mayoite aim: leaders (managers), they showed, through communications (social skill), could manipulate participation (informal organization) to produce a superior group climate (morale) thus enhancing satisfaction (integration) with the group life (social system) and improving performance (output).

Application of these notions in an industrial milieu was achieved first in a series of experiments carried out at the Harwood Manufacturing Company just after the Second World War. The findings supposedly established that if managers involved difficult employees in the planning and execution of technical changes the employees' antagonism to change would be overcome. The title of the best-known report of the study, 'Overcoming Resistance to Change',[4] suggests optimism and practicality – and management bias. However, there were serious methodological flaws in the best-known study; and its findings were not altogether consistent with those of the less-well-reported study.[5]

The trouble with action research of this kind is that it tends to be based on a single case and many variables are not controlled. Local factors may also complicate interpretation; and, by definition, most field experiments cannot be adequately replicated, if only because of the time variable. The Harwood findings seem plausible enough. However, we are certainly not given sufficient information about the local context. Shortly after the group-decision experiments the workers struck over a unionization dispute with management. The successfully 'changed' groups were as pro-union as their colleagues. To explore the suggestive Harwood findings fully, work of a systematically comparative nature was needed.

In the years after 1947, this was carried out on the grand scale, funded initially by the Office of Naval Research, by the Survey Research Center (S.R.C.) of the Institute of Social Research at the University of Michigan. It was here that Lewin transferred from his Research Center for Group Dynamics at M.I.T., which had collaborated on the Harwood Studies. The aim of the S.R.C. was to integrate the efforts of psychologists, sociologists and anthropologists involved on the study of groups – an aim almost identical with that of the Tavistock Institute of Human Relations founded in Britain at the same time and with which it maintained close links. Neither foundation completely succeeded in achieving this integration of social scientific research. Much of the S.R.C.'s early work was similar to, and as trivial as, psephology; much of the Tavistock Institute's was impaired by its concern with psychoanalysis.

The S.R.C.'s first major study examined clerical workers in the office of the Prudential Insurance Company in Newark, New Jersey. The productivity and morale of a large number of working groups were checked against the personal characteristics of their supervisors. Important differences were detected: supervisors in charge of high-production groups were found to be rather less arbitrary and authoritarian.[6] This discovery was soon supported by a study of railway maintenance gangs.[7] Though broadly confirmatory, however, a worrying finding was that those railwaymen who were most satisfied with their work were members of *low*-production gangs. This clearly necessitated a more sophisticated formulation of the relationships between high morale, teamwork and productivity. None the less, this material was taken to show that the attitude and behaviour of supervisors were more significant for production than were the attitudes of the worker. A similar negative relationship between productivity and close supervision was established in a study of work-teams in the Caterpillar Tractor Company.[8]

Studies such as these enabled the construction of a broad profile of the successful supervisor, and hence the design of practical supervisory training courses to impart or nurture the desired virtues – abstention from close supervision of work which men can be entrusted to supervise themselves; refusal to nag constantly about the need to get the work out; willingness to help out in rush periods; readiness to take a sympathetic interest in the men's personal worries; concern with explaining instructions instead of barking them out in an authoritarian manner; and maintaining discipline, for instance over time-keeping, by persuasive rather than punitive actions. In the late 1940s there was a mushrooming of courses which claimed to cultivate these leadership practices.

Unfortunately they had a less solid foundation than the reports pouring from the S.R.C. at this time suggested. Critics were quick to point out, for example, that a finding that high productivity is associated with relaxed supervision is ambiguous. If simple causality is assumed, which itself is dangerous, relaxed supervision may be viewed as an *effect* of high production rather than its cause. High morale amongst workers may similarly be the precondition, if not the precise cause, of a democratization of leadership. Studies undertaken more recently have provided considerable evidence for these interpretations. In fact, old-fashioned autocratic supervision maximizes production more often than the enthusiasts of the democratic style care to admit.[9]

To give them credit, the main S.R.C. researchers soon began to entertain such doubts themselves. In the railway-gangs study, too, it was postulated that the kind of leadership behaviour any supervisor can adopt may depend on his relations with his own superior. A study by F. C. Mann of an electrical utility[10] drove this point home: the degree to which supervisors implemented good human relations was ultimately dependent on the attitudes of higher management.

Such findings by no means invalidate the human relations credo, but they do suggest that studies of the work-group and its leader in microcosm must be supplemented. And they indicate that democratization must spread to all leadership levels in the organization. (This line of reasoning was adopted by the 'neo-human relations' theorists of organization.)

By the early 1950s doubts were beginning to creep in about the managerial value of cohesive groups. For example, the interactionists Arensberg and Horsfall, in a study of four seven-man teams in a shoe factory, had showed that the employees had adopted a method of equalizing production between fast and slow teams, thus frustrating the management's incentive scheme; the more cohesive teams were also the more restrictive.[11] Cohesiveness came to be seen increasingly as a somewhat ambiguous property, though some studies continued to provide evidence that the involvement of cohesive groups in minor decision-making could increase production, cut turnover and weaken the power of a trade union.[12] But in 1954 we find an S.R.C. student exclaiming: 'We emerge from this study with some new ideas, but mainly with considerably increased respect for some old ones ... The popular admonition to supervisors that they should develop a cohesive team, if carried out indiscriminately, may merely lend force to the divisive influences within the larger organization.'[13]

It is surprising that critics of human relations as a practical movement have not paid more attention to this psychological wing. Many of the most frankly manipulationist textbooks on human relations were produced by industrial psychologists, not sociologists, in the post-war period.[14] Although these manuals paid considerable, often critical, attention to Hawthorne and the work of the Chicago School, they paid even more to the early Lewinian and S.R.C. studies. A whole brood of managerially oriented organization theorists followed in their footsteps, though these 'organizational psycho-technologists' (their work will be dealt with in the next part) reintroduced the problem of formal organization, as a software technology, and adopted a rather different psychological methodology.

These developments occurred at a time when Mayo's thought in particular was coming under devastating attack. How could the psychological Mayoites and their psycho-technological successors have ignored this onslaught? The answer is that they did not ignore it, but believed that their work was innocent of the charge of portraying managers as an élite. This defence rested upon their preoccupation with democratic leadership. The goals of efficiency and participatory democracy, they maintained, were consistent – indeed, functionally interdependent. No managerial élite was required, merely some very simple training and re-education for élitist, autocratic supervisors and managers. They had squared the circle.

Not surprisingly, then, even the interactionist Arensberg, when he took up the cudgels to defend human relations against the jibe that it was an ideological plant sociology – a set of parables about an élite (managers) and 'aborigines' (workers) – based his defence largely on the discoveries of these psychologists. He and his associate were replying to the classic attack by Clark Kerr and Lloyd Fisher mentioned in the introductory chapter of this book.[15] 'What irony,' ran the defence, 'it may well be when we finally learn, with empirical proofs rather than moral homilies, that the best way to manipulate man to organizational goals is the very representative democracy these economists think they are defending.'[16]

The irony of this reply itself will not be lost on those who have read the foregoing section on *Applied Anthropology*. Arensberg overlooked a central contradiction in the work of the psychological Mayoites which stems from their methodology as much as anything. As we noted at the outset, Lewinian psychology, so powerfully drawn (or should it be 'adducted') towards physics, overlooks the voluntarism of human action. Man responds to forces. Managerial social skill consequently consists of exerting forces which will shape the workers' behaviour. This could perhaps be characterized as 'plant physics: the magnets and the pins'; but its connection with genuine industrial democracy is remote.

16

OVERVIEW

Human relations was in many ways a surprisingly diverse approach – certainly more so than either Taylorism or human factor psychology. But this diversity – this elasticity, even – becomes apparent only when the equation between Mayo and the movement is discarded. Once this has been done, even the message of the Hawthorne studies becomes equivocal.

This relative fluidity complicates assessment of the approach overall. When its inseparable ideological and practical dimensions are also scrutinized the task becomes almost unmanageable in a book like this. Latter-day champions of human relations will therefore find many challengeable generalizations in what follows. My commentary should have indicated a grudging sympathy for them. Reaction against human relations has become counterproductive because it is today so uncompromising. But Warner's, Whyte's and even Roethlisberger's and Dickson's writings still repay a critical reading.

Detailed arguments already given for such individual rehabilitations will not be repeated here; nor will specific complaints against value-bias, ethical lapses or technical failures in method and explanation. In an overview of human relations such variations are important only in so far as they support or contradict a general explanation of the approach and its development.

Human relations emerged in the mid 1930s in America because Myersian psychology was incapable of handling 'social man', because Mayo was a gifted publicist, because Harvard had become a leading sociological centre, and because American management faced novel problems of social control and legitimation. Although the Myersians were sensing the significance of the social factor by the late 1920s, their 'trained incapacities' and lack of resources prevented them exploring it. Unrestricted by disciplinary boundaries, in fact by any scientific caution, Mayo eagerly propagated 'helpful' new ideas. These depended on the work of Henderson and Parsons at Harvard in discovering in nineteenth-century sociology and contemporary anthropology an image of man and society which stressed supposedly irreducible social elements in collective life. The depression had unveiled social antagonisms, stimulated unionism, promoted government intervention in industry and generally rendered workforces less tolerant and respectful of managerial authority.

All these factors interacted, but Harvard sociology and the depression did so particularly closely; and of them the socio-economic crisis was the dominant partner.* Harvard sociology was designed to provide, and attracted young middle-class intellectuals who sought, renewed faith in American institutions, especially American capitalism.[1] 'As a Republican Bostonian who had not rejected his comparatively wealthy family,' a typical recruit, George Homans, has explained, 'I felt during the thirties that I was under attack, above all from the Marxists.'[2]

Inbuilt conservative bias and the sociologistic tendency to represent all collective phenomena, especially economically induced problems, as essentially social – these the human relations perspective acquired almost automatically from Harvard's functionalist social thinkers. But human relations inherited empirical and practical concerns from industrial psychology which most early functionalists

* A full account of these predisposing conditions would also require an examination of the impact of the rise of fascism and the consolidation of Soviet rule.

despised. These concerns, reinforced by Mayo's clinical bent, produced one of its sustained methodological faults, its pre-occupation with the plant. Its treatment of industrial conflict as a local, or plant, problem stems from this obsession with cases as much as from wider prejudices.

Changing socio-economic conditions, disagreements between its theoreticians and critical reactions all partly account for its diversification from the late 1930s onwards, and each factor is difficult to isolate. However, the concern with supervisory skill and communications in the early 1940s, and acceptance of unions as legitimate partners with management later in the decade, reflect awareness, if not approval, of new industrial realities. Whether such changes would have occurred without the stresses of war-time production and the growth of organized labour no one can say. The fact that the two developments coincided is none the less suggestive. Even more so is the rapid decay of the approach with the spread, and relative failure, of human relations training for supervisors.

Arensberg's case demonstrates that theoretical controversy within human relations could be lively. In his hands, social man almost disintegrated. His technocratic justification for research and manipulation, his enthusiasm for a hard methodology and his eagerness to peddle the purported skills of applied anthropologists were likewise barely consistent with Mayo's own thinking. Promising so much to managers, apparently better able to deliver it thanks to interactionist social engineering, and like other early industrial sociologists rising rapidly to enviable academic power, Arensberg's role in provoking the reaction against human relations has been underestimated.

A full account of this reaction would be interesting but only a few points can be made here. It began earlier than is often supposed, in the mid 1930s, and the first critical fire was brisk and accurate.[3] After a relative lull during the war, it began in earnest. Between 1946 and 1950 nearly all the conventional charges against the school were systematically pressed: neglect of unions; managerial bias; acceptance of manipulation; inadequate treatment of industrial conflict; failure to relate the factory to the wider social structure; and fear of anomie.[4] Surprisingly, however, no very careful examination was made of the empirical reliability of key human relations investigations. Not until the 1960s did Carey show that the Hawthorne studies, upon which so much human relations theory depended, were too incompetently executed to demonstrate very much at all.[5]

The edge of earlier criticisms was often blunted by the critics' failure to discriminate between the various branches of human relations, and their frequent resort to guilt by association. Any target which had a remote association with Mayo was subjected to a kind of intellectual carpet-bombing.[6]

Some of the venom in these attacks naturally reflected revulsion against the political import of human relations. But in my view leftist critics, such as C. W. Mills, were relatively measured in their observations.[7] It is noteworthy that the definitive assaults on human relations were to come in the 1950s, that is after the adoption of the technological implications approach by industrial sociologists, and the widespread failure of human relations training schemes, from an economist, Clark Kerr, and a business commentator, W. H. Whyte, with implicit political positions decidedly right of centre.[8] The rage and sarcasm of these attacks, it is worth remarking, centre on human relations' suspicion of traditional American values, especially market values such as the legitimacy of high monetary incentives and competitiveness.

Few human relations exponents answered any of these complaints directly. When they did so, their replies tended to be feeble or intemperate.[9] Their readiness to accept the rational element in the criticism is difficult to judge. In my view, Whyte's 'educability' is shown by his gradual shift towards technological implications and his re-examination of economic incentives. But perhaps he is an exception. Writers of influential textbooks on human relations in the 1950s continued to babble about supervisory skills and the potency of communications as if very little had changed.[10]

In some senses, very little had. Industrial students turned their attention to technology and formal organization as crucial influences on workers' behaviour. But attention still remained fixed on the plant (or organization) as the main unit of analysis. Similarly, manipulation could still be advocated, though by changing technology (as hardware or software) instead of supervision. These core concerns of the human relations approach were retained. But it is noteworthy also that the fullest elaboration of the new approach was to be made outside America, where human relations lacked an academic infrastructure.

PART IV

SOME METHODOLOGICAL
AND
THEORETICAL CONSEQUENCES
OF THE
TAVISTOCK INSTITUTE
OF HUMAN RELATIONS

TIME FOR
A CHANGE

Two important revisions in industrial studies occurred in the 1950s. First, technology supplanted the human relations climate as the favourite variable for explaining industrial behaviour. Second, industrial sociology – the most distinct, developed and coherent branch of inquiry – was all but wound up, in name anyway: increasingly, analysts referred to themselves as 'organizational sociologists' or 'organization theorists'. This substitution occurred more rapidly in America. But work done in Britain did much to encourage it.

These two developments were linked. Those technology theorists whose work most immediately suggests methods of improving industrial performance were Woodward and the Tavistock Group in Britain and Sayles in the United States. They did not picture technology as a direct influence on behaviour but rather, as operating through the medium of an associated work organization which is more (in the Tavistock case) or less (in that of Woodward) variable. The prospect was therefore raised for the managers of a firm, in itself an organization, of modifying work-methods and work-relationships, that is, its internal organization, either to achieve a better 'fit' between technology and organization or to capitalize on organizational choice.[1] Alternatively they might be better able to take account of the behaviour of their workers which was technologically influenced in formulating an industrial relations policy or making production engineering decisions.

Another set of writers, the so-called neo-human relations school,* emerged at this period to advocate the adoption of certain organizational reforms in the workplace, though upon empirically less solid foundations. A final group of students, heavily imbued with the functionalist theory of orthodox sociology, were seeking to develop and apply the insights of classical theorists such as Weber and Michels to organization and bureaucracy. These forces tended to focus attention upon in-plant phenomena. The links between organizational performance, organizational structure and organizational behaviour achieved new prominence because it appeared they could be studied, and manipulated, with new precision.

The core of the technological implications approach is an assumption, and usually some demonstration, that technology and work-behaviour are intimately related. Writers have varied in their views of this relation, and this is best shown by examining their contributions. In doing so it is instructive to note their varying treatment of the following questions: (i) what is the nature of the technology–behaviour link – is this direct, or does it operate via the organization of work?; (ii) to what extent is behaviour a sheer response, a reflex, to a given technical or organizational milieu; is some individual interpretation of the milieu allowed for?; (iii) what is meant by the term 'technology'? Does it refer to plant, equipment and productive processes, or is work organization *itself* included? One can argue, for example, that managing systems are themselves a consciously applied technology: the popular term 'administrative machinery' is a suggestive analogy.

Because of their priority, and because they led to the largest sustained research effort and the most ambitious theoretical scheme, it is important to note first the studies of coal-mining undertaken by the Tavistock Institute of Human Relations in the late 1940s. The title of a celebrated article of 1951 by Trist and Bamforth, 'Some Social and Psychological Consequences of the Longwall

* Alternatively, the 'organizational psychologists', or 'self-actualization school'.

Method of Coal-Getting', indicates their orientation.[2] It was to be pursued in a research programme in the pits lasting almost ten years. It was put to the test by Rice[3] in the culturally exotic setting of India, and it emerged so impressively that, ever since, Tavistock analysts have tended to overlook its limitations.

A full discussion of the Tavistock's other early industrial studies and research philosophy has been provided by Richard Brown.[4] The Institute was founded in 1947 as an agency for psychologists with interdisciplinary inclinations to make available to industry the expertise they had accumulated on personnel and other problems in the war. An important early study was of joint consultation in the Glacier Metal Company, whose managing director, Wilfred (now Lord) Brown, was an enthusiast of applied social science. The mining studies, also commencing in the late 1940s, were initially concerned with 'the conditions likely to increase the effectiveness of the "dissemination of information" about new social techniques'.[5] Fortunately the researchers seem to have interpreted this brief liberally.

Bitter conflict had marked the industrial relations of British coal-mines between the wars. Nationalization had been expected to reduce this conflict, both in its overt forms and in those of absenteeism, labour wastage and low productivity. This did not happen. Medical observers of the mines, however, had for twenty years been noting an increase in morbidity and psychosomatic illness amongst colliers, which at least one related to growing anomie as confidently as any Mayoite.[6] This period, however, had also seen the displacement of traditional 'hand-got' mining organization by the Longwall method. Older miners often expressed for the former system a nostalgia that did not seem to be compatible with the great difficulties of the work-methods they had experienced.

Aware of these paradoxes, and that tentative modifications of the normal longwall organization since nationalization had sometimes been 'accompanied by impressive changes in the social quality of the work-life',[7] Trist and Bamforth set out to identify those technical features in the traditional and the conventional longwall systems which might produce different human consequences. Bamforth had spent eighteen years at the coal-face himself.

Whatever the technology employed to win the coal certain features of coal-mining as a productive operation make it distinctive. First, the underground situation is dirty, dangerous and dark. Second, geological variations constantly threaten the smooth flow of operations. Third, operations logically divide into an endlessly repeated three-phase cycle, namely: (i) *preparation*, cutting the fresh coal in the seam; (ii) *getting*, removing the cut coal from the seam and the coal-face; (iii) *advancing*, moving forward machinery and the pit-props supporting the roof, into the gulf created by extraction, to prepare for the next cut.

In the days of 'hand-getting' the technology available at the face was rudimentary, consisting of little more than hand tools such as picks, shovels and, later, pneumatic drills; metal tubs were used to remove the won coal and feed it into the haulage system. Work was organized in the so-called 'single-place' form on a 'bord and pillar' layout.* Briefly this consisted of creating square pillars of uncut coal by driving tunnels into the seam at intervals of about forty yards; 'places' of six to eleven yards in length were then allocated on each set of pillars to small teams of miners.

The team of about six miners was self-selecting. Because of the general use of a three-shift system, two of its members would be at work on any one shift. Each member was a composite workman; that is, he had to acquire all skills required at the face before he stood a chance of selection into one of these small groups of 'marrows' (mates). Each marrow group of six colliers was paid a lump sum related directly to output, and could divide the proceeds as it agreed, taking account of internal variations in experience or effort. Its relation to wider management was almost that of a sub-contractor, and in matters of discipline and output it was virtually self-regulating.

It could be claimed that this form of organization was well fitted to the technology available and the unique features of the underground situation. Within limits, each team could set its own pace. This was satisfying to its members and convenient to management

* The Tavistock mining research eventually covered several coal-fields, and local terminology varies. Here, that used in *Organizational Choice* (Trist *et al.*) will be followed.

from many points of view: for example, the flow of coal from the face as a whole was fairly even throughout a shift, thus avoiding jams in the haulage system to the surface. Again, if geological difficulties were encountered, each collier possessed the full experience to meet them in both the technical and psychological senses; and if the cycle of operations was delayed on one shift, the oncoming pair of marrows could take up where the foregoing pair had been forced to halt. The deputy (first-line supervisor) stood largely in a service relationship to the group, which accorded well with the collier's independent, egalitarian spirit.

Longwall layout was introduced into the mines from about 1900 onwards. It seemed necessary for the exploitation of the new moving conveyor belt. Pillars and places were abolished and continuous faces of up to several hundred yards attacked. This was accompanied by a mass-production factory philosophy: 'the work is broken down into a standard series of component operations that follow each other in rigid succession over three shifts . . . so that a total coal-getting cycle may be completed once in each twenty-four working hours'.[8] The production engineering logic of an elaborate division of labour thus eradicated the tiny marrow group of all-round craftsmen and installed task-groups of specialized workers tied to particular operations on a particular shift.

Such changes were at odds with the miner's belief both in general equality, since it created a new status system tied to job gradings and tasks, and in status dependent on composite skill, which disappeared. Management was faced with new, and severe, problems of supervision and co-ordination. The cycle and shift groups were no longer self-regulating. They bitterly resented efforts to regulate them from 'outside'. But unless the general task of a given group was completed on its given shift, control was lost because the oncoming shift was specialized in different operations and was neither willing nor able to tackle the unfinished work. Given the unpredictability of underground conditions the pattern of operations became a bad-tempered struggle from crisis to crisis with frequent stoppages.

Almost invariably longwall faces yielded an average output far below their theoretical potential. Absenteeism and sickness rates climbed. These effects were masked by the general conflict between workers and management, and the powerful economic weapons which management possessed, in the bitter 1920s and hungry 1930s. The post-war situation made them more apparent.

In 1951, the Tavistock workers were not yet ready to formulate a detailed model to account for this contrast between traditional and longwall methods, nor to propound organizational solutions. 'As regards the longwall system,' they note, 'the first need is for systematic study and evaluation of the changes so far tried. It seems to the present writers, however, that a qualitative change will have to be effected in the general character of the method so that a social as well as a technological whole can come into existence.'[9]

I shall discuss the later stages of these studies in a later chapter. For the moment, two features of Trist and Bamforth's approach are worth noting. Firstly, they undoubtedly distinguished varying social and psychological *concomitants* of the two technical systems. Secondly, they saw these as mediated by the organization of work. They did not claim that the technical apparatus necessarily produced certain human effects directly, nor that it entailed a specific form of organization. In this respect their outlook, unlike that of many other technology theorists, was not rigidly determinist or behaviouristic. The writers considered in the next chapter were less cautious.

TECHNOLOGICAL
TOPOGRAPHICS

Almost simultaneously with the first stages of the Tavistock coal-mining studies the fieldwork for what was to become an equally important contribution to the exploration of technological factors as influences on work was being undertaken by Walker and Guest in the United States. This was to be written up as *The Man on the Assembly Line*,[1] and Walker's and Guest's monograph of 1952, soon followed by a companion, *The Foreman on the Assembly Line*,[2] rapidly became, and to some extent remains, a key point of departure in discussions of the relation between technology and the worker's experience of his job situation in the large mass-production factory.

Reading this monograph today it soon becomes clear that the authors were conscious of breaking new ground but were not altogether sure how to tie in their findings with previous work, or what tradition of industrial studies they were working in. There is an amazing scarcity of reference, even critical, to the work of the human-relationists, though the results of the study plainly indicated that human-relations theory needed revision. They had, however, evidently studied Georges Friedmann's critiques of 'technicism'[3] – a growing source of inspiration to English-speaking industrial students at this period, as translation made them more widely accessible. But it is noteworthy that the most lavishly referenced previous work is that of the Myersians Wyatt and Fraser. However, Walker's and Guest's theoretical discussion is always low-keyed. They seem to have hoped that their results would speak for themselves.

Thus we are not presented with any ambitious theoretical scheme. After all, 'the new geography of man-at-work has received so little scientific study'.[4] In this 'geography', however, the machine is to be seen as a commanding feature. 'The machine will be surveyed less as a tool of production than as a part of the topography of a man's workplace, and mass production not as an engineering method but as a code of law governing his behaviour and way of life in the factory.'[5] It is also worth noting at this point that adjustment is viewed as an 'elementary problem area', and leads to the question: 'To what degree can – or should – men be "adjusted" to the new environment of machines, and to what degree is it possible to adjust or rebuild that environment to fit the needs and personalities of men?'[6]

The research results were derived from interviews with 180 auto-workers from 'Plant X'. The vast bulk of this sample were assemblers of one kind or another, and nearly two thirds were in machine-paced operations. Plant X was a newly built plant in a previously non-industrialized area. Only one in ten of the respondents had previous experience of machine-paced repetitive work. Walker and Guest recognized that these facts might affect their findings, but in a psychological rather than sociological manner. (They talk of their population being possibly less 'conditioned' to mass-production than workers in, say, Detroit.) Indeed, although some of the best-known sections of the monograph are those where they outline the impact of technology on social relations in the plant, the investigation was essentially a study of *attitudes* towards mass-production work, of responses to its salient features.

This bias is not immediately apparent. After arguing that the three key features of assembly-line work (programming of production, mechanized handling and fractionalization of work operations) yields a modal job which is machine-paced, repetitive, unskilled, fractionalized, unchallenging and monotonous, they picture the worker's total job situation as consisting not merely of the work itself (and its pay, physical surroundings and promotion opportunities) but also of relations with workmates, with supervision, and with the union. Thus social factors were certainly investigated. But only about one quarter of the report was devoted to them. The chapter which deals with the behavioural consequences of the working system is a bare eight pages long. When the authors note, then, that 'The technological factors of automobile assembly work affect the worker, both directly and indirectly. They affect him directly through the immediate job, and indirectly by modifying the basic organizational and social structure of the plant',[7] it should be understood that they really are discussing *psychological* effects on the worker.

The findings themselves can be briefly summarized. Machine-paced work was found to be thoroughly disliked, ranking first of the three most disliked features of the work mentioned spontaneously. These other features, repetitiveness and lack of challenge, however, are clearly related closely to machine-pacing. Evaluations of a particular type of operation correlated highly with its objective mass-production characteristics.

Hardly surprisingly, the work itself was the least liked aspect of the total job situation and money was the best liked feature. Three quarters of the sample claimed to work at Plant X solely for its high pay, which was sometimes a 50 per cent increase on their pay in previous work. The work was regarded as steady, and was also liked for this reason particularly by the men's wives. However, the variation in reward between different jobs was small. This reflected company and union policy, but also the homogenizing effects of the production system. A further consequence of this sameness of the work were the relatively poor opportunities for promotion. Yet many workers felt their chances for promotion were in fact higher in Plant X than in their previous jobs, and only a fifth expressed any frustration over their hopes of promotion. Most respondents aspired to transfer to jobs 'off the line', which were sought less for higher status or earnings than as an escape from pressure and monotony. But chances of making such transfers were generally low.

The findings on the social side indicated, in brief, that less than half of the sample experienced frequent social interaction on the job. It was prevented not only by environmental interferences such as noise but by the layout of the line itself. Since this varied from one shop to another to some extent, opportunities did occur to talk with a few workmates quite often, and in rare instances men could be said to belong to teams whose functionally interrelated tasks permitted some social cohesion. But few respondents were conscious of belonging to any identifiable workgroup, and some were social isolates. The investigators suggest that lack of social contact represented an important deprivation – at least, 'those who were members of true teams spoke of their group interaction in positive and cheerful terms'.[8]

The findings about relations with management figures could be described as bimodal. Interaction with foremen, or other first-line supervisors, was generally frequent. An unfavourable assessment of the job itself did not generally affect the tone of relations with foremen. Three quarters of respondents claimed to get on well with their supervisors, and remarks about them were generally favourable. Thus the technology did not preclude a healthy relationship with the foreman.

As for other managers, contacts were typically rare, superficial or non-existent. Walker and Guest obviously feel that this is not desirable. Later they remark that

in so far as the technology of the line keeps the work groups weak and non-functional, it tends by that much to weaken the individual's sense of belonging to a *bona fide* industrial community. There is a close personal work bond between the individual and his immediate boss, but all other bonds either with supervision or with local management are non-personal or impersonal.[9]

Yet their data on workers' assessment of the value of worker–foreman interaction suggest that such relations were not of primary importance. It was thought important to have a good foreman, but factors like pay or the job itself were relatively much more highly evaluated.

One perceives here a more than residual acceptance of human relations doctrine. We have noted that reference to other industrial students is rare, and in fact even Mayo is mentioned only once. But

this reference suggests that the Mayoite assumption of the importance to the worker of membership in a tightly knit work-group is
taken as axiomatic.[10] This reappears in the analysis of the workers'
relation with the trade union. (The plant had been rapidly organized
by the United Automobile Workers, and relations between it and
management were stable.) Although often 'green' unionists, two
thirds of the workers were favourably disposed to the union. The
authors comment:

> The nature of the workers' comments together with other evidence suggests
> that, in addition to its usual bargaining functions, the union met a psychological
> need by counterbalancing in part the sense of impersonality and anonymity
> men felt in their work.[11]

By now the pattern of thinking underlying this study should be
clearer. Technology can prevent the formation of true work-groups
and this frustrates the worker's natural urge for social attachments.
He becomes unadjusted:

> Causes of poor adjustment to the group situation are manifold ... but too
> often overlooked is the fact that technology in any given operational unit may
> be the crucial factor in determining the character of the social relationships
> for any individual or for a group of individuals.[12]

But unlike a later writer (Sayles, see Chapter 20 below) with an
otherwise comparable view of the deterministic nature of technology
Walker and Guest are relatively uninterested in its effects on
workers' behaviour.

Their brief chapter on this is little more than a discussion of
quit-rates and absenteeism: these are high in the automobile
industry as a whole, and in Plant X quit-rates correlated with the
number of mass production features in the job. Despite their
respondents' statements that machine-pacing was the most disliked feature of the work, and the men's suggestions for improving
the work by introducing more rest-pauses and the chance to vary
their work-pace (by building 'banks', or 'working up the line'),
Walker and Guest see the main problem as one of overcoming
some kind of psychological starvation:

> We suggest that the sense of becoming de-personalized, of becoming anony-
> mous as against remaining oneself, is for those who feel it a psychologically more

disturbing result of the work environment than either the boredom or the tension that arise from repetitive and machine-paced work.[13]

Thus, although one must certainly agree with their claim that 'one of the interesting results of our study . . . is a fairly clear picture of the *kind* of social interaction a moving-belt technology permits and also the kind it denies',[14] it is appropriate to remark that they uncritically assume that this interaction is insufficient to satisfy some natural psychological need, and do not give adequate attention to the patterns of behaviour which may be associated with it. They are, as it were, unconsciously glancing over their shoulders for the approval of Mayo's ghost.

These unacknowledged affiliations may be detected in their justification for the main nostrums they suggest for mitigating the deprivations of the assembly-line. These – job-rotation and job-enlargement – are viewed as being likely to increase adjustment as much by increasing the extent of social interaction as by reducing boredom and monotony. Their call for experiments to determine how far jobs can be redesigned to permit more social contact, and recommendation of group incentive schemes (a direct echo from Wyatt and Fraser, and Mayo), exemplify a similar faith in the virtues of teamwork. But such remedies ignore the possible implications of the orientation of workers to the job. This had already been sketched by Dalton,[15] though it is to be explored more thoroughly elsewhere.[16]

None the less, by focusing on the notion that workplace phenomena might be significantly influenced by the technical apparatus of production, this study is a watershed in American industrial studies. Again, there is a worthy humanitarian impulse behind the call for job-rotation and job-enlargement. These devices are the analogue of the participative leadership of the psycho-technologists (see next chapter). The bait for management is likewise the prospect of higher productivity, or, at least, reduced administrative costs.

Neither set of devices have quite lived up to expectations, especially economic expectations, but they have certainly led to minor alleviations in the monotony of mass-production work.[17]

ORGANIZATIONAL
PSYCHO-TECHNOLOGY
AND
THE SELF

An important school of writers whose work in a number of respects accords with the technological implications approach became influential, especially in the United States, in the later 1950s. Frequently they are referred to as the 'neo-human relations' school, or as 'organizational psychologists'.[1] Much in their work certainly justifies the first title. The second embraces a more heterogeneous group of contributors than those whose work will be examined here.

For these analysists I prefer the term 'organizational psycho-technologists', on three counts: (i) they view 'conventional' formal organization as a set of techniques embodying specific psychological assumptions held by its designers; (ii) they assert that this form of organization generates individual psychological distress; (iii) they offer technical organizational prescriptions to improve matters. They may also be characterized as a group of essentially kindly men who have interpreted the psychological formulations of A. H. Maslow too selectively and too zealously.

Maslow suggested that human behaviour is driven by distinct sets of needs or motivations.[2] In order of importance, these are: physiological need, safety, love, esteem and self-actualization. A kind of ratchet mechanism governs the quest for fulfilment of these needs. To simplify, when a man is hungry his overriding obsession is food; but once this need has been satisfied his behaviour will be governed by a search for safety. Failure to gratify the next set of needs results in frustration, and eventually in pathological symptoms. If, however, the objects of the class are attainable, they become powerful motivators, and the appetites of those fortunate enough to obtain them will graduate to a higher set still. A lucky minority will even succeed in satisfying their needs for self-actualization. The latter signifies a sense of personal worth and achievement, a realization of one's human potential.[3] Maslow was careful to qualify this general theory of behaviour by noting the need to investigate modifying factors, including 'the role of association, habit and conditioning' and 'the relation between needs and cultural patterns'.[4] Enthusiastic followers have been less guarded.

Douglas McGregor is a case in point. His views are conveyed, with almost embarrassing sincerity, in his *The Human Side of the Enterprise*.[5] Acknowledging his debt to Maslow, he distinguishes three major classes of need: physiological, social and self-fulfilment. Self-fulfilment is especially important, but McGregor argues that coventional organizational structure and practices totally ignore it. The 'theory' which lies behind this form of organization is called Theory X, and is pernicious. Its assumptions are that workers are passive, indolent, unambitious, self-centred, resistant to change and gullible, and therefore that the manager's task is to coerce and manipulate them by any means at his disposal. Practically the only acceptable assumption of Theory X, in fact, is that management has a basic right to organize the enterprise to pursue economic goals.

Indeed, it reappears as the very first term of Theory Y, which is healthy, and otherwise directly opposed to Theory X in all its assumptions. This tells us that employees are indifferent to organizational goals only because experience so teaches them; that all are capable of at least some personal psychic development; and that management must so structure the organization that employees' private goals coincide with the needs of the organization (We are not told whether organizational needs are also hierarchically ordered;

or whether organizations too become frustrated and aggressive if their needs are not met!)

Theory Y, in fact, is more of a programme than a theory. Mc-Gregor uses it to argue against conventional forms of organization, pleading for the spread of job-enlargement, participative leadership and decentralization of organizational power in general.*

Rensis Likert, a more empirically minded writer, likewise views prevailing organizational structures as self-defeating and unacceptable. Higher management, who apply the logic of line organization and job specialization, must be held responsible for this. Such neat organizational geometry is characterized by flows of information and advice, each in its private channel, from a group of subordinates to a common superior; reverse flows of orders and instructions issue from the superior to each subordinate. Group activity within each such organizational segment is thus prevented, reducing collaboration and delaying the transmission of information.

Yet, Likert claims, much research demonstrates a link between high production and the practice of general, delegatory and considerate supervision. Successful organizations are staffed by personnel with attitudes favourable to one another. They do not rely merely on financial incentives, but tap such powerful motivators as desire for status, recognition, approval, security and new experience. They thus become 'tightly knit, effectively functioning social systems', where there is good communication, participation in decisions and sensitivity to others.[6]

Such findings purportedly become comprehensible in terms of the needs hierarchy, which suggests other structural changes. Organizations should be restructured as a series of interlinked collaborative groups. The critical role of group leaders as the link-pins of the organization must be recognized. Participative groups demand leaders whose own bosses accept and operate the participative philosophy, and they will only do so if their own superiors in turn accept it. Thus, participation should be practised from top to bottom. It will not only improve performance because the cohesive group is superior to the individual as the basic work

* He also relies for his limited industrial evidence on the early studies of the Survey Research Center.

unit, but it will enable organization members to perceive the importance of the organizational 'mission'. To get this message across, the manager must relate it to the individual aims and views of his subordinates. Participative groups enable him to appraise these aims quickly.

Since both of the foregoing writers are highly prescriptive, and over-selective in their use of evidence, I shall not discuss their ideas in any detail. It is fairer to assess the school as a whole with reference to Chris Argyris, its most sophisticated member.[7] Argyris's starting point is 'an assumption that human beings are need-fulfilling, goal-achieving unities. They create various types of strategies to fulfil their needs and to achieve their goals.'[8] An organization usually takes the form of a pyramid. Yet these structures conflict directly with the individual needs of their members. Individual and organization are strongly opposed.

This conflict is usually severe, because in 'our culture' – and Argyris's partial escape from the imputed universalism of the Maslovian scheme should be noted – we acquire certain expectations. As we grow up we are encouraged to proceed from a state of dependence to independence, from passivity to activity, from a narrow to a broad choice in our behaviour, from casual interests and amusements to those which are sustained, from a short to a long time-perspective, from indifference towards social rank to positive status-striving, and from sanctions on our behaviour which are imposed by some external agency to internal self-regulation. In short, we progress from irresponsible childhood to responsible adulthood, and learn to associate lack of responsibility with child-ishness, and its possession with maturity.

Yet a person's condition in most work situations is one of dependence and constraint. Several factors that create this condition can be distinguished. 'The formal organization-structure is the first variable (includes technology).'[9] Usually associated with this are directive leadership, and managerial control measures such as budgets, quality control, time-and-motion study and rate-setting. As we descend the organizational hierarchy the more severe the constraints stemming from these sources become.

Dependence produces frustration and tension. These are resolved either through absenteeism, quitting, apathy, defensiveness, the creation of informal groups or claims for higher wages. Moreover, the organization is directly responsible for many other social evils, since people come to 'accept these ways of behaving as being proper for their life outside the organization'.[10] For its part, the organization seeks to repress these responses, especially the formation of informal organization, by tightening the formal structures. This closes a circuit of positive feedback.

As an example of the process in action Argyris has cited the case of the 'X Y Z Plant'. Manual recruits to this organization were carefully screened by the personnel department to detect any disposition to rock the organizational boat. Those passing were assigned either to highly skilled or low-skilled working categories. In terms of supervision and economic rewards, the situations of both categories in the plant were more or less comparable. But the highly skilled group worked on more challenging and absorbing jobs. In interview, distinct differences in predisposition between the two became apparent. The highly skilled showed themselves much more concerned over the quality of their work, more interested in it and more conscious of their 'self-worth'. But they were far less concerned with money. Argyris asserts that these predispositions were generated *after* entry to the organization; they were a response to the conditioning effects of the work situation. But his evidence for this claim is indirect, and in my opinion inconclusive.

Where the nature of the work situation bars self-actualization, a strong informal organization comes into play. This can undermine the authority of supervisors, who become passive. Although they acknowledged that production performance was good, the X Y Z management disliked this style of supervision, which they regarded as a sign of weak character. They therefore put pressure on foremen to be more 'go-getting' and to constantly inspect the workshops. Workers enjoyed this attention, but the foremen resented it. Argyris asserts that their dissatisfaction was shown in agitation for more money, status and control, and an increased tendency to contract out of active leadership. This intensified managerial pressure on them and the frequency of workshop tours. Management, however, were generally pleased with workers' behaviour, which they attributed to the carefully selective hiring policy. Thus, Argyris proposes, the managing system, like the technology, 'coerces psychologically different employees to behave in a similar manner',[11] and the entire system is self-reinforcing.

Five observations on the work of the organizational psycho-technologists are worth considering. Firstly, the status of the 'needs hierarchy' concept is uncertain. If we assume that needs are real how can their existence be proved? As with all such psychological concepts no direct method is available. We are obliged to resort to indirect methods. We can say, for example, that if a man is observed to pursue status, that suggests he has a need for status. But this is unsatisfactory: to say status is sought because of a status-seeking propensity reminds us of the explanation that opium makes us sleepy by virtue of its dormative properties. We can argue just as well that if status is sought, it is not necessarily as an end in itself, but as a means to other ends, e.g. more wealth, power, etc. How many needs are there, in fact? None of these writers seems able to agree. (These difficulties recall the arid disputes between instinctual psychologists.) Again, are the needs, and their imputed ordering, universal and innate? Comparative data suggest they are not. And if we accept some cultural variation, as Argyris does, we must still be careful. The expectations that he suggests are implanted in 'our culture' are perhaps those which guide child-rearing in suburban America, but not all Americans live in suburbs (or rely on Dr Spock's admittedly influential child-rearing manual).

How sound are the assumptions on which much of this work rests? It is true that there is evidence of an association between repetitive work and high absenteeism, quit-rates and comparable indices;[12] and even between low occupational status and poor mental health.[13] But an explanation in terms of frustrated needs or expectations – particularly non-financial ones – is far from being the only plausible one available.[14] If widespread frustration and dissatisfaction exist – and some writers question their supposed extent[15] – they may be as much the product of conflicting social value systems as a sum of individual responses to deprivatory work situations.[16] A recurring theme of the psycho-technologists which this and the previous objection throws into question is that frustrated higher needs breed an obsession with cash rewards. This doctrine is obviously attractive to management but its scientific foundations are fragile.

These writers are highly selective in their use of evidence, especially of that which bears on their proposals for organizational reform. Much of it derives from the studies of work-groups undertaken by the Survey Research Center, especially its early studies. We saw earlier that S.R.C. workers had modified their early conclusions drastically by the mid 1950s.* Moreover, all of this work has serious methodological defects; it is therefore unsatisfactory to base sweeping generalizations on it.

These writers repeatedly muddle their practical, ethical and scientific obligations. Clearly men of goodwill, they are genuinely concerned with the well-being of all groups in the organization, and eager to remove destructive stresses. But equally obviously, they are very concerned about efficiency and profitability. This makes suspect their whole analysis, which tends to show that a fortuitous concurrence exists between individual and organizational needs, and that management can accept their programmes with confidence. This is very reminiscent of 'classical' human relations. To their credit, however, they are more critical of prevailing management practice, and more specific in their prescriptions, than were their predecessors. All the same, the impression remains that science, however unconsciously, is once more the servant of power.

Further, their concentration on the individual-organization nexus has led them to ignore comparisons between organizations, and the influence on organizational form and performance of environmental factors. This might seem a minor omission. In fact, given their commitment to organizational effectiveness, it is critical. To take one example, the kind of overlapping-groups structure advocated by Likert as universally efficient is not supported by the work of investigators like Burns and Stalker.[17] If effectiveness is the overriding goal such a structure may be appropriate only in a rapidly changing environment. A more general modification is suggested by Woodward's work, which we shall discuss shortly. Recent experimental evidence has further weakened the internal

* See Chapter 15 above.

prescriptions for effectiveness themselves.[18] One cannot say simply that they overestimate the range of organizational choice, however; there are only two basic choices available. Management has generally chosen wrongly. The 'correct' choice, their own, is in fact a rigid prescription.

It is disagreeable to end upon a totally negative note, and I think it is fair to endorse a point made about these writers by David Silverman. Unlike many organizational theorists they do not view the worker as a being who merely *responds* to technology or formal organization. He brings with him certain needs and expectations which also affect his behaviour at work. In other words, their polemic is implicitly anti-behaviourist.[19] It is wrong to derive such needs from Maslow's extremely general and rather conjectural philosophical psychology

TECHNOLOGY
AND
AGGRIEVED
GROUPS

All-embracing structural prescriptions find little place in Sayles's *Behavior of Industrial Work Groups*;[1] neither does 'self-actualizing man', who is ousted in favour of a kind of collective *homo economicus*. This seems the first major industrial study to have capitalized on W. F. Whyte's numerous asides and marginalia on the effect of technology on work-group behaviour. (Whyte and Chapple receive generous credits in the Preface.) It was undertaken on an ambitious comparative basis: data on 300 'groups' in thirty plants were collected over a four-year period. Moreover, Sayles set out to examine and explain *behaviour*, i.e. actual patterns of activity, rather than to splash around in the pleasant, but usually shallow, waters of attitude research.

Sayles concentrated upon behaviour of a specific kind, namely grievance activity: evidently, high grievance activity tends to identify those sections of an organization where tension and conflict have become marked. Sayles's starting-point is that certain plants or shop departments, or sections of them, have a reputation in both managerial and union circles for being troublesome, despite changes in management policy, turnover or changes in supervisory style. Others are noted for their quiescence. He tries to show that such 'groups' are largely a product of the technology.[2] Four kinds of 'groups' – apathetic, erratic, strategic and conservative – are delineated. Actually Sayles has caused untold confusion by clinging to the term 'group' here. These are not real groups, but ideal-typical patterns of grievance behaviour, to which the observed behaviour of actual interest aggregations variously approximates. He makes this plain enough,[3] but would have done better to have employed a term like 'pattern' throughout the book.

The 'patterns' are reasonably self-explanatory. The *apathetic* is marked by quiescence, disunity, suppressed discontent, lack of leadership; aggregates showing it are typically poorly led, low-paid and low producers. The *erratic* is characterized by inflammability, inconsistent grievance pressure and sudden switches in loyalties; departments in this category are centrally led, as fickle in output behaviour as in grievance activity and disliked by management. Continuous pressure on management, planned activity, high internal unity and high productivity mark the *strategic* pattern. A *conservative* pattern is one of restrained pressure to achieve concrete objectives which follows a regular, cyclical path; aggregates showing it tend to have high job-status and good output.

Actual departments or shop segments approaching a given pattern, Sayles claims, show 'a striking similarity in technological characteristics'.[4] For example, aggregates with a conservative pattern will typically be highly paid craftsmen employed on skilled, self-supervised work, either highly concentrated in their own building or ranging over the whole plant, with only the most general supervision, to undertake maintenance duties. Sayles calls the latter 'scatter groups'.

But technology – whether in its hardware or software senses – does not operate directly. Rather, different technical milieux must be seen as enabling or restricting a given pattern: 'We believe that a group's behaviour in the plant is a product of its *inherent ability to function in a certain way*.'[5]

Two important sets of factors are explored: those which tend to distinguish an aggregate from other 'groups' in the plant; and those which bear on the internal structuring of the segment or aggregate. On the first count nine factors are discussed – the segment's status in the plant, its size, homogeneity, discretion in work, compactness, sex-composition and hours, the degree of repetitiveness in its work-functions and how far they are essential to the plant as a whole. The general conclusion is that activity is influenced most by the segment's status, the indispensability of its work and its size and homogeneity.

Size and homogeneity taken together appear particularly important. The larger the group and the more homogeneous the tasks of its members, the greater the likelihood of its mobilizing to press grievances. Sayles here introduces his interesting concept of 'resonance':

> What seemed essential for verbalizing complaints and uniting people to 'right them' was some reinforcement or *resonance* factor. Where this reverberation was provided by people having identical experiences, each one could hear his own grievances repeated and magnified.[6]

This process is analogous to those depicted on a wider canvas in theories of class-formation or, at an intermediate level, of unionization – for example, in Lockwood's *The Black-coated Worker*.[7]

Turning to factors affecting the internal organization of an aggregate – such as internal task-differentiation, promotion chances, frequency of interaction, the work-flow, etc. – Sayles finds that: 'Technology also shapes the relationships within the work-group, and thus the structure of the group itself.'[8] For example, where job skills are very mixed, status and sectional interest are against concerted action. Again, in an otherwise homogeneous department, technical arrangements may create 'islands' of workers whose highly interlocking task-structure encourages separatism and cliques.

Taking both inter-group and intra-group factors together, the following associations appear. A high degree of grievance activity is shown by workers with fairly high or middle-status jobs, high indispensability of function and considerable control over their own performance; a low degree of activity is linked to very high- or very low-status jobs. As to the form of activity, unpremeditated action occurs amongst crews or assembly-groups with interdependent work-operations; and deliberate, predictable activity in segments with individual and independent jobs, though sometimes also in very homogeneous teams and crews, or groups on short assembly-lines.

At this point Sayles approaches a technologically determinist viewpoint. He notes:

> Upon reflection it appears as though all of our relevant variables are related to the technological system designed by the company to organize the work process ... We recognize that many persistent industrial relations problems have their *roots* in the technology of the plant. We are in the habit of attributing these to individual worker or manager characteristics ... However, this study also suggests that the social system *erected* by the technological process is also a basic and continuing *determinant* of work group attitudes and actions.[9]
> (The italics are mine.)

But in fact he recognizes quite well that although technology may influence the patterns of intra-plant industrial conflict, it cannot initiate it. For 'these technological factors are really *enabling conditions*. They do not explain what sets off a spate of aggressive activity, what brings it to a halt, and what are the personal motivations involved'[10] (Sayles's italics). The motivations introduced are rather unambiguously economic in character.*

Groups constantly compare their status and earnings and: 'In a sense the groups we have been talking about resemble the purely selfish economic men of classical theory.'[11] This makes the industrial relations of the plant inherently dynamic.

Two things about this analysis are worrying. First, Sayles veers towards a dubious holism in his view of the work-group. A group may act as if it were a unity, but his own analysis shows that the degree of such cohesion is most variable. Second, the reference points for reward comparison are all intra-plant. This tendency to exclude extra-plant sources of motivation and comparison must be questioned. But Sayles perceives positive virtues in it. Too much theorizing in industrial sociology, he asserts, has concentrated on broad occupational groups. When we look at interest

---

* A scheme for interpreting how individual economic aims coalesce into a group-based form is summarized in diagrammatic form on page 105 of *The Behaviour of Industrial Work Groups*. Broadly, this is reminiscent of Whyte's scheme in *Money and Motivation*. It is also recognized that leadership may be necessary to articulate grievances, but this is not pressed.

groups at the plant level they do in fact behave as wider occupational groups supposedly conduct themselves.

Taking the point that the worker will interpret his general occupational situation by reference to an immediate work-situation, why should this exclude an examination of action in terms of wider occupational identification? Such an exclusion reintroduces plant sociology. Few workers, after all, live and die in the service of one firm. Sayles's own analysis suggests that members of many occupations will find themselves in technical milieux which, though in different firms, will be comparable. Similar problems and objectives will thus recur for them throughout industry. Sayles seems too eager to play down this possible extension of resonance.

In his general discussion of research and theory on groups in industry Sayles emphasizes the limitations of Mayoite thinking about the link between teamwork and productivity. This hypothetical quest for social equilibrium ignores simple economic interest as a group unifier and motivator. We should focus on intra-plant interest aggregates, and: 'To repeat, this is not the traditional concept of the informal group seeking conformity with established norms of conduct. These are much more free enterprise units, interacting in a struggle for maximization of utility.'[12] The interest aggregate is thus often involved in a triple disloyalty – to management, to the union, and to fellow workers.

Here, a quite legitimate reminder of the rational basis for industrial conflict is taken to excess: the plant must be viewed as a war of each (aggregate) against all. Let us consider why. Sayles was writing at a time of intense reaction against Mayoite human relations, and passes up few chances to upbraid the founder's ghost.[13] But he none the less regards himself as a reformer *within* human relations. This (and the subtitle of the book, *Prediction and Control*) explain his concern with the plant.

Sayles accepts a commitment to assist administrators to manage with greater sophistication. If technology causes conflict, it is futile to blame it on hot-heads or agitators, or hope to eradicate it by communications. With some understatement he notes that 'this report should have some significance for the industrial engineer'.[14] He also, correctly, I think, reminds managers that the logic of technological causation cannot be overlooked when ogling the alluring philosophy of participative management. Rather, the administrator should devote extra attention to likely trouble-spots. The 'administrator', incidentally, does include trade union officials; if Sayles is a manipulator he is an impartial one.

The main fault of this study lies in its tendency, despite the lavish use of comparative material, to concentrate attention on the plant, to regard it as a closed system, rather than in its 'technological determinism'. Sayles's position on the latter score is more ambiguous than diagrams entitled 'How technology shapes work behaviour'[15] and other fanciful lapses suggest. Certainly, too, his use of the term 'group' is unsound, his data over-represent certain industries and he underplays the influence of incentive systems on group cohesion. But it is his underestimation of the link between in-plant and out-plant phenomena which I find most disappointing. Even at a practical level this could lead to poor management. Faced with an aggrieved group, a manager, or union official, might decide there was no real grievance; that the agitation was a sign merely of inter-group rivalry aggravated by technological factors. But of course the pressure could originate in the community experiences or reference operations of the workers concerned.

But though this contribution is something of a sociological failure, it fails interestingly and usefully. Sayles unquestionably demonstrated that technology has *some* important effects on in-plant behaviour, and provided an important reminder that workers' actions have a rational basis. The book also counteracts some of the careless prescriptions of the organizational psycho-technologists. For this, its own value-position is almost excusable.

MANAGEMENT ORGANIZATION
AND
TECHNICAL EVOLUTION

Just as Sayles sometimes comes close to asserting that technology determines the cohesiveness and militancy of work-groups, Joan Woodward all but claims that it dictates management organization (and to a lesser degree, the tone of intra-plant human relations).[1] Woodward's work thus challenges the assumptions of classical human relations and organizational psycho-technology alike. But it also exposes the phoney universalism of classical administrative theory. Publication of her early findings brought excited responses from teachers of administration, especially in Britain, where 'management' was on the point of taking off into rapid growth and acceptance as an academically respectable subject, and the timing of *Management and Technology* appeared particularly tasteless.[2]

Since reports of Woodward's work in South Essex are easy to obtain and read, and some readers will already know it, I shall provide only an outline here. A survey of a hundred firms, virtually a full census of industrial plants with over a hundred employees in this area of Britain, conducted mainly in 1954–5, showed that the wide variations of formal organization discovered could not be related immediately to size, industry or effectiveness. In about half, standard principles of administration – prescriptions about the line of command, span of control, etc. – had been applied in some form: their application in no measure guaranteed success.

But distinct patterns began to emerge when firms were grouped according to their technology. Woodward's conception of technology at least at this time, was not rigorous: in some contexts it denotes merely tools and equipment, i.e. hardware; in others it seems to refer mainly to working methods and managerial control systems, i.e. software; but generally it appears to denote a mixture of the two, called the 'production system' or the 'system of techniques'.

Eleven production categories were established and firms allocated to each classification.* Adjacent categories were then telescoped into three major classes: unit and small batch, large batch and mass, and process production–system groupings. Both the detailed and the general groups were, however, used as more than purely heuristic classes; indeed, they embodied a developmental theory of industry:

It will be seen that the systems of production given [above] form a scale; they are listed in order of chronological development, and technical complexity; the production of unit articles to customers' individual requirement being the oldest and simplest form of manufacture, and continuous-flow production of dimensional products, the most advanced and most complicated. Moving along the scale ... it becomes increasingly possible to exercise control over manufacturing operations, the physical limitations of production being better known and understood.[3]

Distinct association between certain broad features of formal organization and technology, that is, the type of production system, were detected (e.g. a lengthening of lines of command, an increase in the ratios of managers and clerical workers to production personnel, a narrowing of the chief executive's span of control) as technical complexity increased: 'Therefore the main conclusion reached through this research project was that the existence of the link between technology and social structure ... can be demonstrated empirically.'[4] Further, the most 'successful' firms in each major production category possessed structural features which approximated to the median values for each dimension of organization which could be quantified. For instance, in process production the median

* The number of categories in fact varies between Woodward's reports.

value for the number of levels in the management hierarchy was six; those process firms which had six levels were much more likely to be successful than those which had four or eight.

Woodward commented: 'While at first sight there seemed to be no link between organization and success, and no one best way of organizing a factory, it subsequently became apparent that there was a particular form of organization most appropriate to each technical situation.'[5] This appears to put paid to traditional administrative theory. However: 'Within a limited range of technology this was also the form of organization most closely in line with the principles and ideas of management theory.'[6] This may well be because the exponents of 'classical' management theory have been practitioners themselves mainly within this branch of production (in fact, mass-production) and have generalized their experience onto all industry.

Now such findings clearly undermine the human relations and organizational psycho-technological verities in so far as they indicate that the effectiveness of a firm relates to the fit between its production system and its formal organization, and not necessarily to managerially manipulated informal organization or to participative, interlocking teams. And they bring severe discomfiture to exponents of classical administrative science. But do the South Essex data do much else? Personally, I do not think so. Though Woodward usually described her studies as a contribution to industrial *sociology*, they are so only indirectly, when taken together with the findings of other writers. They are unsociological because they offer relatively little behavioural or attitudinal data about the groups of workers staffing these organizations which can be used in a comparative way to identify the possible influence of technical factors on intra-plant social structure and action.* Woodward herself admitted that even the association established between technology, organizational form and performance cannot be explained in causal terms.

* She does suggest that a technical system has effects on managerial *personalities*, and hence on behaviour. But her data are impressionistic and throw little light on the possibility of differential recruitment or self-selection. See ibid., pp. 79–80.

There are two obvious reasons for this. Firstly, the initial assignment was to verify the 'laws' of administration, not to study and explain industrial behaviour. Therefore the data collected, which derived from broad indicators of formal organization, related almost entirely to formal organizational properties. Only the most superficial behavioural information – for instance, on industrial relations 'climates' – was gathered for the full sample of firms. Secondly, no fixed definition of technology was adopted. Again, Woodward herself concedes 'the lack of a satisfactory instrument for measuring technology', and wonders: 'Is the control system a further dimension of technology?'* If it is – and I believe there is a good case for considering it as such – then it should be included consistently. In the Essex studies it appears sometimes to be included, at least implicitly, and other times is treated either as an aspect of formal organization or as a separate variable. One result is some logical difficulty with the whole thesis: the proposition that organization varies with technology is less arresting in so far as technology *equals* organization, and vice versa.

In this regard, it seems a pity that Woodward did not follow through more systematically her own numerous *aperçus* about the relation between the nature of the product and that of the production system. Her scale of technical complexity or advance is equally a scale of product standardization and predictability: as these increase so, generally, will the complexity of the equipment used in manufacture, that is, the hardware aspect of technology; likewise the control system, the software aspect, will become more highly structured and specific. These two modes of technology, however, are not necessarily related, though they may usually be so empirically. Thus, 'technological advance' becomes an ambiguous term. One can envisage for example the development of a highly structured and specific control system to programme the construction of a unit article, without any comparable improvement in tooling. Likewise, an advance in tooling could occur without an equivalent advance in programming know-how.

* Ibid., p. 249. Control systems themselves may be considered largely as social products: the textbook principles of organization are an obvious instance, and recognized as such by Woodward.

Such considerations throw into question the evolutionary aspect of the scale of technical complexity. Woodward pictures process firms as approximate examples of the most sophisticated production technology – automation. But such a judgement has a hardware bias. One can envisage a unit production firm – in Woodward's scale it would fall at the rudimentary stage of technical development – installing a computer system that prescribed in great detail job allocations and timings for each contract. In a software sense such a firm would also be automated – and one would certainly anticipate changes in its organization – and probably in its industrial relations 'climate'.

Admittedly, Woodward became aware of such prblems, and was developing more sophisticated measures of production systems at the time of her premature and tragic death.[7] Work such as this is of the greatest importance, whether or not (and it now seems increasingly unlikely) the general automation of manufacturing is imminent or even possible. However, it must be linked very closely to studies of workers' attitudes and behaviour which take into account out-plant influences. Such studies demand a sophisticated understanding of society as a socio-economic whole, especially if they adopt an evolutionary view of the development of industry. Blauner's work, which I review in the next chapter, provides an appropriate reminder of this requirement.

TECHNOLOGY AND 'ALIENATION'

Robert Blauner's *Alienation and Freedom* is an ambitious comparison between certain objective conditions of work in various industries. Though he recognizes that the economics of any industry, its division of labour and its social organization are significant, Blauner stresses that the 'most important single factor that gives an industry a distinctive character is its *technology*'.[1] Technology, for Blauner, is essentially machinery, i.e. hardware.[2] Though he recognizes the possibility of some organizational choice in the design of work-roles and relationships, Blauner is less interested in technology's influence on these features of the work-situation, or upon workers' behaviour, than in its implications for what he calls workers' alienation.

'Alienation,' Blauner maintains, is 'a general syndrome made up of a number of different objective conditions and subjective feeling-states.'[3] These refer to four kinds of satisfaction or deprivation a work-situation can create, and are denoted by the terms *powerlessness, meaninglessness, isolation* and *self-estrangement*. Each, Blauner asserts, can be operationalized. For example, *powerlessness* can be gauged by examining how far workers can control their conditions of employment, for instance through unions, or – much more important to Blauner – regulate the work process itself, their pace of work or their working methods. Lack of control over managerial policies or finished products are not considered: Blauner points out that American workers express no interest in such aspects of power. (His reasoning here is contentious.)

Meaninglessness refers to the immediate significance a work-operation or product can have for a worker. Some products, such as shoes, are more immediately meaningful than others, such as computer memory-banks. *Isolation* refers to 'absence of a sense of membership in an industrial community'[4] such as the plant in particular – though Blauner concedes union loyalties may mitigate isolation too. *Self-estrangement* is maximized when work denies a sense of wholeness and identity. In one sense it is a product of the three other dimensions. But it also arises when work is not 'highly integrated into the totality of an individual's social commitments';[5] that is, when it is not a central personal, social or religious value, but merely a resented means to other ends.

Using various rough measures for each dimension Blauner assesses the typical level of alienation in four industrial environments – printing, cotton-spinning, automobile-making and petro-chemicals. Each of these industries employs a characteristic technology; in turn, craft, machine-tending, mass- and process-production. (They are thus very similar to Woodward's three broad types of production-system.)

Printing emerges with a low score for alienation. The printer sets his own pace, escapes management pressure, chooses his own techniques and is supported by a powerful union. He exercises a complex skill, enjoys plentiful social contact during work, and has a high job-status. He identifies closely with his work. Automobile workers, as one would expect from the work of investigators such as Walker and Guest, suffer extreme alienation. Mass-production denies control, minimizes meaning, increases social isolation and prevents any sense of self-actualization.

In process-production, alienation is once more abated, thanks to the technology. Petrochemical workers work in prosperous, technically advanced plants where many of the operations are automated. Except during crises when pipes fracture or reactions go critical they largely control their pace of work and are free to move around engaging in pleasant social intercourse. Organized in teams responsible for the safety of the process and quality of the product, process workers attain considerable understanding of the chemical reactions whose progress they monitor. This, he insists, inculcates a sense of belonging, achievement and responsibility, which is reinforced by close contact with highly educated and modern-minded managers.

The foregoing industries allow Blauner to build up a strong argument for technologically determined alienation. Objective features of the varying work environments can be correlated – at least to some extent – with workers' subjective feelings (as reported in attitude-polls: we shall come back to this point).

However, Blauner's machine-minding textile workers present a problem. With minimal control over their highly repetitive, monotonous and gruelling work, subjected to autocratic supervision and with little social contact during work, it would seem likely that the machine-minders would experience considerable self-estrangement. But subjective indicators suggest the reverse. Apparently the machine-minders were relatively satisfied with their work. Blauner explains this by pointing to out-plant attachments. His material relates to mills in small, tightly knit rural communities in the southern states of America. Observers have suggested that southern mill-workers form a kind of industrial caste in which notions of submissiveness and fatalism dominate the subject's world-view. In this deviant group, then, subjective alienation is held at bay by community loyalties and values.

But if objective alienation can be neutralized by out-plant factors, Blauner's technological determinism largely collapses – at least, if he wishes to retain a correlative subjective dimension to alienation. Alternatively – and this is more important – it obliges us to abandon the whole conception of alienation as a property of industrial environments rather than of the prevailing socio-economic formation as a whole.

Actually, Blauner's indicators for self-estrangement (subjective alienation) are less than convincing. Presuming such a complex structure exists, measuring it would involve the construction of, for example, elaborate scaling devices to be administered in extensive depth interviews. Blauner, however, relies mainly on a job-attitude poll conducted over a dozen years before he wrote his book. This asked workers such questions as whether their work interested them, whether they would pick the same job again, and so on. It is hard to believe that Blauner could take this as valid evidence for self-estrangement. But he does, if rather selectively. (Some of the poll findings seem to contradict his thesis.)* In fact all the poll really demonstrates is that workers in different industries expressed varying amounts of satisfaction with their work when questioned by a pollster.

Since Blauner undoubtedly does distinguish important objective variations between industrial environments, his confusion over subjective alienation might charitably be disregarded. However, his aims are rather more grandiose. In brief, he believes his analysis indicates that technical progress will reduce alienation. Since industrialism commenced, he argues, alienation has described an 'inverted-U curve', i.e. non-alienating craft work was superseded by alienating machine-minding and mass-production, which in turn will be superseded by tomorrow's automated industry of which non-alienating process work is an advance example.

Whether such optimism is warranted by the technical and economic realities is beside the point. Likewise, no one who takes Blauner's evidence as a whole would deny that automated industry would remove some of the deprivations of contemporary mass-production work. What is misleading is his assertion that technological advance alone would reduce *alienation*.

Blauner's use of this concept is thoroughly naïve and unhistorical, though highly fashionable. In the 1950s, Anglo-Saxon sociologists were rediscovering Marx's early writings. In them, Marx revised the traditional philosophical concept of alienation and centred his own 'naturalistic humanist' philosophy upon it.[6] His concern with the concrete led him to analyse the man–machine relationship as one aspect of human alienation. Discovery of the humanistic young

* For example the Roper data indicated that no less than 49 per cent even of printers were unsure that they would, or said they would not, choose the same occupation again; 82 per cent of textile workers asserted that they found their work nearly always or mostly interesting: see ibid., pp. 202–4.

Marx excited academic sociologists not only because these early writings are in themselves extremely suggestive but because they were presumed to bear little relation to his more controversial mature thought. Alienation supposedly disappeared in Marx's 'ideological' political economy.

In fact, the reverse is true. Marx's examination of political economy was a stage in his uncompleted philosophical programme. His work as a whole can be viewed as an exploration of, and search for a solution to, the problem of human alienation. Be that as it may, it is a violation of Marx's work, and of the philosophical tradition against which he reacted, to represent alienation merely as a matter of a worker's experience of a socio-technical situation. Deprivations suffered in that situation are naturally a facet of a worker's alienation. But the conquest of alienation requires the dissolution of capitalist relations of production, which permit the appropriation of surplus value by private owners or dictatorial state agencies, and their replacement by the ownership and control of the means of production, and of the product, by producers as a class. (Even such changes as these would be the necessary but not sufficient conditions for true self-actualization.)*

If Blauner had accepted the full connotations of the alienation concept his textile workers would have presented fewer problems. Their subjective lack of self-estrangement, far from mitigating their objective alienation, demonstrates the extent of their genuine alienation. Their failure to perceive the full extent of their deprivations in work stems from acceptance of values which serve not their real interests but those of the employers who exploit them. To over-simplify, they are victims of false consciousness.

I resign myself to the likelihood that many readers will regard this as an arrogant value-judgement. Defence of it would go beyond the scope of this chapter. But I think two things are indis-

---

* The importance of this qualification has not been fully recognized by critics of Marx, and possibly still less by 'official' Marxists, until recently. The single most important reason is that Marx's completed work fails to elaborate on it. However, it is a central theme of the programme outlined in his re-discovered – and increasingly influential – *Foundations of the Critique of Political Economy (Grundrisse)*. See K. Marx, *Grundrisse*, trans. M. Nicolaus, Allen Lane, 1973; Penguin Books, Harmondsworth, 1973.

putable. First, when an industrial sociologist utilizes empirical data about particular industrial situations to speculate on the future of society he should possess an adequate model of that society as a whole. Second, he should avoid concepts such as alienation if he is not prepared to grasp their overall meaning.

Blauner lacks any explicit model of the socio-economic whole, though the image of convergent industrial society lurks elusively in his text.* And he reduces the concept of alienation to a set of rough measures for deprivation in work. To distinguish the varying amounts of different kinds of deprivation experienced by workers in a range of socio-technical environments – and he does this admirably – was a considerable achievement. To equate this with alienation is at best misleading, though it is eloquent of the limitations of the social scientific tradition in which he was working.

* See Chapter 28 below.

23

'ORGANIZATIONAL CHOICE':
THE MAKING OF A MYTH?

None of the writers whose work we have reviewed assert, or can demonstrate, that technology – whether understood as hardware, software or both combined – uniquely determines behaviour. Yet all endow it with a primary explanatory value, whether they are examining psychological deprivation, the level of intra-plant conflict, management effectiveness or alienation: in so far as a technology demands a typical pattern of organization (if a profit is to be made) it creates role-determined behaviour.* The demands of the technology permit only marginal adjustments to the entailed system of work-roles, through job-enlargement, rotation, etc.† Such conclusions are gloomy for managers eager to reduce industrial unrest and for humanitarians committed equally to the dignity of man and the profit motive.

Hence perhaps some of the excitement over the development of

* The work-role itself being a determined pattern: see J. Woodward, 'Industrial Behaviour – Is There a Science?', *New Society*, October 1964.

† Writers persistently claim that more could be done along these lines. But few specific radical proposals are made, whether thanks to lack of production engineering expertise or to socio-political caution. Hopes for general alleviation have consequently been linked to the arrival of an extremely ill-defined automation.

the concept of the *socio-technical system*; for a crucial feature of such systems is that: 'Unlike mechanical and other inanimate systems they possess the property of "equi-finality"; they may achieve a steady state from differing initial conditions and in differing ways.'[1] A full explanation of this statement will appear in the course of this chapter. Briefly, it claims that organization can be significantly varied without a change of technology, and with results which will put happier smiles on the faces of workers and cost-accountants alike. I believe, however, that it can deliver much less than it promises, and can be interpreted as an attack on the trained incapacities of production engineers and as an advertisement for social scientific industrial consultants. Nevertheless, if it is misleading, it is interestingly so; and much of its spuriousness has been given to it by those who have received it with enthusiasm rather than by its original proponents.

It is convenient to examine it by referring to the book *Organizational Choice*. This a full report of the research undertaken by Tavistock investigators in the Durham mines. I began by reviewing its early phase and the direction of the researchers' thought. It is instructive to end by examining their thinking in its highly influential, mature (though not final) form. (To be fair to them, the Tavistock investigators have been modifying their ideas lately. But they have been overtaken by others who are more influential – at least, as theorists.)

The empirical core of the book consists of the comparative studies of conventionally and 'compositely' organized mining teams working on longwalls. Word of informal experiments with some kind of composite organization had been coming to the researchers' ears since the pilot work in 1950. Such longwall organization is, ideally, composite in four senses: the workman is enabled to acquire a wide range of face-skills; work-groups are self-selected and share out preferred and disliked tasks equitably; they receive a bonus to be shared equally in addition to their flat-rate pay; and they proceed to the next phase of the cycle, which is in three phases, when opportunity offers, and not merely when a shift changes over. Note that such arrangements partly reproduce those of traditional organization and depend on its associated values.

To test the notion that composite working might be at least as productive as, and probably more harmonious than conventional organization, two depth studies were made: between a composite and a conventional team; and between two composite teams, one being more composite than the other. The measures used to test the consequences were rather simple, and clearly environmental factors could not be fully controlled. This was especially true of the geological one; allowance was, however, made with expert advice.

In sum, the composite group produced more, went absent less, maintained their cycles, sometimes even forging ahead of them, and also expressed higher work satisfaction. These results were reinforced by those for the variably composite teams: the more composite had marginally better records for output and absenteeism. Moreover, the relations between the composite groups and management altered significantly, as the authors note in an almost lyrical passage.* Further experimentation demonstrated the importance of the principle of self-selection into teams.†

The main concept used to explain these results is that of the *socio-technical system*. It is based on this logic: any productive system embraces a given kind of equipment and layout and a work organization: the technology sets limits on the form of this organization, but the latter has certain social and psychological properties independent of the technology. For example, given longwall technology, one can choose between conventional and composite organization: the socio-psychological consequences of the two were shown to vary importantly. Though one can examine the socio-psychological properties of systems at a multitude of levels, from that of the individual worker to, in this case, that of the National Coal Board, certain convenient boundaries can be distinguished: here, the boundary surrounding the primary work group was chosen. But we should remember that this boundary is not hermetic:

---

* 'The first difficulty is letting go the traditional managerial controls over the primary group; the second over accepting the consequent rise in the level of work now required within management. To surmount these difficulties, however, is to replace job alienation in the worker by task-oriented commitment . . .' ibid., p. 130.

† This conclusion is entwined with many qualifications, however: see ibid., p. 213.

on the social dimension, the primary work-group is a component of 'seam society' as a whole, and its relation with this larger collectivity affects its behaviour.

Constraints other than technology and wider socio-psychological attachments must, however, be taken into account. In the words of Rice: 'A socio-technical system must also satisfy the financial conditions of the industry of which it is a part. It must have economic validity.'[2] Thus the productive system has three key dimensions which are all interdependent: the technological, the social and the economic. Yet each of these possesses its own scale of independent values. To pursue one set of these and ignore the others is to invite trouble, if not disaster; more formally, optimizing along one dimension does not produce optimal results for the system as a whole. Overall system optimization usually implies sub-optimizing along each dimension.

In more concrete terms this means, for example, that if you set out exclusively to maximize profits the workers will resent it and/or your equipment will become outdated; that if you introduce technical change too quickly you will generate resistance to change in organization and probably go broke into the bargain; the latter will also happen if you pay the workers too much and permit the cosiest form of social organization. Such realities, it must be said, perhaps with the partial exception of those relating to the social dimension, were not unknown to entrepreneurs and economists of the firm before the creation of the socio-technical system concept.

It is claimed that this systems approach is impartial, and that its logic does permit significant choice, by those with decision-making power, on at least two distinct levels: that of the whole organization and that of the work-group. At this first level, in theory, managers could favour profits and ignore technological innovation and the workers' socio-psychological wellbeing. But because of the interrelation of dimensions this would in fact work only where competing organizations were equally non-innovating and where worker dissatisfaction was contained by, say, a high level of unemployment.

Alternatively, they could ignore economic considerations and concentrate on maximizing worker satisfaction. This policy, however, would require external subsidy. Given a market economy it is clear that there is in fact little choice at this level: the organization would need to make at least a normal profit to continue. Granted such an assumption, it is hard to view the systems notion as much more than a sophisticated defence of the economic status quo.* And, in fact, these theorists see its greatest potential as a guide to organizational choice at the work-group level (the cycle-group here), where greater optimization on the socio-psychological dimension may be possible.

As they state it: 'It is the socio-psychological system which affords the greatest opportunity for either formal or informal change at the level of the cycle-group – in such matters as altering the pattern of work-group organization.'[3] As we have seen, such change proved possible, and promoted further socio-psychological optimization. But it also promoted further economic optimization. Consequently the question arises whether organizational choice is really a choice at all. Surely it is a prescription for better organization? Is the improvement in socio-psychological 'climate' the real gain sought, or is it merely, by happy coincidence, a necessary precondition of more productive arrangements? If the latter, the socio-technical concept may be seen as a device for helping production engineers to discover better 'best ways'.

Possibly, some of the ambiguities which appear here may be the result of the industry chosen: the durable culture, and the dangers, of mining give socio-psychological factors an unusual importance. In other industries the choice, that is, discovery, of a different, that is, more effective, organizational form might result in an increase in output but a reduction in worker satisfaction. How would the Tavistock group view this result?

Clearly, they are to some extent concerned with what they call 'social health' as an end in itself. My prediction is that, in the

---

* That is, a status quo dominated by market forces and governments committed to preserving them. Trist and his associates criticize miners who resist further mechanization for their unrealistic attitude: 'Its unreality is that by slowing down the rate of change it increases the threat from uncontrollable forces in the external environment, such as a competitive oil industry, so that in the end there is no gain in security' (ibid., p. 269). Perhaps, however, such forces are uncontrollable only in so far as one refuses to consider the extension of socio-technical principles to society as a whole.

situation just described they would be prepared to make the best of a bad job by offering their services as brokers of 'adjustment'. What is the evidence for this? Readers are referred to the closing chapters of the book. In my opinion these: (i) show a growing preoccupation with the priority of economic and technological objectives; (ii) betray a tendency to patronize the miner, whose resistance to change is both deeply psychological and reinforced by 'the unanimous character of local rationalizations' (shades of Mayo at his most Paretian); and (iii) can be viewed as a soft-sell for Tavistock manipulatory skill in changing organizations.

Many of these passages are blatantly 'manipulationist'. We are told, for example, that: 'As always in the experience of the research team' the adoption of 'group methods of learning' produced 'a massive shift in attitudes'.[4] Though composite organization is the organizational *sine qua non* of progress towards higher mechanization, miners themselves often resist it. Such a failure to perceive what is good for them is overcome by 'working through' their anxieties in the 'permissive atmosphere' of officially organized unofficial ' "working conferences" whose specific object is to permit attitude change to take place'.

This certainly leaves me wondering whether in the real world there is scope for very much organizational choice at all. In so far as this study condemns the conventional wisdom of mass-production engineering it is of course salutary. Too often, work organization reflects the unthinking application of engineering logic, to the detriment of both the worker and output. Rightly enough, the Tavistock investigators have pointed out that this organization may be less often dictated by the technology than by the production engineer's prejudices. But the notion that choice of organization is possible, given a specific technology and the need to show a profit, is in my view somewhat deceptive. In *Organizational Choice* what is shown is how a more *effective* form of organization, not simply an alternative, was introduced by some highly accomplished consultants.

24

ASSESSMENT

Underlying uniformities are evident in the studies examined. To begin with, technology is given priority in the explanations, whether taken in its hardware or software senses or both, though what is explained varies from attitudes towards work, actual worker behaviour, alienation, to organizational efficiency. Next, Blauner partially excepted (and the Tavistock group in their later studies), analytical attention is fixed firmly within the organization.* This focus upon the organization mirrors the preoccupation with technology. So does another common strand: the behaviourist tendency of this approach. Behaviour or attitudes are conceived as a *response* to the technical, or socio-technical, features of the work environment. (The psycho-technologists partly avoided this, and so did Blauner. But the motivations which the former attribute to workers are excessively generalized.)

* The recent involvement of the Tavistock group in the Norwegian Industrial Democracy Project has, as Trist rightly claims, 'given a new dimension to socio-technical studies' since the latter have been applied to 'what ordinarily would have been treated as a political problem'. See E. L. Trist, 'A Socio-Technical Critique of Scientific Management' in D. O. Edge and J. N. Wolfe, eds., *Meaning and Control: Social Aspects of Science and Technology*, Tavistock Institute of Human Relations, 1973.

Some less evident features should be noted. Most of these writers exude a certain air of confidence and optimism. Its origins seem twofold. Firstly, since technology, the main explanatory variable, is an objective feature of work situations, knowledge of industrial behaviour can presumably be given a concrete, positive basis. Secondly, this gives rise to the supposition that behaviour and attitudes can be altered in predictable ways, by more enlightened production engineering or – rather less easily – by redesigning formal organization. Grounds certainly exist for these convictions, though they are less firm than these theorists conjectured.

These considerations suggest that although the new approach successfully exposed some errors of human relations, its originality (and attributed value-freedom) are easily overstated. Technological exigencies might override managerial social skill; but worker compliance could be brought about by more direct means, i.e. by redesigning the work-process. At any rate, paramount concern with the plant was retained, and so was the preoccupation with applications. Manipulation was not urged so blatantly upon managers, but it was openly offered.

In another sense, the 'advance' was less a failure to advance than a definite regression. The behaviourist element is strongly reminiscent of human factor industrial psychology and, rather less so, of Lewinian field-theory. This reversion should not be a total surprise. Some of the problems addressed, for example, the monotony of assembly-line work, were directly inherited from the Myersians. (Walker's and Guest's study of automobile workers has a candidly acknowledged debt to the Myersian *opus*.) The psycho-technologists likewise drew much of their empirical ammunition from early Lewinian studies.

Amongst the Tavistock group, both traditions were influential. Though it went through a vaguely Mayoite phase, British industrial psychology never completely abandoned its hard methodology. When the Tavistock Institute was formed, this tradition was blended with Lewinian field-theory – and to some extent, and fortunately only temporarily, with idiosyncratic borrowings from psychoanalysis.

If so many of the vices of plant sociology were preserved, why did technological implications never arouse the same antagonism as human relations? Several factors should be considered. Systematic examination of the technological variable was novel and the new generation of analysts accepted – indeed helped to promote – criticism of Mayo's thought. The approach never became an organized movement like human relations. (Its exponents even lacked a generic name until the mid 1960s.[1]) Also, it lacked a pre-eminent theorist or ideologue eager to promote it. Potential critics were denied an Aunt Sally.

It is useful to recall also the attraction of industrial students in the 1950s towards organization sociology. This branch of structural–functional theory seemed to offer a more promising line of advance at the time than the revision of a discredited, and apparently moribund, industrial sociology.[2] Several of the writers discussed regarded themselves as organization theorists, and their work can be – indeed, is typically – accommodated in that artificially created specialism.[3] To put it bluntly, dog does not eat dog.

Finally, though the approach lacked an individual leader, it effectively had, indeed, still has, a collective one – the Tavistock group. As a theoretical pioneer and keeper of the faith, this group has displayed remarkable inventiveness and dialectical agility. Personally, I regard many of its members' recent schematizations as quite mystifying; but this is a private opinion and may be thoroughly misguided. What is sure is that the target has always been intellectually mobile and well armoured in current awareness. Good industrial consultants keep abreast of the literature and these are very good consultants.

Accounting for the emergence and main properties of this approach in a more general way presents some difficulties. (Biographical and other information bearing on academic relationships and individual thinking is scarce and 'sensitive'.) Any explanation must therefore be somewhat indirect, and be based upon what the approach failed to do as well as its achievements.

It is always tempting to view any progress in social science as the result of logic alone. Technological and organizational constraints do have an important bearing on workers' behaviour, and they had not been explored systematically by human relations, though

Roethlisberger and Dickson were certainly aware of them.* Since they bear directly on the ability of workers to form groups and of managers to exercise supervisory skills, their investigation might be thought a purely logical and otherwise unprompted revision of human relations. A progression of this very kind can plausibly be read into the work of W. F. Whyte.†

However, human relations had suggested the need to explore many other aspects – industrial conflict, community attachments, union affiliations, and so forth. These equally logical extensions were not given so much attention as technology.

Quite noticeably, the route chosen was also the least disruptive to human relations thought. The logic which governed this choice almost certainly had more to do with institutional and personal inertia than with purely reflective reason. By the early 1950s industrial sociologists constituted a major scientific community in America. The academic gate-keepers had risen with human relations. It would have been unnatural, though refreshing, for them to have encouraged any revision but the least radical one possible.‡ This is not to insinuate any conspiracy, individual or collective, to indoctrinate or suppress. Scientific originality is seldom curbed so deliberately. The process is altogether more devious. (Broadly, I accept that part of Kuhn's work which describes it.[4]) When American industrial sociology accepted the technological approach it did so because it was least upsetting to established theory and established theoreticians, and was simultaneously a minimal concession to the critics of industrial sociology outside the discipline.

In Britain, the perspective was adopted more readily in part because industrial sociology was *not* institutionalized. British industrial students were few and scattered, and from the early 1930s had rather casually imported many of their ideas from America. There was no native human relations 'industry' to speak of, whether

* See Chapter 13 above.
† See Chapter 14 above.
‡ As noted above, even writers such as Sayles regarded themselves as reformers within the human relations camp. The acceptability of the work of the organizational psycho-technologists and the Tavistock group to latter-day human relations enthusiasts should be evident.

academic or practical. When moves to promote one were taken after the war,* investigators adopted the ideas which most suited their immediate aims – often without understanding them fully. Such amateurism often produces rapid and original results because the borrower is not hampered by the 'trained incapacity' of the professional. (Later, when the amaetur has generated his own concepts and theories, atrophy may set in.) At any rate, the theoretical initiative seized by the Tavistock researchers in the early 1950s can usefully be viewed as the reward of the uninitiated. (The Liverpool group of British industrial sociologists, though less influential than the Tavistock group, also produced some excellent 'amateur' work in the 1950s.[5])

One cannot, however, fully explain the popularity of the technological approach at the time solely in terms of academic structures. This was a period of unexpected economic stability and growth, relative industrial tranquillity, rapid technological progress and growing working-class affluence. Internationally, coexistence replaced cold war. In Western countries, where the labour movement seemed to have lost its radical vitality, consensus politics were discovered, and writers like Daniel Bell proclaimed the 'end of ideology'.[6] The planner and technocrat were supplementing – even supplanting – the politician. An industrial sociology which explained the conflict and dissatisfaction that persisted within industry as the product of technological factors, and promised an industrial social engineering allegedly uncontaminated by sly managerial manipulation, could hardly have harmonized better with the technocratic optimism of the decade.

These socio-economic conditions naturally did not determine what the technological theorists thought and wrote; but they helped to exclude any examination of wider influences on workers' motivations and behaviour. They also promoted a certain climate of opinion – amongst young investigators, academic influentials, industrial leaders, the administrators of research funds and government officials eager to promote industrial harmony and growth – which unquestionably affected what theories seemed relevant and

* For example, by the formation of the Tavistock Institute and the appointment of Elton Mayo as a consultant to the Labour government.

valid. The theories, in their small way, reinforced the prevailing but ultimately unwarranted optimism. No one should deceive themselves, then, that the technological implications approach was free from ideological contamination.

PART V

ACTION
APPROACHES

INTRODUCTION

Human factor psychology and technological implications viewed the worker as a passive being who responded to his physical or technical surroundings. Taylorism and human relations attributed to him paramount drives – universal economism and universal sociability respectively. But all these approaches neglected or dismissed socially patterned motivations which derive from the worker's out-plant experiences and attachments. Obviously, though, work and community involvements interact, even when workers themselves vociferously deny any connection between the two spheres.

Action approaches to industrial behaviour, which I shall refer to generally as actionalism, attempt to explore the work–community nexus and to incorporate socially generated and distributed aims, attitudes and actions in the model of the worker and explanations of work behaviour.

By the late 1960s, actionalism was being systematically promoted by a number of British and French students of industrial behaviour as a method which corrected the biases of the technological implications approach (a behaviourist tendency to view workplace social phenomena as a bundle of reactions to technology), and of organization theory in general (a presumption that all organization members do, or should, share the aims attributed to organizational leaders). These recommendations, the most important of which will be reviewed here, reflect the conviction that industrial studies must be given a genuinely sociological foundation before they can usefully proceed further.

What an action approach broadly entails requires further explanation. In general sociology it derives pre-eminently from the methodological recommendations of Max Weber.[1] Societies tend to be studied either as abstract systems of institutions, role-patterns, etc., or as the collective artifacts of purposeful human action, which in turn inject meaning into characteristic activities.[2] The first image represents society as something independent of man, the second as man's product. Both tend also to presume that the social element in collective life is not only distinguishable but logically separable from others: this is debatable.

Neither image claims absolute validity. Ideally, study of society should integrate system and action perspectives. However, the magnitude of this task is discouraging. Followers of Weber adopt the second approach. In practice, this demands not only that the typical social actions of typical social actors be determined, but also the meanings actors typically attribute to their actions; i.e. an examination of socially distributed subjective motivations is regarded as an essential part of any analysis of patterned conduct.* Generally, actions are presumed to be rational – at least as far as the typical subject is concerned. The purpose, or goal, of the action may seem irrational in the observer's eyes, and the means adopted to achieve it equally so. Actors act, however, in accordance with their own interpretations or definitions of the situation. The observer must therefore try to project himself into the actor's situation; if he succeeds, he will achieve a sympathetic understanding of observed acts, not merely a set of statistics about their relative frequencies and causal connection with other acts or social properties.

Achievement of such an identification with subjects is seldom straightforward, but its implications for industrial studies are

* This clearly need not exclude, though it precedes, an examination of the individual psychology of the motivations of particular *persons*.

obvious. Consider the bank-wiring men in the Hawthorne Studies. Roethlisberger and Dickson interpreted their restriction of output as a means of resisting technical changes which would upset group stability. But little effort was made to view the situation through the bank-wiring men's eyes. This would have involved sensitive study of their backgrounds and current attachments outside the plant. Very probably, this would have led to the adoption of an explanation that was in fact finally rejected – that restriction of output served wider social and economic interests.

In other groups of workers, different backgrounds and loyalties might have resulted in different behaviour. This is precisely what is shown in an early study by Dalton of 'rate-busters' and 'restricters', where readiness to respond to incentives closely matched varying social backgrounds and values.[3] Actionalism, in fact, existed in industrial sociology long before it was systematically propounded and consciously advocated. There are even traces of it in *Management and the Worker*. Some of these informally actionalist studies deserve brief mention if only as a reminder that the orthodoxy of previous approaches was not universally accepted.

Without any question the most impressive is Chinoy's *Automobile Workers and the American Dream*, a study of the inconsistencies between the harsh realities of the automobile workers' situation and the American success ideology.[4] Chinoy states that 'men need more than the satisfactions derived from predictable patterns of social interaction on the job from working with a "good bunch of guys". They seek in their jobs to satisfy desires derived not only from their co-workers but also from family and friends and from their experience as members of the community and wider society.'[5] 'Desires' implanted by the 'wider society' stress ambition, inventiveness, responsibility, leadership, independence and material success. Every aspect of mass-production factory-work denies their realization.

Aspirations, consequently, must be redefined in terms of more modest objectives (promotion to a slightly less monotonous task, the purchase – in the indefinite future – of a small business), projected onto children or deflected into the acquisition of showy consumer goods or some similar domestic project. Chinoy suggests that the adoption of specific aspirations follows the life-cycle: by the time they near retirement, success means little more for most workers than ensuring security in their old age. The processes outlined involve constant redefinition of the subject's situation and objectives, as desires clash dynamically – and depressingly – with reality.

Chinoy's portrait of typical worker motivations could hardly be less like that drawn by the Mayoites. Workers suffer less from failing to discover tribal intimacy in the workplace than from the fear of being, or feeling, stigmatized as social failures. Their redefinition of the success ethic results in what has been called a 'subordinate value system' of the wider society – a 'negotiated' version of the dominant value system.[6] Chinoy notes that this can be viewed as an aspect of, and an attempt to escape, their alienation in a society with highly structured inequalities and equally refined dominant ideologies which deny, but covertly justify, such inequalities. (His use of this concept antedates Blauner's by several years and is much more literate.)

Gouldner's studies of industrial conflict in a gypsum-mine also represent a major anticipation of actionalism.[7] In explaining the origins of a wild-cat strike, and the functioning of various 'patterns of bureaucracy' (i.e. organizational arrangements), Gouldner constantly contrasts the varying orientations towards work of managers and workers generally, and of different kinds of managers and different categories of workers. These typical outlooks are related to varying social origins, community ties and other wider influences. Though they guide the adoption of certain managerial practices and the workers' reaction to being managed, ongoing experiences themselves modify to a certain extent outlooks and conflict strategies. The result is a subtle analysis of processes of conflict and cooperation in the plant which (unlike those of 'interactionists' like Whyte)* is not abstracted from a wider social context.

Gouldner undertook another study in the mid 1950s in which varying orientations towards work even more explicitly guide his interpretation.[8] This showed how 'latent social roles' (i.e. effective outlooks and identities – actor orientations) underlie the attitudes

* See Chapter 14 above.

and actions of personnel occupying similar formal roles in an organization. Though the group studied, the staff of a small American university, was non-industrial, Gouldner's primary distinction between 'cosmopolitans' and 'locals' provided a fruitful comparative tool for the examination of the managing and professional cadres of organizations as a whole. Similar kinds of distinction were being toyed with by other organizational sociologists at the time, but they did not link varying orientations with individuals' non-organizational attributes as carefully as did Gouldner. Dalton's study of industrial managers is an outstanding exception.[9]

None the less, by the end of the 1950s a very substantial body of work had accumulated which recognized, in one way or another, that organizational behaviour could not be accounted for without paying some attention to factors outside the organization – whether these were community affiliations, social origins or national culture.[10] There was a lack of some systematic formulation of an action perspective; one which spelt out its methodological assumptions and delineated its potentialities as an instrument for industrial investigation and theorizing. In the next chapter the first, and most influential, attempt to do so will be examined.

MIDDLE-RANGE
ACTIONALISM

It is probable that this chapter will be the least objective in the book. The Luton studies, whose industrial component I shall characterize as an example of middle-range actionalism, were a contribution to a major sociological – indeed, socio-political – controversy (the *embourgeoisement* of affluent workers), and have become a subject of controversy themselves.[1] The occasional sharpness of the debate hardly encourages a balanced view. For me, the problem is worse because I was employed as a routine field-worker on the studies. Such an involvement works against neutrality and even a correct understanding of the material. It is best to draw attention to this openly at the outset.

Even the sharpest critics of the Luton research regard it as the most important contribution to British industrial sociology of the 1960s. My only quibble with that is the qualifier 'industrial'. The researchers themselves described the monograph reporting the industrial data, *The Affluent Worker: Industrial Attitudes and Behaviour*, as a by-product of the larger investigation – a 'more or less unforeseen' one at that.[2] But in fact the distinction of the Luton studies rests as much as anything on the linkage of research in the workplace and the community to investigate the sort of problem which lies at the heart of empirical sociology – or should do.

In the late 1950s many commentators – academic, political and journalistic, especially those combining these attributes – were concluding that affluence in Western countries was leading to the incorporation of prosperous manual workers into middle-class society.[3] In Britain, the conservative victory in the general election of 1959 seemed powerful indirect confirmation for this *embourgeoisement* hypothesis. In 1963, however, David Lockwood and J. H. Goldthorpe, largely by means of a careful analysis of the concept of class and the supposed processes of *embourgeoisement*, were able to discredit this thesis largely on logical grounds alone.[4]

Lockwood and Goldthorpe had been attracted to Cambridge University, where the Economics Faculty was making a less than enthusiastic attempt to meet suggestions that sociology should be added to the syllabus and research promoted. Both had researched in the sociology of work previously; Lockwood was author of a minor classic (*The Black-coated Worker*) dealing with the class-consciousness of office workers, and Goldthorpe had studied friction between supervisors and coal-face workers in British mines.[5] Neither of these studies could readily be characterized as contributions to the technological implications approach, though Lockwood emphasizes the bureaucratic organization of offices as one precondition of the unionization of clerks, and Goldthorpe recognizes the technical organization of mining as a contributory factor in supervisor–worker conflict. Rather more important to the matter in hand, I believe, is that both studies embodied historical perspective, particularly an awareness of changing socio-economic conditions. In this sense, they are less sociological than the kind of work which began to appear in Britain in the later 1960s as sociology expanded and became more professional.

When their 1963 article appeared the work of testing the *embourgeoisement* hypothesis empirically was already well in hand in Luton. Discussion of the choice of this town, and of other key methodological decisions, cannot be pursued here.* In brief, if affluent

* Other comparable towns *were* considered. Luton was not chosen simply because of its accessibility from Cambridge, as has been claimed.

workers in Luton remained essentially working-class it seemed improbable that *embourgeoisement* could be occurring elsewhere on any scale. The project as a whole was, in fact, designed very carefully to test not only the central hypothesis but subsidiary aspects of it. In my opinion this was done about as well as the four* investigators' awareness of available literature (which was extensive) and financial support (which was less so) permitted.

The nature of the industrial data sought illustrates this attention to associated aspects of the *embourgeoisement* issue. Workers from varying socio-technical settings (mass-production, batch-production and process-production) and with varying skill levels were deliberately sampled, because technological implications theory indicated that some settings might better facilitate *embourgeoisement*. Process plants, in particular, had been widely portrayed as locales where, relieved of an 'alienating' environment, workers who were so disposed might assimilate the values of the technologists and managers in whose company much of their work was done. (In some process plants nearly everyone seems to wear a white coat. It is easy to read too much into this.)

In fact, the collected data suggested hardly any significant differences attributable to socio-technical settings, and relatively few related to levels of skill.† Patterns of attitude and behaviour showed remarkable consistency between the three work-forces sampled, but the prevailing syndrome was especially pronounced amongst the mass-production workers of Vauxhall Motors, the British subsidiary of American General Motors.‡ Much of the material on these assemblers is directly comparable with the findings of previous studies of automobile workers, and some of it was reported before *The Affluent Worker* itself was published.[6] Particular attention has therefore been devoted to it. At this stage, exposition will be simplified by following this practice.

Although they typically described their fragmentary, machine-paced tasks as boring and monotonous, and there was little oppor-

---

* The influence on the design and execution of the studies of Bechhofer and Platt, the two junior investigators, was considerable.

† Highly skilled workers were somewhat less instrumental in certain respects.

‡ The sample of process workers, it is worth noting, was fairly small.

tunity for in-plant sociability, the assemblers' evident deprivation of intrinsic satisfaction from their *work* apparently did not lead to any marked dissatisfaction with their *jobs* as a whole. Neither frustration of some hypothetical inner need for self-actualization nor production pressures provoked any general desire to seek other work or any deep, brooding hostility towards management.* On the contrary, the assemblers expressed broad satisfaction with their jobs as a whole. Indirect indicators of dissatisfaction such as absenteeism and turnover were low and consistent with these subjective appraisals. Two additional facts are relevant to this finding. First, most of the sample had held jobs at least equivalent, and sometimes substantially higher, in skill and responsibility before joining Vauxhall; and alternative work was readily available in Luton when they were polled. Second, open industrial conflict was virtually absent: unlike other British motor firms Vauxhall was then celebrated for its freedom from strikes. (Some local union activists disparaged it – significantly – as a 'cabbage-patch'.†)

What explains the apparently paradoxical coexistence of objective (and subjectively sensed) deprivation with objective (and subjectively claimed) satisfaction? 'Satisfaction' here is evidently not contentment, nor need it be construed as resignation. In the Luton team's view its nearest equivalent is practicality. Asked what kept them at Vauxhall the vast majority replied 'the money' without hesitation; and indeed they had been sampled precisely because their earnings were above the British industrial average of the time.‡

Contrary to some allegations, however, Goldthorpe and his associates did not regard the Luton workers as classic 'economic men' whose dissatisfactions were crudely bought off by an open-handed employer. After all, other British car-workers were equally money-oriented and although the majority were better-paid they

* The survey interviewing technique adopted would not necessarily readily detect such hostility.

† This term refers to the rural origins of many of the workers as well as their newness to industrial work and lack of militancy at the time.

‡ These earnings, however, were hardly spectacular by motor industry standards, and involved shift-work and overtime. None the less, respondents often replied to the question as though it was particularly naïve.

made ready use of the strike weapon. All industrial workers – indeed, practically anyone who works – is by definition economistic in greater or lesser degree, in a market economy especially. To claim that money lay at the heart of the Luton workers' industrial motivations would have been true but trivial.

Goldthorpe and his associates, rather, suggest that the assemblers' economism is one aspect of a broader instrumental orientation towards work which is linked with a privatized community existence. This syndrome is endowed with specific features. The Vauxhall assemblers in particular were thought to display an unusually intense instrumental–privatized orientation to work. (In fact, they were initially characterized as deviant: later, and more contentiously, this was revised to 'proto-typical'.)[7]

The intensity of the assemblers' instrumental–privatized orientation is suggested by much interview, and some rather sparse observational, evidence. For example, though technical factors, as well as managerial policy, debarred tightly-knit work-groups, the assemblers expressed no hankering for solidaristic attachments at work of any kind. Jovial familiarity was expected; but, as their own maxim went, 'Mates are not friends'. This held true for out-plant life also. Similarly, foremen who left them alone were strongly preferred. Meddlesome friendly human relations supervisory styles, no less than the autocratic varieties, seem to have received adverse reactions. Work, then, was not a place where social intimacy was either expected or sought. It formed no part of the workers' 'effort-bargain'.[8]

This calculating dissociation recurred in their more general image of the firm. Somewhat ritualistically, the majority affirmed that the organization was comparable to a football team; and, rather more alertly, that it was a better employer than most others they knew. This belief in team-work certainly implied no positive moral identification with management. Rather, it acknowledged an overlap of economic interests. Some members of the team (work-study men in particular) were portrayed as less than consistently sporting players. And if most workers kept a well-trained eye on the profitability of the firm, this was not to rejoice in the score-line for its own sake. The bargain acknowledged management's right to manage; but it excluded exploitation and profiteering. Industrial peace was strictly conditional.

Unionism, too, was apparently regarded in calculative terms. Few assemblers viewed it as an expression of working-class power and social solidarity, or as a means of worker-participation in management, let alone an avenue to eventual workers' control. There was little interest in union affairs at branch or higher levels. However, at workshop level interest was livelier. The shop-steward was regarded as a mixture of auctioneer, news-bearer and solicitor. Joining the union was a method of increasing security and bargaining-power mainly at this very local level.

Goldthorpe pointed out in preliminary reports of these findings that they cannot be understood as responses to the socio-technical setting of work or to supervisory practices. Nor is it easy to portray them as the product of partly satisfied and partly frustrated universal human needs. A solution of the explanatory puzzle would be to assume that the calculativeness which apparently marked the assemblers' attitudes and behaviour at work governed their entry to that kind of work in the first place. They could be viewed as a highly self-selected group.[9]

Entry to an occupation, Goldthorpe argued, is rarely random. Even in semi-skilled work considerable choice exists under conditions of full employment. Workers will shop around for a job which provides a mixture of rewards which matches most closely an ordered set of personal priorities. Thus, while some social types will demand a good deal of intrinsic interest from their work task for example, or plentiful opportunities for social interaction on the job, others will give such rewards a low weighting and earnings a much higher one. As a result, like-minded (and like-situated) individuals will concentrate in the work-forces of certain organizations (or in certain workshops). Goldthorpe's methodological conclusion is 'that in *any* attempt at explaining and understanding attitudes and behaviour within modern industry . . . orientations to work which employees hold in common will need to be treated as an important *independent* variable relative to the in-plant situation.[10] In other words, if we want to understand what goes on inside factories we must look outside them.

The question naturally arises of where we look outside, and what we look at. Where, to put it bluntly, do 'orientations' come from?* At this point the Luton team were themselves faced with considerable difficulties in locating the sources of instrumentalism, as they candidly acknowledged in a frequently overlooked disclaimer:

What accounts for the fact that . . . our affluent workers reveal such a markedly instrumental approach to their work-tasks, their work associates and their work organizations? Answers to questions of this kind are, in any circumstances, hard to establish; and moreover, it is at this juncture that the difficulties which stem from our study being a more or less unforeseen by-product of a larger investigation become particularly acute. In a number of respects we lack what would be the most useful and relevant material.[11]

Very tentatively, they distinguished several factors apparently associated with heightened instrumentality: position on the life and family cycles; the character of Luton as a community – or rather, a non-community; experience of downward social mobility; and level of skill. Crudely stated, an argument which arranges these factors logically might run as follows. Young married men of lower skill who have experienced downward social mobility relative to their kin have higher than average financial commitments and feel a need to compensate for their loss of standing with relations. This requires that they carry out unpleasant but highly paid work for long hours and restrict their non-work activities to the family circle. This instrumentalism at work and privatization outside it may be reinforced (or at least, not diluted) by the character of the community – in the case of Luton a 'town of migrants' in which persons of their own type predominate.†

The Luton researchers could hardly have made plainer the conjectural nature of this explanation.[12] It is merely consistent with

* In an important sense, of course, they derived in part from the research process itself, in that they were inferred from answers to a particular set of attitudinal and behavioural inquiries.

† Reinforcement may also have occurred in the workplace. In accord with the generally insufficient attention given in the study to in-plant social processes, this probability was not examined in any depth, as Bechhofer has acknowledged. See F. Bechhofer, 'The Relation between Technology and Shop-Floor Behaviour' in D. O. Edge and J. N. Wolfe, eds., *Meaning and Control*, Tavistock Institute of Human Relations, 1973.

their available data and is not the product of irresistible statistical correlations or backed by systematic observation. Whether or not it is a valid conclusion is not a point that can usefully be discussed here. The same goes for most of the other empirical findings, especially about *embourgeoisement* itself. (Minor shifts in habits and values towards a possibly more middle-class pattern were detected. These far from unambiguous normative changes aside, the Luton workers remained decidedly working-class.)*

Untoward consequences often follow indirectly and largely accidentally from major investigations, and this could be said of the Luton studies. The main misunderstanding they have promoted derives from the use of the action frame of reference to make some sense of the industrial data. The nature of this misunderstanding revolves around the concept of orientations towards work and the manner of their explanation. From an uncritical reading of *The Affluent Worker* it might easily be supposed that the task of the industrial sociologist reduces to delineating the orientations which predominate in a particular work-force and correlating them with a number of other easily measured social characteristics. Any differences in work attitudes and behaviour could presumably then be explained in terms of varying out-plant characteristics. Numerous industrial phenomena could be subjected to this treatment. The result, however, would be a proliferation of sociologistic middle-range theories, which abstracted the phenomena from their wider socio-economic context on the one hand and ignored their internally dynamic aspects on the other.[13]

It is ironic that the Luton studies which, as a whole, were concerned very much with an aspect of the wider socio-economic structure, and with social process, should encourage such a tendency; but it could be said that they do. To a large extent, they do so accidentally; because they relied predominantly upon survey techniques and because many of the industrial findings were quite unexpected and *The Affluent Worker* was indeed an 'unforeseen by-product'.

---

* Though something of a non-event for sociologists, this finding was an important one which is still ignored or resisted by politicians and others who for their own reasons continue to insist that 'we are all middle-class now'.

Survey questionnaires have several serious weaknesses. The range and richness of the data collected depend upon the questions put to the respondent, as well as upon his honesty, memory and verbal skill. They also project a static image of social reality. We cannot, therefore, be at all sure that *The Affluent Worker* reports *the* attitudes and behaviour of the workers polled: it gives inferences about *some* attitudes and behaviour from respondents' reports.* The investigators acknowledge this, but do not pay sufficient attention to the second problem. Admittedly, since high instrument-alism is (cautiously) linked to position on the family cycle, by implication its intensity is variable. But the suggestion here is that orientations change, if at all, only in line with out-plant factors, not through experience at work itself.[14]

It may be empirically true that the orientations of the Luton workers were highly stable, and were formed and modified exclusively by out-plant factors. What is unwarranted is any suggestion that this applies to *all* workers. W. W. Daniel, in an otherwise somewhat eccentric commentary, points to the very real danger that actionalists risk suspending their analysis at the factory *entrance* just as previous researchers have done at its exit.[15]

Many studies of strikes certainly indicate the possibility of quite dramatic changes of orientation stemming from in-plant experiences.[16] Further, when orientations are changed externally there is a very real risk of sociologistic reduction in identifying the origin and agency of the change. Warner and Low, whose study of the 'Yankee City' strike was reviewed in an earlier chapter, finally decided that the workers' loss of social status in the community was a crucial out-plant determinant of their unionization. In fact, however, much of their own analysis demonstrates that any such cause was a mediating factor at most: the real origins of the change lay in general socio-economic change and immediate economic crisis.

In fact, this excellent but perverse study linked the out-plant change with in-plant change. The two were inseparable modes of the wider socio-economic transformation of which the situation

* Even if much more sophisticated measures (especially of attitudes) had been employed, severe problems of validation would have remained, especially in view of the paucity of observational data.

in 'Yankee City' itself was a purely local, precise instance. A reading of this classic study along the lines suggested earlier is an instructive reminder of the inherent dangers of middle-range actionalism as it is frequently comprehended.

I must leave readers to decide for themselves exactly how far treatment of the Luton industrial data, and the method recommended for industrial sociology, actually fell prey to the risks I have sketched. Some further, more general, comment is, however, in order.

The instrumentalism of the Luton workers is contrasted with a solidaristic manual worker orientation. A solidaristic orientation is ascribed to traditional workers.[17] The traditional worker (like his instrumentalist successor) is an ideal type – an artificial construct to aid analysis. But such a construct must depend ultimately upon a sound empirical reference. Though they certainly treated cautiously the evidence then available, the Luton team accepted the traditional worker's historical (and residual contemporary) existence. Lately, however, historical and other evidence has seriously questioned the extent of his ascribed solidarism, and even his existence.[18] Pronounced instrumentalism is by no means a recent syndrome; and workers in traditional industries such as shipbuilding appear to be far less collectively minded than sociological folklore once insisted.[19]

This throws great doubt on the speculation that the Luton workers were proto-typical in their degree of instrumentalist–privatization. Although they undoubtedly differed in some respects from other groups of British workers, both historical and contemporary, it now seems dangerous to ascribe their distinctiveness to this property.*

Was the suggestion that these workers were proto-typical derived from the adoption of the action perspective itself? I shall leave this particular question to others.[20] But it seems most probable that such risks do exist for investigators who embrace a middle-range actionalist approach to industrial behaviour. Instrumentalism, or any comparable syndrome, is not a property that arises purely from social experiences and social relationships, though it may be

---

* Proto-typicality could nowadays be argued on other grounds perhaps; for example, in terms of the workers' *situation* as employees of a large trans-national organization in an industry whose future is becoming cloudy.

mediated by them. Its origins must eventually be sought in the constitution of the socio-economic order as a whole. It cannot arise independently of that structure, whose stability it may promote or threaten. Industrial sociologists may not feel it is their task to undertake sweeping societal analyses. But, at the very least, their studies should be designed and reported in a manner which will allow others to do so.

This demands that they adopt some model of the socio-economic whole, or at least declare their chief assumptions about it. The Luton team did not altogether shirk this task. In the final volume of the 'affluent worker' series (*The Affluent Worker in the Class Structure*) they contrast liberal–pluralist and neo-Marxist conceptions of industrial society and its evolution, but refuse to accept either. They envisage a 'relatively open' future.[21] Up to a point such scepticism is healthy. Determinisms of all kinds have hampered social science. But in my view their agnosticism derives from an excessively sociological mode of thought.

From the first, they had acknowledged that their predictions were conditional upon the continuance of the stable growth of Western economies.[22] Even in the Britain of the mid 1960s such a continuance seemed probable. Changes since then suggest that the economic dimension should be given more attention. It seems absurd to me that the Luton team should be faulted for having failed to predict the specific dislocations currently evident in British capitalism in particular, and Western capitalism generally.[23] None the less there is an important lesson here. If sociologists are to make predictions (and a 'relatively open' future *is* a prediction) about major social processes, such forecasts should be better grounded in contemporary economics. The tendency of the Luton material as a whole is against this, and the middle-range actionalism it promoted has a sociologistic bias which could exclude it altogether.

Against this must be set the renewal of interest in the subjective rationality of the actor. No satisfying explanation of industrial events can dispense with this altogether. But the attention paid to the subject's personal rationality can easily be taken to excess. In the following chapter the risks will be illustrated.

PHENOMENOLOGICAL
ACTIONALISM

Middle-range actionalism fails to encourage investigators to situate their analyses of worker orientations and behaviour within an explicit model of society. More evidently, it discourages examination of the processes whereby orientations are modified by experiences in work. The brand of actionalism examined in this chapter seeks to rectify this second defect. But in doing so it diverts attention even further from the first.

Excessive stress on actor orientations, or on subjective definitions of a situation, may suppress consideration of the underlying objective properties of the situation in which action occurs. Occasionally, some such stress may be a useful antidote to explanations which exaggerate the influence of objective features of the work situation, such as technology or formal organization. None the less, such factors do operate, if only as constraints upon possible actions.* Less directly still, but no less importantly, the worker's general situation in society possesses distinguishable objective characteristics

* The terms 'action' and 'constraint' are often ambiguous. F. Bechhofer, 'The Relation between Technology and Shop-floor Behaviour' in D. O. Edge and J. N. Wolfe, eds., *Meaning and Control*, Tavistock Institute of Human Relations, 1973, provides a valuable exploration of this issue.

which must not be disregarded. The study of interpersonal, and inter-group, processes cannot be abstracted from this wider context. Stated otherwise, actors are not sovereign in defining and acting in accordance with their definitions of the situation; and subjectively rational action may be objectively irrational.

It is not arrogant or patronizing for investigators to acknowledge this at least in principle. Indeed, unless they do, social study can offer no important generalizations. Men are never completely free to define their situations independently of structural constraints, to identify their objective interests fully, or to act completely rationally as a result.* They may struggle to do so, and the ultimate value of social science lies precisely in assisting these efforts. Misplaced sympathy for subjects may result in a sentimental exaggeration of their freedom and rationality, and indirectly assist their continued suppression.

These issues will be raised again. They have been brought to prominence by the recent vogue for radically subjectivist styles of sociology – symbolic interactionism, ethnomethodology and phenomenology.[1] Exponents of these styles seek a philosophical grounding for their methods in the phenomenological social thought of Alfred Schutz. Whether Schutz's philosophy is truly phenomenological is disputed, but his admirers suppose it is and I have characterized the radically subjectivist approach accordingly.[2]

Its advantages for industrial studies have been argued with great skill and clarity by David Silverman, its leading British exponent, in his highly persuasive book *The Theory of Organizations* – a slightly misleading title since no comprehensive theory of organizations is actually offered.

His objective of seeking 'to draw out the implications for study and theory building of a view of social reality as socially constructed, socially sustained and socially changed'[3] is essentially a

---

* This has been expressed more epigrammatically: 'Men make their own history, but they do not make it just as they please; they do not make it under circumstances chosen by themselves, but under circumstances directly encountered, given and transmitted from the past.' K. Marx, *The Eighteenth Brumaire of Louis Bonaparte* in *Karl Marx and Frederick Engels: Selected Works*, Lawrence & Wishart, 1970, p. 96.

methodological one, and it involves a critical appraisal of the assumptions of conventional organization theories.

Silverman's superb critique of three variants of the prevailing image of organizations as systems underscores its tendency towards reification, i.e., the supposition that organizations are living entities with pseudo-biological needs (for survival, stability or growth).[4] Organizations, as such, can have no such needs, nor can they take actions independently of their human members.[5] Ascription of such qualities is partly an unwarranted extension of everyday speech, and partly a value-judgement – the most important needs or actions which theorists attribute to organizations as entities are either suspiciously similar to those of organizational *leaders*, or those which a business consultant believes will improve efficiency. In sum, the systems image depends upon logical confusion, un-warranted practical convenience and ideological thinking.

Conventional definitions of organizations are therefore suspect. The claim that organizations are social units which possess goals obscures the variety of aims which their members, including their leaders, pursue in practice.[6] Likewise the hierarchical, formal nature of organizational relationships is easily overstated. Actual working arrangements are much more fluid than organizational charts or manuals suggest; and anyway, other social units can be hierarchical and formal.

Silverman, however, maintains that though such definitions are inadequate we cannot ignore the commonsense division between organizations and other collectivities or social networks. Moreover, founders of organizations characteristically prescribe initial objec-tives, rules and formal structures; and their successors constantly reassert or replan these in a deliberate manner. The controllers of an organization at least, do not take its everyday life for granted.[7] Because of this conscious drive from the top to organize and re-organize, which may be resisted from below or have other typical undesired or unforeseen consequences, the study of organizations can be a specialized area of sociological investigation.

However, the method of investigation advocated by Silverman – an action approach – is identical to the one he believes is desirable in sociology as a whole. Blending the methodological prescriptions of classical and modern writers, Silverman accepts a radical distinction between natural and social science.[8] The latter should concern itself with patterned human action whose subjective meaning is derived from society but changed by experience of interaction with others. This formulation brings out the paradoxical aspect of social living, i.e. that the social world is a human creation yet is experienced as 'given'. If society creates the subject (by giving him identity and his actions meaning), the subject concurrently creates society through his actions and, less directly, through changed perceptions of his social circumstances.

Perceptions and meanings are socially distributed. Some are shared by all members of a given society at one historical moment, but many vary from group to group. In studying organizations, attention must be fixed upon typical patterns of member-involvement, typical actions, and the consequences of such actions, both intended and unintended.[9] These will depend upon members' varying social values and definitions of their situation in the organization, which in turn derive from varying 'biographies' and the history of the organization. Action in organizational situations may engender changes in involvement, aims, and definitions of the situation.

The stress here is quite clearly on charting social processes and explaining them in terms of subjective – though typically subjective – actions and definitions of the situation. Reworking some standard material, Silverman suggests the possibility of classifying organizations in terms of their 'predominant meaning-structures', the varying member involvements, the strategies utilized to further members' sectional aims, and power – or rather, the 'relative ability of different actors to impose their definition of the situation on others'.[10]

The emphasis here on how meaning-structures originate, operate and change is significant. It reappears in later sections of the book in an increasingly distinct form. Because 'the special role of the sociologist is to understand the subjective logic of social situations', Silverman insists, theorists should be wary of imposing their own definitions on the situations they study. Supervision which is apparently authoritarian, for example, might be construed by workers merely as interference or even as leadership.[11] Still more provocatively, Silverman asserts that 'when the definitions of a relationship change even where the original physical behaviour patterns remain, the relationship has in a very real sense changed'.[12]

To be sure, these more contentious ideas intermingle with many sound reminders about the limitations of conventional research techniques and instruments, and about the risks for social scientific theory when theorists simple-mindedly ape natural science. There is no question, either, but that Silverman deflates conventional organization theory with a hiss which one could wish was audible in the editorial offices of the *Administrative Science Quarterly*.

But serious shortcomings offset this valuable commentary. Silverman's treatment of power, society and the role of the investigator illustrate the central misconstructions that his essay encourages.

Organizations are created to marshal, express and apply power; their internal structure embodies differences in power and is closely related to systematic variations of power in society as a whole. Silverman by no means overlooks these facts, but in some respects his conception of power is bizarre. His recommendation seems to be we pay less attention to how much power organizational actors actually possess than to how much they believe they possess, i.e. to their definition of their own, and of others', power position.[13] Moreover, actual power should apparently be considered as a resource which enables a group to impose its definition of the situation, not its will, upon the less powerful (or presumably upon those who underestimate their power).

Certainly such perceptions should be taken into account. Likewise, organizational factions and strata undeniably engage in propaganda wars to impose certain viewpoints, holding in reserve more effective weapons such as strikes, sackings, slow-downs, black-listings, etc. But personally, I find the procedure of always viewing the exercise of power through the medium of definitions of the situation somewhat roundabout and potentially misleading.

It may be true that 'He who has the bigger stick has a better chance of imposing his definitions',[14] but the power-holder does not need to modify a subordinate's perceptions to have his way. For example, bosses of underpaid workers who strike usually plead that the firm cannot afford higher wages, and may threaten dismissals unless work is resumed. Any resumption of work usually depends more upon such threats than upon any acceptance of the managers' expectation of insolvency. It is probable that, in any case, the conflicting groups possess a very similar definition of the situation, i.e. whoever has the 'bigger stick' can coerce his opponent. The matter of deciding who has this stick involves practical rather than intellectual procedures.

To continue with the example, as like as not the cloudy representation of the financial situation offered by management will be largely fictitious. In propaganda battles, the definition of the situation that a group urges others to accept is rarely its own but a distortion whose plausibility can be enhanced by resort to other forms of power, for example, control over the issue of vital information. Ability to impose definitions of a situation is part of that situation. Useful investigation proceeds by examining such situations first. Examination of actor-definitions of them is important, but secondary.

Reversing the procedure involves particularly severe risks. Critics of subjectivist sociology correctly point out that it is one thing to take the actor's definition of the situation into account, but quite another merely to take it.[15] The latter procedure leads one towards a largely relativistic social world of disembodied perceptions and actions. An analogy with human relations theory suggests the consequences for industrial studies. Investigators would produce a series of stories or anecdotes much along the lines of those of 'interactionists' like Whyte;* but instead of explaining them in a vocabulary of 'sentiments', 'activities' and so on, they would rely on varying actor-definitions. A 'Logic of Definitions' would succeed the 'Logic of Sentiments', with little gain to science.

To be fair to him, Silverman senses the risk and faces the question of where orientations, definitions and meanings originate. 'One valid answer,' he claims, 'would be that meanings are given to men by their society and the past societies that preceded it'; furthermore social reality 'is "pre-defined" in the very language in which we are socialized'.[16]

This suggests a somewhat mechanical view of collective life much

* See Chapter 14 above.

at odds with the dynamic perspective Silverman advocates otherwise. He attempts to resolve the tension by arguing that social reality is *empirically* stable but intrinsically 'precarious'. Unless they are constantly reinforced by the words and deeds of others, 'taken-for-granted' assumptions about the social world are discarded or transformed. Since there is an element of discretion in our performance of a role, patterns of interaction can mutate; in their struggle to make sense of these innovations people generate new meanings.

There are several unanswered questions here. If discretion exists in role-performance, are these variations purely random or are they influenced by other factors? If so, what is the nature of these factors and do they operate systematically? If some action is meaningful only after the event, as a result of retrospective rationalization, and is otherwise based on unquestioned assumptions, has Silverman exaggerated the rational component in action generally?

At one point he indeed comes close to endorsing a quasi-Mayoite image of the actor. 'The fact that the stock of knowledge upon which action is based tends to change rather slowly,' he suggests, 'reflects the vested interest we all have in avoiding anomie by maintaining a system of meanings which daily confirms the non-problematic nature of our definitions of ourselves'.[17]

It seems to me that most of the foregoing queries, and this astonishing suggestion that social actors *choose* conformity, are created by a refusal to recognize the importance of objective social constraints on human freedom. Seeking to establish an image of the actor as liberated from these constraints, Silverman can only explain the fact of social order in terms of some hypothetical drive towards conventionalism.

A provocative rephrasing of the last quotation might go as follows: 'The fact that social actors fail to perceive and act upon their objective human interests reflects the success of dominant class members in perpetuating their privileges, thanks to their socio-economic power and their allies in government, the state apparatus, political parties, trade unions, the mass media and education.' Beside Silverman's subtle formulations this may sound crude, but it has far greater verisimilitude.

My guess is that he would not bother to challenge it either. The radical relativism and subjectivism which permeate his methodology seem to apply to other social theories – even to systems theory. He goes so far as to comment that 'it would be foolish to suggest that any view is better than any other or that each person ought necessarily to be interested in the conclusions of the others'.[18] Actually, this agnosticism is logical enough within a phenomenological framework. Scientific theories are presumably higher-level definitions of the situation, and must therefore be respected for their subjective rationality.

Schutz's thought, which underlies phenomenological actionalism, has been aptly summarized as follows:

> There is no social structure and no structure of history beyond those determined by the interests of some social scientist or historian or other. In particular, Schutz's 'phenomenological' sociology and history are the only social sciences: they are not dependent upon some other structural science. The effect of Schutz's humanism is a speculative empiricism of the surface phenomena of social formations in which social structures and historical events are reduced to givens which govern but do not appear in the analysis.

The writer (B. Hindness) also provides this useful reminder: 'If some of Schutz's followers in sociology use the "commonsense" categories of a somewhat more radical audience that in no way alters the general character or the scientific status of their stories.'[19]

Regrettably, this applies all too well to Silverman's phenomenological actionalist approach to industrial behaviour. His demolition of systems theory is salutary. His reminder that the social relations and micro-politics of workplaces have an important element of change, however, is cancelled by his refusal to locate these phenomena within an explicit model of present-day society.

Most disturbing of all is the inability of this method to disclose inconsistencies between subjectively rational actions and objectively rational interests. Indeed, it actively obscures such contrasts. Though promoted by a kindly respect for the dignity of the individual, such humanism is somewhat unsophisticated and in so far as its explanations of the disagreeable features of social existence procures reconciliation with them, potentially irresponsible.

HISTORIC

ACTIONALISM

Taken together, the types of action approach so far reviewed remind us that industrial behaviour is subjectively rational; that industrial relationships have a changing, dynamic aspect; and, above all, that actions and attitudes in work are inseparable from wider social attachments and identity.

Beyond that, their usefulness is restricted. For phenomenological actionalists, society seems to be a quite nebulous entity, which exists only by agreement amongst actors. Even obstinate social facts may, apparently, be transformed by actor definitions, or defined away altogether. Middle-range actionalism is down to earth – but too much so. Industrial behaviour is linked to a very limited range of social attributes, and no compelling image of society itself is proposed.

In this chapter the variety of actionalism propounded by Alain Touraine in his book *Sociologie de l'action*, which attempts to link work phenomena with a complex theory of society, will be examined. Unfortunately, Touraine's book is not available in English and is rather difficult. (In the words of one follower, Touraine's writing 'can be as confused as it is brilliant and original'.)[1] But the struggle to understand it is rewarding, if only as a reminder of the magnitude of the tasks which now confront social science. It will be helpful to say something about these first.

Studies of a particular social sphere should relate to an image of society as a whole. In industrial studies it is tempting but inadequate to meet this requirement by establishing a simple division between a group's in-plant and out-plant situations. Although this can approximate reality by showing interaction between the two spheres (i.e. orientations acquired outside work affect work behaviour; experiences at work create orientations which affect out-plant behaviour; etc.) the simplicity of the separation is excessive and therefore misleading.

A subject's work situation is inseparable from his total situation in society. Entry to a given kind of work and typical experiences in it may or may not develop a subjective sense of identity in an individual, but they and a great number of closely related social experiences express an objective social identity. Such identities are not randomly but systematically distributed throughout society and are one – and possibly the most important – embodiment of social structure. It is difficult and inadvisable to reduce them in any way.

Analysis of particular phenomena requires some conception of society which penetrates beneath its surface properties but can none the less deal with those properties adequately. These two requirements are inseparable. Functionalist approaches to the problem, which represent any given social structure as a set of abstract arrangements which permit the continuance of that society, certainly pursue generalization. So do structuralist perspectives which portray societies as equally abstract systems of signs and meanings. Both of course derive from, and are applied to, the study of actual societies. But their logic demands that concrete social forms should be treated as instances of a set of universal principles.

Because these principles purportedly apply to every society, no society is necessarily more advanced than any other, though it may be more complex. Likewise, internal tensions are under-estimated because a society which was not relatively well integrated would by definition not exist. No major element of structure governs the form of all others or is the product of non-social –

for example, economic – forces. Neither perspective, then, can convincingly explain social change. Functionalists mutter about inherent impulses to adapt or integrate better; structuralists conjecture a gigantic human game with innovation.

Investigators who deplore the submersion of the concrete in an abstract scheme, who hold that structural elements are ordered in importance and that conflict is a critical social fact, and who insist that social analysis must embody historical perspective, consideration of economic factors and some notion of human progress, have until lately usually embraced some form of vulgar or deterministic Marxism. Such perspectives offer few advantages over their bourgeois competitors. Adoption of crude images of economically determined class conflict historically evolving in a unilinear direction merely leads to scrutiny of particular societies for evidence which upholds the basic thesis.

In the early 1950s, some adherents of each perspective began to modify their approaches to a certain extent. Functionalists began examining conflict, the economic basis of society and social change; Marxists paid more attention to the superstructure (surface social relations) and even began to express doubts about the 'necessary' evolution of capitalism into socialism as a result.

Revisionists in each camp repudiated abstract schemata in favour of more factual analyses of contemporary industrialized societies. Consequently, two major kinds of substantive theory became available, for which 'industrial society' and 'technological society' are convenient descriptive terms.[2]

Broadly, theories of industrial society assert that advanced industrialism functionally demands a continuing measure of social inequality but high social mobility. Ideologies which contest this, whether from principled egalitarianism or principled élitism, must be abandoned for the sake of efficiency. The logic of industrialism allegedly overrides societal differences stemming from national traditions or formal political systems, producing a structural convergence of all advanced societies in the long term.

Adherents of the technological society theories accept much of this. Capitalism is no longer portrayed as self-destructive. Class domination may be perpetuated thanks to economic planning and technological innovations which guarantee material security for the masses. Manipulation through advertising and the mass media generates false consumer needs which can then be gratified to produce false satisfactions and false loyalties to the system. Domination is perpetuated on the pretext of technological necessity. This applies equally to 'state-capitalist' Eastern bloc countries, where bureaucrats, technocrats and party *apparatchiki* constitute a new class unsympathetic to social democracy. Convergence upon totalitarianism is a global tendency produced by the exploitation, and the cult, of technology.

Both theories exaggerate the present extent of convergence and, quite possibly, the capacity of capitalism to surmount its economic problems. Curiously, too, the technological society theory is if anything less economically determinist than its bourgeois partner. Be that as it may, both discourage a view of society as a humanly created entity over which a measure of human control can be exerted to secure genuine progress. It is in the light of this latter deficiency that Touraine's work, a discussion of which follows, should be understood.

The particular relevance of Touraine's contribution to the theme of this book is that in *Sociologie de l'action* he links societal analysis directly to the study of work. In fact, the latter extends ideas which Touraine advanced in a much earlier work, *L'Évolution du travail ouvrier aux usines Renault*.[3] It will, then, be helpful to approach *Sociologie de l'action* by way of *L'Évolution*.

Published twenty years ago, when Touraine was about to embark upon a period of intensive empirical research in French industry, *L'Évolution* reports an investigation of varying socio-technical settings in the Renault car factories. Because of this, and even more probably because only a few badly translated extracts are available in English,[4] it is usually regarded as a contribution to technological implications theory. It supposedly confirms Blauner's and Woodward's conjectures that the craft organization of work (which Touraine calls Phase A) and automation (Phase C) have comparable social consequences, whilst mass-production (Phase B) produces alienation.

Undeniably such interpretations could be read into it by those only superficially acquainted with it. However, Touraine had trained under Georges Friedmann. Many notions in *L'Évolution* certainly reflect the searching thought of his mentor on socio-industrial issues.[5] Others go well beyond it, and indeed alarmed Friedmann himself. It is therefore remarkable that Blauner in particular did not take direct issue with Touraine rather than cite his study as confirmation of his own extravagant speculations.

Touraine certainly argues that work as a whole is evolving from Phase A (craft organization) to Phase C (automation). But the social charactcristics of these two systems present a sharp contrast. The Phase A worker was incorporated in a tightly knit craft group which jealously policed its internal status distinctions and prerogatives with respect to other groups, thus maintaining general divisiveness throughout the plant. Phase C integrates work processes throughout the plant, and instrument-monitoring and information-recording operations supplant the direct manipulation of the product. Individual adaptability and flexible group relations, rather than manual skill, become prerequisites for the operation of the complex automated work-system. Such work derives meaning neither from its intrinsic interest nor from narrow group-memberships, but from wider social reference-points – the overall social relations of the plant, pursuit of a particular life-style outside work or a domestic project, or wider social attachments and values.

Phase B (mass-production), far from being the polar opposite of the two other forms, is, Touraine contends, similar in many respects to Phase C. It is a contradictory, transitional phase wrongly supposed to be typical of industrialism. Under it, progressive standardizatiou and rationalization of work occurs. These changes temporarily aggravate its dehumanizing properties but are the prerequisite of Phase C. Touraine further asserts that, in Renault at least, Phase B extended the job hierarchy, thus enhancing overall opportunities for upward plant mobility: under craft production, many labourers failed to attain journeyman status.

By eradicating a rigid job-structure Phase B facilitates transition to Phase C. Since work is a purely technical experience, value can be injected into it only by reference to wider social values. The persistence of craft work prevents the emergence of such standards, because beside it Phase B work naturally appears meaningless. By sentimentalizing the former we despair unnecessarily about the deprivations of the latter. In Touraine's view this is quite misguided because 'work which, from a technical point of view, *has no meaning* – is sheer inhumanity – derives its one and only significance from the social milieu and the social value system to which it is related, in such a way *that there would in fact be nothing in common between two working systems which made an appeal to quite distinct evaluative standards*'.[6]

Until automation is generally applied, mass-production work should be rationalized to reduce technical pressures by designing jobs which call for minimal attention. This will eventually facilitate the social reintegration of complete work-forces after the temporary turning-point of mass-production has been passed.

The nature of this reintegration will naturally depend on a revision of society's conception of work as a whole. How this will be achieved is not very carefully specified. But Touraine adamantly denies that advanced technology evokes a universal emotional or social response. If work experience is technologically determined, it is so under craft production, not under mass-production or automation. As he puts it:

This study of the Renault factories should have indicated that the prevailing form of the technical environment, far from signifying the domination of technical factors and their at least partial autonomy with respect to the social conditions of work, supplants that autonomy which on the contrary characterized the craft system of work, and subordinates the meaning of work entirely to its social conditions.[7]

In his preface to *L'Évolution*, Friedmann rather anxiously described these conclusions as 'a little daring', and Touraine could certainly have discussed how a general shift in social attitudes towards work might be procured. But he evidently recognized a link between the content of general social philosophies of work and the properties of the socio-economic whole. New meaning cannot be generated independently of structural innovation: he is most certainly not a phenomenological actionalist *avant la lettre*.

After a period in which his work closely resembles, and antedates,

British middle-range actionalism,[8] Touraine returned to the problem he addressed in *L'Évolution* of linking micro-studies of the work situation with macro-sociological analysis. *Sociologie de l'action* is a reprise and extension of these concerns.

Earlier I noted that this book is not easy to read, and I can do no more than sketch my own interpretation. Touraine hypothesises a dynamic link between work and society. Work is the cradle of novel forms of social action and new values, both for the individual worker and for society. Society, in fact, may be conceived as a 'collective worker' which through its productive operations may acquire self-awareness and a sense of purpose – an implied historic project – and therefore become a 'historic subject'. Neither any one individual nor society as a whole necessarily achieve such awareness, though all members of society unconsciously participate in the historic subject; and in particular epochs it may be closely identified with a particular social formation (e.g. the working class).

In identifying the historic subject, the analyst's main criterion is its potentiality for promoting human emancipation. Touraine explains: 'The study of the historic subject is, above all, a sociology of *freedom*, it is always a quest for the movement by which, simultaneously, the forms of social life are constituted and contested, organized and sublated [*dépassé*]'.[9]

Functionalism and structuralism, preoccupied with static systems of conduct, values and signs, are methodologically inadequate for such analysis. So too, Touraine argues, is Marxism, which is over-speculative, deterministic and over-reliant on the (possibly vanishing) proletariat as a historic subject. Sociology should be concerned with the genesis of social values, and this implies study of the 'orientations of action' which, 'far from imposing a sociology of the "inner life" can and should be studied in action'.[10] Action becomes historic in so far as it results in 'creation, innovation and attribution of meaning'.

New meaning and new action are generated through work. Work transforms society, or facilitates transformation, by altering the material basis of existence, and by modifying man's conception of his needs and identity, that is, his human nature. But work entails some system of social relationships; and, for Touraine, a society, the 'collective worker', can achieve self-consciousness by reflecting on its productive system just as his experience of work may contribute towards the individual worker's self-image. Societies which acquire a 'historic consciousness' of their needs, identities and emancipatory potentialities become true 'historic subjects'.

Some poetic licence must be granted Touraine to grasp what he means by the historic subject. Apparently, it must be apprehended largely through a series of paradoxes and exclusions of meaning. 'The historic subject is no more a concrete actor than it is the collective consciousness of God,' he explains. 'It defines a certain relation of a society – a collective worker – with itself, a relation defined by the capacity of that society to comprehend its environment as its product, its artifact.'[11]

Such a capacity is a variable partly dependent upon a society's level of economic development. But Touraine rejects the Marxist, or rather, vulgar Marxist, relationship between the material basis and the social superstructure. His basis, so far as he accepts the notion, denotes neither the material forces nor the social relations of production, but the extent of a society's self-awareness. Such awareness may be inferred empirically by examining the objectives and deprivations of work, the norms of social institutions and the content of symbolic systems (e.g. language, the arts, mass communications). Society, Touraine claims, 'transcribes' the effects of its work into novel institutions and symbols. Consciously or unconsciously, it projects its self-image in so doing.

Touraine seems to believe that industrialized societies have reached a stage of considerable self-consciousness as historic subjects. Advanced technology is transforming production systems; problems created by the social relations of the workplace intermingle with all others; and the state increasingly intervenes to promote technological change, to regulate the economy and to plan social life. Work has become a totalizing force.

This, he argues, is something of a pardox. Work as sheer economic necessity is becoming less important precisely when the social element in, and social consequences of, work relationships bulk larger. Likewise, the technical rationalism which underlies work organization is becoming increasingly evident in the community as a whole. A piquant result, he alleges, is that a genuinely scientific study of society – which must begin with work – becomes feasible for the first time in history. 'If the sociology of work was born with the industrial revolution,' he claims, 'it could not become scientific until work had become social [i.e. societally encompassing], until the notion of society once more took on a meaning, before the appearance of industrial societies, that is to say, which organize the control of the collectivity and its technical and economic activities.'

To some readers the inferences which might be drawn from these allegations will seem either absurd or sinister. Is Touraine seriously suggesting that industrialized societies have arrived at the threshold of 'authentic' history? Or is he claiming that it is the state nowadays that embodies the emancipatory historic subject in its purest form?

I believe Touraine is stating that industrialized societies all possess the capacity to become self-liberating historic subjects, and that state power can be used to this end. These developments are possible – even probable – but by no means inevitable. He distinguishes between an industrial civilization, a pattern upon which societies are converging, and industrial societies. Though the latter are all 'sublations' or '*dépassements*' of class societies they vary enormously among themselves.

Such variations seem to arise from numerous dialectical processes. I am by no means sure that the nature of these processes can be made clear by me, or by Touraine, but I will do my best. Work expresses two universal, necessary but opposed principles or motions: one towards creation, the other towards control. (Touraine argues, and I am inclined to agree with him this far, that these basic properties constitute a fact rather than a philosophical conjecture: what can be deduced from such a fact, however, is uncertain.)

A productive act performed by an isolated producer necessarily implies some drive to create. A completed product breeds a sense of achievement, a 'proud consciousness'. Likewise the producer seeks to control his act of production and his created product. Yet production also involves recognition of the need to produce to survive; and the product must be consumed, or traded for others which will be consumed. The struggle with nature and the inevitability of consumption generate a 'submissive consciousness'.

'Creation' and 'control' are, then, in Touraine's scheme of things, inherently ambiguous activities. Any productive act, whether it is individual or collective, tends to evoke two currents of consciousness in those who perform it, and these two currents run contrary to one another. It is, as it were, by examining the motions of the sediment swirled along and eddied by these opposing currents that we can infer the 'projects' actually pursued by historic subjects. More prosaically, any such examination will always reveal a conflict between a desire for material progress on the one hand and a desire for greater freedom on the other.

In society, submissive consciousness reappears as 'constitutive consciousness' – an emergent central value-system to which persons must subordinate their selfish impulses. Some groups – the 'masters' – identify with the constitutive consciousness more closely. Thus the proud consciousness of workers is repressed and class-struggle – or rather, a 'dialectic of social classes' – results. Rejecting soapbox Marxism, Touraine indicates additional complexities. Progressive and reactionary elements coexist in all class formations. Politically radical workers may be social reactionaries, voting Communist one day and abusing blacks the next.[12] 'Masters' likewise may be economically go-ahead but socially repressive (as in Nazi Germany), or the reverse.

Consequently, a '*double* dialectic of social classes' ensues; and, from this, Touraine deduces that 'all classes, all social groups are at every moment carriers of the historic subject . . .'[13] (Similar double dialectics are detectable in the life of organizations, political parties, etc. All embody the productive embattlement of the forces of creation and control.)

When we analyse society at the highest level of abstraction, Touraine proposes,

the terms 'creation' and 'control' can be replaced by those of 'development' and 'democracy'. Development is more than [economic] growth and, *a fortiori*, than expansion. It is the transformation of society by work. Democracy is not an institutional mechanism . . . it is primarily the awareness, freely formed and expressed, of the legitimacy of ways of utilizing the product of individual and collective work.[14]

(Touraine also describes democracy as an attempt to overcome various alienations which the quest for economic progress creates.)

The motion towards democracy is manifested in 'historic social movements'. Unable to participate effectively in the historic subject as individuals, people form appropriate organizations. Touraine's classic example of this is the labour movement. Unfortunately, he asserts, it fought a sectional crusade and economic advance has removed many of the alienations against which it struggled.

In future the historic subject will embrace all groups in society because the battle for subsistence will have been won, because work will become an increasingly voluntary and social activity, and because development will be promoted by governments. Henceforward, societies will 'cease to be historical and become historicizing; they are not in history – they make history'.[15]

In some countries, Touraine acknowledges, totalitarianism could ensue, for 'this evolution favours Machiavellian activity by the state as much as social democracy'. Totalitarianism can certainly wear a pseudo-democratic, populist mask. None the less, he maintains that material abundance stimulates demands for further individual freedom – somehow; he is altogether vague about what will replace the labour movement as the vehicle of democratization.[16]

This is such a complex and contradictory essay that detailed comment must be excluded here. Its fundamental weakness is a confusion of aims. Touraine states at the outset that his study 'seeks to avoid both doctrinaire thought and the simple description of contemporary industrial societies; it has no other ambition than to define the elements of a method'; but at the end he announces that 'actionalism in sociology is not a doctrine but a theory'.[17] As Touraine moves from methodological discussion to substantive theory, a substantial measure of doctrine seeps in. Suggestions for the successful analysis of contemporary industrialized societies give way to an actual analysis.

This analysis, it seems to me, borrows very heavily indeed from the convergent industrialism thesis discussed earlier in this chapter, and to a lesser extent from the technological society jeremiads of Marcuse and his followers. Touraine was writing in the mid 1960s, when both of these plausible doctrines were widely accepted. But he is reported to have repudiated many of his ideas since then.[18]

The optimism which pervades much of *Sociologie de l'action* does indeed read curiously in the light of intervening social and economic events.

The formal and substantive failings of the book cannot be disregarded, but in a sense they are unimportant beside its intentions. To recapitulate, these were: to sketch a sociology of historic change which can neverthless account for social order in any given period; to demonstrate that change derives from the evolution of production but is not a direct outcome of technical or economic advance; to show that change can facilitate genuine human progress ('emancipation'); to provide criteria for judging it; and to demonstrate how 'the internal contradictions of socio-economic systems provide the mechanism for change which becomes development'.

Eric Hobsbawm, not Touraine, is the author of this latter phrase, and it appears in a critique of vulgar-Marxist social theory in which Hobsbawm welcomes the current renewal of social scientific interest in history. His main specifications for a historical sociology are precisely those Touraine seems to have had in mind when he planned *Sociologie de l'action*.[19]

The task of developing a suitable paradigm, which is pressing, presents enormous difficulties. Touraine deserves great credit for attempting it and failing so suggestively. It is of course disheartening that a social scientist of his calibre and experience should fail to give his insights real substance and coherence. His borrowings, conscious or otherwise, from the received thinking of the early 1960s on the nature of industrialized societies is a further reminder of the insidious plausibility of those theories.

This problem will be raised again in the final chapter. Some general comments on actionalism will serve as a useful preliminary, and follow in the next chapter.

ACTIONALISM:
COMMENTARY

Worker responses to the objective features of a work situation – technology, organizational constraints, power relations, changes induced by the market or by technical innovation, etc. – are mediated by socially structured subjective aims and perceptions. Action approaches may therefore be viewed, potentially at least, as a step towards full understanding of industrial situations.

The large resources devoted to the study of behaviour in work organizations in America, and the adoption of informal action perspectives by investigators such as Dalton and Gouldner, make it surprising that the approach was not formulated there rather than in Europe. In fact, a systematic argument laying stress on actor orientations as a factor in organizational dynamics was put forward by Etzioni around 1960.[1] But Etzioni was trying in the main to show that organizations spontaneously struggle towards an internal balance of social relations which makes them more effective in achieving their imputed goals. These mysterious adaptive reflexes supposedly demand congruence be established between the kind of power utilized by organizational controllers to secure the compliance of lower participants and the orientations towards that power of the latter.

Etzioni, then, introduced actor orientations merely as an adjunct to a systems conception of organizations which, despite its appearance of novelty, contains all the flaws of that perspective – reification, tautology, mystification.[2] Nothing could illustrate more plainly the subordination of American industrial studies to applications-oriented organization theory and the capacity of this orthodoxy to suppress or distort new insights.

Structural functionalism in general sociology, of which organization theory is an offshoot, never commanded the same following in Europe. Before 1960, sociology was little more than a fringe subject in Britain, its exponents being concentrated primarily in the London School of Economics. Functionalism was viewed sceptically there. (Lockwood was one of its foremost critics.) When British higher education was expanded rapidly in the 1960s, sociology was chosen as a major growth-point – a decision later regretted by the authorities – and it was mainly students trained at the L.S.E. who became sociology teachers.

Though suspicious of American 'grand theory', British sociologists lacked any agreed substitute and continued to admire American research expertise. The Luton investigation was really the first major British empirical study whose design and execution rivalled American professionalism. It also embodied a measure of theoretical originality. Whilst the *form* of actionalism put forward was no doubt influenced by the nature of the industrial findings, the germs of the approach are amply evident in the main investigators' previous work, especially in Lockwood's *Black-coated Worker*.

The Luton monographs went directly into the required reading lists for British sociologists not only because they tackled a major contemporary issue, but because they did so with an evident fluency of theory which offered some alternative to functionalism. For industrial sociologists in particular they represented an exemplar in research technique and an apparently ideal antidote to the failings of prior approaches.

Phenomenological actionalism has not had a comparable impact on industrial studies, and the likelihood of its doing so appears slight. Radical subjectivism in sociology has also been developed in opposition to functionalism. More generally, it has been connected with socio-political opposition to the status quo – spontaneous, rebellious opposition, it should be added, not systematic confrontation. Specializing in the study of deviants, marginals, neurotics, minorities and social isolates, its adherents develop intense sympathy with their subjects and revulsion against the injustices done them by straight society. Functionalism, which implicitly equates social normality with social usefulness and necessity (and, by extension, with sanity and virtue), quite naturally disgusts this type of investigator more than most.

Regrettably, rejection of this particular perspective typically involves the rejection of any social theory which does not centre upon the authenticity and rationality of subjective experience. Likewise, the critique of social scientific research technology, which begins with a valuable attack on attempts to mimic the procedures proper to natural science, frequently degenerates into a repudiation of anything resembling scientific procedures or assumptions. If there are no social facts independent of individual experience, it is argued, there can be no science of them and the paraphernalia of quantative investigation and inference are deceitful.

Much of this harmonizes well with a more general mood which developed rapidly in Western countries, but particularly amongst American middle-class youth, in the 1960s. Reasoned pessimism mingled with fashionable despair, and considered anarchism with puerile rebelliousness. A far from insignificant ingredient in this amorphous counter-culture was the popularity of psychedelics. Without undue exaggeration, subjectivist sociology may be viewed as an alternative (or as a supplement) to the exploration of 'inner space' made possible by acid tabs. It can offer many comparable revelations, but self-indulgent impotence is as likely a result as authentic enlightenment.

Intellectually, subjectivism is also an oppositional alternative to Marxism; and its popularity must be read partly against the disarray of Marxist scholarship, which remains plagued by dogmatism on the one hand and adventurism on the other.* The majority of 'Marxist' attempts to exploit the rebelliousness of the 1960s (notably Marcuse's), or to incorporate subjectivism, have failed

* Or both, as in the writings of L. Althusser.

embarrassingly.[3] It is also worth noting that subjectivism demands far less intellectual (and other) self-discipline, and is the kind of socio–cultural stance which presents the establishment with no insurmountable problem of containment.

The particular social, economic and political conditions of the 1960s which were so hospitable to subjectivism do not seem likely to be perpetuated in the present decade. In both Britain and America, however, its exponents have gained a foothold in academic social science. It will therefore probably continue as a minor force to be reckoned with. But its inadequacies are becoming more apparent as the situation which created its fashionability disappears. These inadequacies are better recognized in studying a sphere such as work, where the structured realities of collective life impinge insistently on behaviour and attitudes, than in the *demimondes* cherished by the subjectivist.

Some readers might be tempted to dismiss Touraine's historic actionalism as a 'typically French' brew of pretentious, ungrounded speculation. Actually, French industrial studies since the war have for the most part been 'typically Anglo–Saxon', i.e. heavily empiricist. In *Sociologie de l'action*, Touraine remarks of his generation of French sociologists: 'Men of the left hostile to doctrines, men of science haunted by the great questions of the past and all the revolts and revolutions, we sometimes preferred to seek in the most rudimentary empiricism, in the limited investigation, in blind erudition, a relief if not a resolution.'[4]

Touraine's actionalism is an open attempt to amend this scholarly withdrawal. Its sweeping holism, however, also reflects the telescoping of socio-economic history in the post-war France of the planners and technocrats. Rapid economic recovery, accelerated industrialization, sudden technological advances, consumer affluence, urbanization, novel domestic and cultural patterns – the battery of interlocking developments which transformed the texture of social life in Western countries after the war took the semi-industrialized French largely by surprise.

For the Americans, industrial society represented an exaggeration of previous trends. In France it seemed to betoken a sudden qualitative change in the pattern of life. The diffusion of the characteristics attributed to industrial society could be read by Americans as an indicator of the prototypicality of their own way of life. Before coexistence replaced cold war this was especially reassuring – hence no doubt one reason for the discovery of industrial society. For the French as a whole, but especially for French intellectuals, industrialism was one of those sudden blessings whose implications merit examination before it can be fully enjoyed.

Touraine is not alone amongst French industrial students in his reintroduction of historical perspective and moral concern into the study of the nexus of work and society. In certain respects, the ideas of his colleagues Gorz and Mallet are more suggestive.[5] But all these writers seem too ready to accept the economic assumptions which underpin the industrial society model and its derivatives.

International monetary dislocation, world-wide inflation, signs of a general fall in the profitability of industry, rising consumer expectations coinciding with the accelerated depletion of natural resources, and other essentially economic problems are currently eroding the credibility of the logic of industrialism as propounded in the 1960s.[6] Social change now seems much less likely to originate predominantly within the superstructure than Touraine, and Gorz, have suggested. State action may of course ward off any serious breakdown in the socio-economic system of industrial society in the coming years. It now seems unwise, however, to suppose with Touraine that such a growth of intervention would, more likely than not, be accompanied by a spread of democracy.

EVALUATION

None of the four kinds of theory outlined in the introductory chapter adequately explains the overall development of industrial studies. But a brief check of their explanatory potential suggests the kind of theory which might be adequate for that purpose. In fact, since such a theory attempts to elucidate social phenomena (i.e. successive efforts to render industrial studies scientific) it should also, if it is valid, suggest how industrial social science itself might be improved.

The positivist model is the least convincing. Industrial studies have conspicuously lacked the gentlemanly disinterestedness and cautious accumulation of proved hypotheses it invokes. The Myersian industrial psychologists, it is true, subscribed to this scientific self-image, and their work proceeded accordingly. But they are exceptional precisely because of this; and even their acceptance of the positivist code was partly tactical. Their leaders could lapse into somewhat unclinical language when they were evaluating scientific management.

Positivist scientific norms have always been urged on social students as something of an ideal. No one could seriously maintain that they have been generally accepted and followed. It is possibly misguided to suppose they ever could be in this branch of inquiry; and the recommendation they should be results from an uninformed impression of the procedures actually adopted by natural scientists.

Kuhnianism probably comes much nearer to the realities of natural scientific practice – the annoyance it has caused some hard scientists suggests that it has penetrated uncomfortably close to truths they prefer not to recognize. But whether it can validly be applied as a whole to social science is extremely doubtful. Kuhn himself originally questioned whether any branch of social science yet possesses paradigms in the sense he intended.[1]

Ignoring this, and helped by Kuhn's flexible conceptualization of paradigms, others have thought otherwise. Friedrichs has attempted to apply his scheme to sociology; Ward has done the same, much more convincingly in the field of economics.[2] Friedrichs argues that paradigms in sociology represent social relations as either cohesive or conflictual. Underlying any paradigm, however, is the self-image of its proponent, who may view himself as an other-worldly 'priest' or as a 'prophet' dedicated to changing the world. Empirically, Friedrichs asserts, 'priests' emphasize social cohesion, and 'prophets' social conflict. (He also talks about a third paradigmatic possibility, 'dialectic', but his remarks about it are quite unhelpful.)

In my view, Friedrichs's elaborations hardly illuminate the history of sociology itself, where some of his supposed 'prophets' were remarkably other-worldly and some of his 'priests' the reverse.[3] In industrial studies, both Taylor and Mayo were clearly 'prophets' but both assumed an essential harmony of social relations.

Yet Kuhnianism does remind us that once a plausible theory has been put forward in the human sciences a good deal of institutionalization can ensue. 'Scientific community' may be a rather strong term for the grouping which emerges, and 'normal science' decidedly so for its activities. But evidently such groupings have existed in industrial studies, and have espoused varying images of the worker and industrial relationships which might be called quasi-paradigms. A certain amount of rowdy debate has usually accompanied the adoption of a new image, though again the notion of 'revolutionary science' seems misleading. In so far then as it refers to some of the mechanisms which promote conformism and restrain originality in a 'scholarly' grouping, Kuhn's theory – which in this respect is scarcely revolutionary itself – aids description in this and other branches of social science.

As an explanatory rather than descriptive framework, however, it is rather inadequate. The fact that new paradigms oust old ones after a degree of resistance and recrimination is much less interesting than the timing of such 'revolutions' and the *content* of the contending images. Such matters are important in natural science. In social science, they are central.

All science aims to further human understanding of reality and, consequently, control over it. This enterprise costs money, and someone, rarely the scientist, must foot the bill. Backers who believe they will be able to utilize the new knowledge, however indirectly, are much commoner than those who do not. Scientists may thus be tempted to present their work in a way which appeals to possible sponsors. In all social science this creates a constant risk that only that work which excites rich or powerful groups will prosper. As for industrial studies, with their obvious practical bias, it is tempting to assert that the content of theories and the timing of their appearance merely reflect the changing problems of control, primarily over their work-forces, faced by managers and industrialists as the economic situation has changed.

Much evidence supporting such a vulgar-Marxist viewpoint is available in this book; and there is no question that the great majority of industrial students have addressed themselves primarily to managerial problems. As the nature of those problems changed, so did theories. However, it is quite idiotic to portray these students as a whole as flexible 'servants of power', tamely fabricating manipulative techniques and pseudo-scientific managerial propaganda.

Most of them sincerely believed in their own scientific credentials, and were well aware that managerial preoccupations conflict with adequate scientific investigation and inference. Myers and Mayo both attacked scientific management theorists on these grounds; and Mayo himself was brought roughly to book by later theorists. It is amusing to note that each new wave of theorists – including the Taylorites – has claimed to be first to avoid management bias. Again, managers often rejected the advice, sometimes quite sound, that its 'servants' submitted for improving efficiency and industrial relations. Taylor, Myers, Mayo and the Tavistock group all experienced greater or lesser customer resistance which vulgar-Marxism cannot explain readily.

Nor, of course, can it really account for the changing content of theories. How can one automatically deduce Arensberg's inter-actionism from the economic situation of the late 1930s, or the Luton group's middle-range actionalism from that of the early 1960s? How, above all, can such an approach explain the growing criticism within social science from the late 1940s onwards of the failings of industrial sociology, and the apparently growing effective-ness of this outcry?

Gouldner's arguments in *The Coming Crisis of Western Sociology* seem relevant here.[4] Unaware of the prejudices acquired during their social training and subtly reinforced in their professional circle, he claims, social investigators produce theories distorted by un-conscious bias. Confident these theories are value-free, they fail to recognize how others utilize them as propaganda or apologetics. Faced with problems which are essentially economic in character they adumbrate theories which represent them as social problems, and therefore soluble through social engineering.

Though concerned with general sociology, Gouldner's basic thesis transposes well to industrial studies for the period since their main strand became avowedly sociological around 1930. Talcott Parsons, the principal target of *The Coming Crisis*, was a member of the same Harvard coterie as Henderson and Mayo. Mayo's 'sociol-ogizing' of the shop-floor consequences of economic malaise is in many respects a precise miniature of Parsons's more grandiose project.

Gouldner's aim is to demonstrate that much sociology has been ideological in the full sense of that term, i.e. a body of ideas which while claiming to explain reality objectively is in fact distorted by presumptions deriving from the thinker's socio-economic origins and position. When these ideas resonate with those of the powerful, the thinker becomes influential, as both Parsons and Mayo did. It seems much more sensible to view the work of industrial students in terms such as these. An ideologically biased theory is not always thoroughly invalid. A non-ideological thinker might salvage elements from it. Likewise, the powerful may utilize its least sound but most reassuring elements as a 'scientific' prop for their actions and privileges. It is in this sense that most industrial students have been servants of power.

Gouldner maintains, however, that not all sociology is, or need be, ideological. Its methods are essentially neutral, and radical sociologists can turn them against the ideologists of academic sociology. Reflexive sociology, which involves such a critique, and a self-administered scrutiny of the critic's own unacknowledged presuppositions and loyalties, will allegedly accelerate the 'coming' crisis of sociology and transform the subject into a powerful tool of social analysis and criticism.

Industrial studies were no doubt 'sociologized' in the 1930s partly because sociology seemed capable of handling phenomena whose essentially economic character thinkers such as Mayo could not or would not recognize. The process was continued with the formulation of organization theory. Opposition to the structural–functionalist orthodoxy implicit in organization theory and technological implications has likewise accumulated. Accordingly, this branch of social science appears to reproduce, in a compressed form, the patterns Gouldner detects in sociology as a whole. (Gouldner, it is worth noting, is a former industrial sociologist himself.)

Gouldner's approach is attractive because it traces the links between changing historical situations and the kind of sociological theory which gains popularity. These situations have a discernible structure which, he obviously believes, can be adequately described and explained in sociological terms – at least, in the terms of the reflexive sociologist with historical insight.

Although Gouldner adds a historical dimension to social inquiry which I believe is crucial, it is significant that he demands a reflexive *sociology*, not a reflexive *social science*. To point this out is not to play with words. The possibility must be considered that much of sociology is to a greater or lesser degree ideological, and therefore can never provide fully adequate descriptions and explanations of social phenomena, although it may provide very plausible ones.

Sociology as an aspirant science of society emerged at the end of the eighteenth-century Enlightenment and the beginning of the industrial revolution. The Enlightenment had removed former supra-human guarantees of social order – to oversimplify, God was dead. Industrialization was transforming old social orders and generating new social tensions and opportunities. A science of society could set itself two main questions: how could society cohere without divine support, and what opportunities existed to exploit mankind's new freedom and material progress to secure further human liberation?[5]

These questions are not mutually exclusive, but for sociologists they soon became so. The briefest explanation for this consists of one word: Marx. Marx insisted that further liberation depended upon producers as a whole gaining control of the productive apparatus, which entailed abolition of the newly emerged capitalist relations of production. All other social institutions, relationships and forms of thought, Marx argued, supported or reflected the exploitative relation between owners of productive wealth and the workers whose labour had created it. In bourgeois society, social order was maintained by class domination.

Domination essentially implied economic supremacy, which was supported politically by state power. But quite plainly it included *moral* supremacy – workers in general might accept the values and beliefs of their exploiters; and both groups typically presumed that such notions embodied immutable and self-evident truths.* Such presumptions were powerfully reinforced when represented as science. Economics, in particular, unconsciously portrayed the relationships and practices of the capitalist mode of production as universal necessities.

Marx conjectured that the logic of the capitalist economy itself progressively fostered a situation which *permitted* the working class to recognize its own exploited condition; this recognition could produce a struggle to abolish class exploitation; experience of this

* In this respect Marx anticipated phenomenological sociology. His aim, however, was to point out the objectively inhuman, irrational component in the subjectively rational, 'taken-for-granted' world of individuals; inter-subjective moral suffocation, moreover, corresponded with identifiable forms of material dispossession and social subjection.

struggle would heighten workers' awareness of their condition. Revolutionary breakdown was therefore highly probable but not inevitable. A different impression was created by many of Marx's *political* utterances; and he died before his analysis of capitalist economic instability had been supplemented by his intended examination of the counteractive forces in the social superstructure. It is incorrect to talk of any of Marx's work as sociology, but what might have been treated as such was never finalized.[6]

Marx's provocative but incomplete thesis rendered him a natural target for critics alarmed by the prophecy of revolution. Sociologists took up the question of social order. In doing so, they jettisoned the Marxian axiom that surface or routine social phenomena cannot be considered separately from their basis, i.e. historically specific configurations of the forces and social relations of production. Social order in bourgeois society was treated by sociologists as one instance of social order generally. The latter was supposedly explicable in terms of universal principles which operated independently within the social (i.e. super-structural) sphere itself.

Thus Durkheim hypothesized a collective consciousness, and later structural–functionalists a central value-system, which attempt to account for social continuity and conformity in an adequate manner. Such constructs certainly serve this purpose quite well. But to explain social tension and social change all manner of increasingly unwieldy supplementary constructs must be introduced. Nor can this type of sociology very readily explain why any given society holds the values attributed to it – except tautologically, i.e. other values would yield another society.

Sociology, then, is marked by its historic attempt to refute Marx. Martin Shaw argues that it is necessarily ideological because of this polemical aim, of which its proponents are not fully aware, and that even radical sociologists like Gouldner cannot perceive how they are subtly perpetuating it.[7] Whether that is so or not, I think it must be accepted that sociology's claim to be able to deal adequately with all social phenomena in its own terms must now be rejected. In fact, this aim has often been abandoned in practice, and notably in the sixties in discussions of industralism.

When they maintained that non-social forces common to all

industrialized economies tend to homogenize social relations, theorists of convergent industrialism facilitated a step of cardinal importance beyond their own methodological and empirical over-simplifications; for they revived a concern with societies as concrete socio-economic wholes that can be ranked in terms of their level of development, which sociology had substantially discarded. But their erroneousness was even more fruitful. The unmistakably wishful projection of trends, discernible in the United States, rested upon the presumption that material changes *demand* predictable changes in social relations, as no less an authority than S. M. Lipset has candidly recognized.[8] They thus inverted the Soviet communist prediction of the inevitable collapse of capitalism only by appropri-ating generous portions of vulgar marxist methodology. In this somewhat curious fashion the errors of convergence theory made it easier to perceive the limitations of both sociology and Marxism as they existed a decade ago.

The greatest impulse to the revision of social scientific theory, however, has probably been the evolution of the capitalist world in the years since then. If oscillation and dislocation in its economy, accompanied by a resurgence of social conflicts, have come to replace the prosperity and tranquillity of the (historically brief) growth era, thereby promoting an unprecedented popular desire for change though not to date any real revolutionary enthusiasm, then that is the surest testimony of all of the incompleteness of these theories. In their dilettante borrowings from Marxism, convergence theorists equated the material basis of society with the productive *apparatus* whilst ignoring the *relations* of production and their persistent effects; and official marxists had ignored the effects of a growing productive apparatus. However, in western countries capitalist relations of pro-duction remain, and it therefore seems eminently reasonable not only to talk of 'capitalist society' rather than 'industrial society' when considering them but to inquire what implications those rela-tions have upon other structures and events.* Indeed, the term 'capitalism' has re-entered vocabulary to a wide extent in recent

---

* In a sense the term 'capitalist society' is less correct than 'bourgeois society' – though the latter also presents difficulties. See G. Lichtheim, *Marxism*, Routledge & Kegan Paul, 1964, pp. 46ff., 154–61.

years notwithstanding the continuing insistence (heard, not infrequently, on the lips of the directors of large and profitable private companies) that we now live under a quite different social regime.

Several objections to this must be recognized. To begin with, since such a course involves accepting and developing Marxian concepts, surely it commits the analyst to 'Marxist' values? I do not believe this is necessarily so at all, except in so far as those values refer to the desirability of an exact knowledge of society. Admittedly the successful practice of that science may demand acceptance of certain human values, but it is a matter of common experience that there are very few who do not eagerly voice their approval of such values anyway. Translating such values into political action is another matter still, but the recent emergence of 'Euro-communism' is a reminder – salutary also for Moscow, Washington and the ultra-left – that marxist thought is not necessarily (or even traditionally) linked to totalitarian programmes.

Next, abandonment of the industrial society model complicates the analysis of non-Western industrialized societies, and undermines apparently fruitful comparisons between them and their Western counterparts. This is absolutely true, but why it should be an objection escapes me. Undeniably, similarities do exist between all industrialized societies, despite the abolition of private industrial ownership in Eastern countries. This should not be altogether surprising since the state in Eastern countries has functioned in many ways as a monolithic, party-controlled and party-benefiting capitalist. In both kinds of society, the mass of the population is excluded from any effective control over its immediate and long-term destinies. Methods of achieving and justifying this exclusion, however, vary importantly and should be the subject of specialized investigation.

Finally, capitalism today is not quite what it was formerly. (A favourite substitute for 'industrial society' amongst convergence theorists is 'post-capitalist society'.) Certainly, a lengthy inventory of significant developments can be adduced – state regulation of the economy, the emergence of large public sectors, welfare provision, the growth of institutional ownership of industrial wealth, more humane management methods, and so forth.

None the less, the core institutions and social structure of capitalism remain: private ownership and control of productive wealth; the production of commodities for profit; markets for commodities and labour; and social class groupings produced by economic function and sustained by inequalities of wealth, income and socio-economic power. These properties are legitimated by a system of beliefs and values which stress individualism, competitiveness, private ownership and the necessity of free markets. The state, despite its interventionist role, operates essentially to maintain the system; state servants can block or modify even moderate reforms of it; dominant groups are better placed to influence state actions informally.[9]

It is equally important to add that the national state increasingly operates within the constraints of supra-national institutions such as the E.E.C., of those set by the activities of the multinational corporation, and – not to put too fine a point on it – of those created by the vicissitudes of the economy and polity of the U.S.A. This 'municipalization' of the nation state raises novel and exceptional problems, which can only become more acute in those European countries where popular majorities in favour of some decisive modification of the system can be produced.

Anyone alert to events in recent years must have some awareness that these realities are connected to those of daily industrial life. Approaches to industrial behaviour which pay no heed to them belong to an epoch in the history of capitalism which has now closed. But if they cannot be fully evaluated before the history of capitalism has itself been finalized, their principal inadequacy can readily be identified: namely, an inattention to the changing forms and consequences of socio-economic exploitation in the production of goods and services, and an inattention in particular to those consequences which generate challenges to the principle of exploitation itself. Yet these challenges, so often futile or irrelevant in appearance, are expressions of the negative aspect of human history which ensures its onward momentum and supplies our opportunities for real progress. However 'technical' his problem, the essential task of the social scientist is to render this process more comprehensible, and thereby, smoother and more fruitful.

NOTES

CHAPTER I *pages 13–28*

1. See W. A. Faunce, *Readings in Industrial Sociology*, Appleton-Century-Croft, New York, 1967, pp. 20–22, for a useful short bibliography.

2. See Faunce, op. cit., pp. 1–11.

3. C. M. Arensberg and G. Tootell, 'Plant Sociology: Real Discoveries and New Problems' in M. Komarovsky, ed., *Common Frontiers of the Social Sciences*, Free Press, Glencoe, Ill. 1957.

4. C. Kerr and L. H. Fisher, 'Plant Sociology: The Élite and the Aborigines' in Komarovsky, op. cit.

5. A. Etzioni, 'Industrial Sociology: The Study of Economic Organizations', *Social Research*, 25, 1958, 303–24.

6. Space limitations prevent a discussion of the work of this interesting group of investigators. (They constituted an important source of professors when British sociology expanded rapidly in the 1960s.) A good example of their approach, which includes a discussion of their other work, is W. H. Scott *et al.*, *Technical Change and Industrial Relations*, Liverpool University Press, 1956.

7. For example, D. C. Miller and W. Form, *Industrial Sociology*, Harper & Row, New York, 1964; E. V. Schneider, *Industrial Sociology*, McGraw-Hill, New York, 1957.

8. D. Silverman, 'Formal Organizations or Industrial Sociology: Towards a Social Action Analysis of Organizations', *Sociology*, 2, 1968, 221–38.

9. Faunce, op. cit.

10. ibid., p. 1.

11. In particular: R. Aron, *18 Lectures on Industrial Society*, Weidenfeld & Nicolson, 1967; C. Kerr *et al.*, *Industrialism and Industrial Man*, Heinemann, 1962; J. K. Galbraith, *The New Industrial State*, Hamish Hamilton, 1967; R. Dahrendorf, *Class and Class Conflict in Industrial Society*, Routledge & Kegan Paul, 1959; H. Marcuse, *One-Dimensional Man*, Routledge & Kegan Paul, 1964.

12. Faunce, op. cit., p. 2.

13. S. R. Parker, *et al.*, *The Sociology of Industry*, Allen & Unwin, 1967, p. 13.

14. T. Burns, ed., *Industrial Man*, Penguin Books, Harmondsworth, 1969, p. 9–10.

15. L. Baritz, *The Servants of Power*, Wiley, New York, 1965; G. Friedmann, *The Anatomy of Work*, Heinemann, 1961; R. Bendix, *Work and Authority in Industry*, Wiley, New York, 1956.

16. J. H. Goldthorpe, 'Orientation to Work and Industrial Behaviour Amongst Assembly-Line Operatives: A Contribution Towards an Action Approach in Industrial Sociology', Department of Applied Economics, Cambridge University, 1964 (mimeo).

17. See H. M. Johnson, *Sociology: A Systematic Introduction*, Routledge & Kegan Paul, 1961.

18. Much of the material in *Counter Course*, T. Pateman, ed., Penguin Books, Harmondsworth, 1972, with some notable exceptions, veers towards such oversimplification.

19. T. S. Kuhn, *The Structure of Scientific Revolutions*, Chicago University Press, Chicago, Ill., 1962.

20. R. W. Friedrichs, *A Sociology of Sociology*, Collier-Macmillan, 1970.

21. A. W. Gouldner, *The Coming Crisis of Western Sociology*, Heinemann, 1971.

CHAPTER 2 *pages 31–41*

1. F. W. Taylor, *The Principles of Scientific Management*, Harper & Row, New York, 1947, p. 19.

2. ibid.

3. F. B. Copley, *Frederick Winslow Taylor: Father of Scientific Management*, Harper & Row, New York, 1923, vol. I, p. 155.

4. See Taylor, op. cit.

5. F. W. Taylor, *Testimony Before the Special House Committee*, Harper & Row, New York, 1947, p. 109.

6. Taylor, *The Principles of Scientific Management*, p. 60.

7. Copley, op. cit., vol. II, p. 197.

8. Especially H. L. Gantt and R. Feiss, with their 'New Machine' movement. See M. J. Nadworny, *Scientific Management and the Unions, 1900–1932*, Harvard University Press, Cambridge, Mass., 1955, ch. 7.

CHAPTER 3 *pages 42–53*

1. See C. S. Maier, 'Between Taylorism and Technocracy: European Ideologies and the Vision of Industrial Productivity in the 1920s', *Journal of Contemporary History*, 5, 2, 1970, 27–61.

2. M. J. Nadworny, *Scientific Management and the Unions, 1900–1932*, Harvard University Press, Cambridge, Mass., 1955, ch. 1.

3. Reprinted in *Economic Studies*, I, June, 1896.

4. F. B. Copley, *Frederick Winslow Taylor: Father of Scientific Management*, Harper & Row, New York, 1923, vol. II, p. 146.

5. F. W. Taylor, *Shop Management*, Harper & Row, New York, 1947.

6. F. W. Taylor, 'On the Art of Cutting Metals', Transactions of the A.S.M.E., 28, 1907.

7. S. Haber, *Efficiency and Uplift*, Chicago University Press, Chicago, Ill., 1964, ch. 4 especially.

8. ibid., pp. 51ff.

9. Too many to list here, a wealth of examples are documented in Nadworny, op. cit., ch. 3.

10. See H. G. J. Aitken, *Taylorism at Watertown Arsenal*, Harvard University Press, Cambridge, Mass., 1960, for a full account.

11. ibid., p. 32.

12. Taylor, *Testimony before the Special House Committee*, p. 21.

13. ibid., p. 43.

14. E. Cadbury, 'Some Principles of Industrial Organization', *Sociological Review*, 7, 1914, 99–117.

15. C. B. Thompson, 'The Case for Scientific Management', *Sociological Review*, 7, 1914, 315–27.

CHAPTER 4 *pages 54–60*

1. Psychoanalytically oriented historians, somewhat surprisingly, have neglected Taylor. A recent essay, while providing some intriguing psycho-biographical information, illustrates well the inherent dangers of this brand of historiography: see S. Kakar, *Frederick Taylor: A Study in Personality and Innovation*, M.I.T. Press, Cambridge, Mass., 1970.

2. C. S. Maier, 'Between Taylorism and Technocracy: European Ideologies and the Vision of Industrial Productivity in the 1920s', *Journal of Contemporary History*, 5, 2, 1970, 27–61.

3. Quoted in R. Bendix, *Work and Authority in Industry*, Harper & Row, New York, 1963, p. 255.

4. G. Friedmann, *La crise du progrès*, Gallimard, Paris, 1936, pp. 76ff.

5. Bendix, op. cit., p. 265.

6. ibid., pp. 257–67.

7. See M. J. Nadworny, *Scientific Management and the Unions, 1900–1932*, Harvard University Press, Cambridge, Mass., 1955, ch. 7–9.

8. ibid. Nadworny points out that many of the 'New Machine's' ideas were revived during the economically troubled 1930s by the 'Technocracy' movement; see p. 107.

9. *The Annals of the American Academy of Political and Social Science*, September 1920.

10. See Nadworny, op. cit., pp. 119ff.

11. ibid., ch. 8.

12. ibid.

13. ibid., pp. 138 *et seq.*

CHAPTER 5 *pages 65–68*

1. E. Farmer, 'The Method of Grouping by Differential Tests', *Fourth Annual Report of the Industrial Fatigue Research Board*, H.M.S.O., 1924.

2. ibid.

3. For a brief historical account see L. S. Hearnshaw, *A Short History of British Psychology, 1840–1940*, Methuen, 1964, pp. 275–82.

4. C. S. Myers, *An Account of the Research Work Carried Out by the National Institute of Industrial Psychology during the Years 1921–34*, National Institute of Industrial Psychology, 1934. Significantly, Myers's plea for support is built around a reference to Bacon.

5. C. S. Myers, *Industrial Psychology in Great Britain*, Cape, 1924, p. 28.

6. ibid., pp. 35–6.

CHAPTER 6 *pages 69–75*

1. ibid., p. 74.

2. E. P. Cathcart, *The Human Factor in Industry*, Oxford University Press, 1928, p. 17.

3. ibid., p. 20.

4. C. S. Myers, *Industrial Psychology in Great Britain*, Cape, 1924, p. 40.

5. E. Farmer, 'The Interpretation and Plotting of Output Curves', *British Journal of Psychology*, 13, 1923, 308–14.

6. See G. Friedmann, *Industrial*

Society, Free Press, Glencoe, Ill., 1955, pp. 70ff.; Collier-Macmillan, 1964.

7. ibid.

8. These are catalogued in an appendix to S. Wyatt, *et al.*, *The Effects of Monotony in Work*, Industrial Fatigue Research Board, Report 56, H.M.S.O., 1929.

9. H. M. Vernon, 'The Use and Significance of the Kata-Thermometer', *Fourth Annual Report of the I.F.R.B.*, H.M.S.O., 1924.

10. H. M. Vernon and T. Bedford, *A Study of Absenteeism in a Group of Ten Collieries*, H.M.S.O., 1928.

11. ibid., p. 50.

CHAPTER 7 *pages 76–81*

1. H. M. Vernon, *et al.*, *Two Studies of Rest Pauses in Industry*, H.M.S.O., 1924.

2. H. M. Vernon, *et al.*, *On the Extent and Effects of Variety in Repetitive Work*, H.M.S.O., 1924.

3. S. Wyatt and J. A. Fraser, *The Comparative Effects of Variety and Uniformity in Work*, H.M.S.O., 1928.

4. S. Wyatt and J. A. Fraser, *The Effects of Monotony in Work*, H.M.S.O., 1929.

5. ibid., p. 2.

6. ibid., p. 5.

7. ibid., p. 43.

8. ibid., p. 40.

9. May Smith, 'General Psychological Problems Confronting an Investigator', *Fourth Annual Report of the I.F.R.B.*, H.M.S.O., 1924.

10. May Smith, *et al.*, *A Study of Telegraphists' Cramp*, H.M.S.O., 1927.

11. M. Culpin and May Smith, *The Nervous Temperament*, H.M.S.O., 1930.

CHAPTER 8 *pages 82–87*

1. S. Wyatt and J. N. Langdon, *The Machine and the Worker*, H.M.S.O., 1938.

2. W. Baldamus, *Efficiency and Effort*, Tavistock Institute of Human Relations, 1961. Baldamus, whose work – regrettably – cannot be discussed here, locates his studies of monotony ('tedium') within a conflictual model of industrial relationships.

3. Wyatt and Langdon, op cit., p. 45.

4. C. S. Myers, ed., *Industrial Psychology*, Home University Library 1929.

5. ibid., ch. 2.

6. ibid., pp. 33–4.

7. ibid., p. 32.

8. E. P. Cathcart, *The Human Factor in Industry*, Oxford University Press, 1928.

9. ibid., p. 93.

10. ibid., p. 91.

11. ibid., pp. 13–15.

12. G. Friedmann, *Industrial Society* Free Press, Glencoe, Ill., 1955, p. 84; Collier-Macmillan, 1964.

13. C. S. Myers, 'The Efficiency Engineer and the Industrial Psychologist', *Journal of the National Institute of Industrial Psychology*, 1, 1921, 168–72; F. and L. Gilbreth, 'The Efficiency Engineer and the Industrial Psychologist – Reply', *Journal of the National Institute*, 2, 1922, 40–45.

14. F. and L. Gilbreth, op. cit.

15. ibid.

16. ibid.

17. C. S. Myers, *Industrial Psychology in Great Britain*, Cape, 1924.

18. ibid., p. 83.

19. ibid., p. 29.

20. ibid., p. 25.

21. E. Farmer, 'The Interconnection between Economics and Industrial

Psychology', *Journal of the National Institute of Industrial Psychology*, 2, 1922, pp. 78–83.

22. Friedmann, op. cit., p. 125.

23. ibid.

CHAPTER 9 *pages 88–96*

1. Interested readers might compare the design of the lighting experiments at Western Electric with similar investigations by I.F.R.B. staff, e.g. H. C. Weston, *et al.*, *The Relation Between Illumination and Efficiency in Fine Work*, H.M.S.O., 1926.

2. E. Mayo, *Human Problems of an Industrial Civilization*, Macmillan, New York, 1946, p. 41.

3. The conference was held in August 1924, in Toronto; see E. Mayo, 'Day-Dreaming and Output in a Spinning Mill', *Journal of the National Institute of Industrial Psychology*, 2, 1923, 203–9; Myers's *Industrial Psychology in Great Britain*, Cape, 1924, was based on lectures delivered at Columbia University.

4. L. Baritz, *The Servants of Power*, Wiley, New York, 1965, chs. 1–4.

5. W. McDougall, *An Introduction to Social Psychology*, Methuen, 1908.

6. O. Tead, *Instincts in Industry*, Small, Maynard, Boston, 1918.

7. Baritz, op. cit., p. 31.

8. D. Scott, *The Psychology of Advertising*, Small, Maynard, Boston, 1908.

9. Mayo, 'Day-Dreaming and Output in a Spinning Mill', 'The Irrational Factor in Society', *Journal of Personnel Research*, 1, 1923, 419–26; 'Irrationality and Revery', ibid., 477–483; 'Revery and Industrial Fatigue', *Journal of Personnel Research*, 3, 1924, 273–81; *Human Problems of an Industrial Civilization*, pp. 40ff.

10. See Mayo, 'Revery and Industrial Fatigue'.

11. See A. Carey, 'The Hawthorne Studies: A Radical Criticism', *American Sociological Review*, 32, 1967, 403–16, for an uncompromising reappraisal of the design.

CHAPTER 10 *pages 97–100*

1. See J. Child, *British Management Thought*, Allen & Unwin, 1969, chs. 3 and 4.

CHAPTER 11 *pages 103–12*

1. L. Baritz, *The Servants of Power*, Wiley, New York, 1965, ch. 5 *et seq.*; R. Bendix, *Work and Authority in Industry*, Harper & Row, New York, 1963, pp. 287ff.

2. Whyte, loc. cit.

3. T. N. Whitehead, *The Industrial Worker*, Oxford University Press, London, 1938, vols. I and II, covers all phases of this 'experiment'.

4. ibid., vol. I, ch. 18.

5. Roethlisberger and Dickson, op. cit., p. 189.

6. Landsberger, op. cit., p. 21.

7. Roethlisberger and Dickson, op. cit., p. 604; their italics.

8. See J. L. and H. L. Wilensky, 'Personnel Counselling: The Hawthorne Case', *American Journal of Sociology*, 57, 1952, 265–80.

CHAPTER 12 *pages 113–24*

1. E. Mayo, *Democracy and Freedom*, Macmillan, Melbourne, 1919.

2. For a short biography, written by an admirer, see L. F. Urwick, *The Life and Work of Elton Mayo*, Urwick, Orr & Partners Ltd, London, n.d.

3. Mayo wrote an essay on this theme before leaving Australia. See ibid., p. 5.

4. Especially in 'The Irrational Factor in Society', *Journal of Personnel Research*, 1, 1923, 419–26.

5. Henderson's fascination with Pareto is documented from first-hand experience in G. C. Homans, *Sentiments and Activities*, Routledge & Kegan Paul, 1962: see 'Autobiographical Introduction'; also B. S. Heyl, 'The Harvard Pareto Circle', *Journal of the History of Behavioural Sciences*, 4, 1968, 316–34.

6. E. Mayo, 'Maladjustment of the Industrial Worker' in O. S. Beyer *et al.*, *The Wertheim Lectures on Industrial Relations, 1928*, Harvard University Press, Cambridge, Mass., 1929. (Interestingly, another participant in this lecture series was J. P. Frey, a veteran of the struggle against Taylorism.)

7. ibid., pp. 167 and 191 in particular.

8. See F. J. Roethlisberger and W. J. Dickson, *Management and the Worker*, Wiley, New York, 1964, p. 389.

9. E. Mayo, 'The Hawthorne Experiment', *The Human Factor*, 6, 1930. Urwick, op. cit., pp. 32–4, provides a useful bibliography of Mayo's many articles.

10. Roethlisberger and Dickson, op. cit., pp. 53–5.

11. ibid., pp. 6off.

12. ibid., p. 133.

13. E. Mayo, *Human Problems of an Industrial Civilisation*, Macmillan, New York, 1946, p. 79.

14. Roethlisberger and Dickson, op. cit., ch. 15.

15. Mayo, *Human Problems of an Industrial Civilization*, pp. 96–7.

16. Mayo, *Human Problems of an Industrial Civilization*, p. 116.

17. ibid., p. 147.

18. ibid., p. 175.

19. B. Adams, *The Theory of Social Revolutions*, Macmillan, 1913; see *Human Problems of an Industrial Civilization*, p. 165.

20. Mayo, *Human Problems of an Industrial Civilization*, p. 171.

21. E. Mayo, *The Social Problems of an Industrial Civilization*, Routledge & Kegan Paul, 1949.

22. ibid., p. 21. Mayo's italics.

23. Mayo in O. S. Beyer, *et al.*, op. cit., p. 185.

24. Mayo, *Social Problems of an Industrial Civilization*, p. 27.

25. ibid., pp. 74–5.

26. ibid., pp. 8off. See J. B. Fox and J. F. Scott, *Absenteeism: Management's Problem*, Harvard Business School, Cambridge, Mass., 1943; E. Mayo and G. F. Lombard, *Teamwork and Labor Turnover in the Aircraft Industry of Southern California*, Harvard Business School, Cambridge, Mass., 1944.

27. Mayo, *Social Problems of an Industrial Civilization*, pp. 93–5.

28. *The Political Problem of Industrial Civilization*, which would have completed his *Problems* triology, was published in an unfinished form in 1947. In it, Mayo expressed frank nostalgia for the Middle Ages.

CHAPTER 13 *pages 125–46*

1. W. L. Warner and J. O. Low, *The Social System of the Modern Factory*, Yale University Press, New Haven, Conn., 1947.

2. A. Carey, 'The Hawthorne Studies: A Radical Criticism', *American Sociological Review*, 32, 1967, 403–16.

3. See F. J. Roethlisberger and W. J. Dickson, *Management and the Worker*, Wiley, New York, 1964, pp.

22, 180. In fact, the original observer was eventually promoted and given the assistance of a *second* observer. It is extremely difficult to establish the chronology of this and associated changes.

4. T. N. Whitehead (*The Industrial Worker*, Oxford University Press, London, 1938), commenting on this, remarks that initially 'it was not clearly realized that full co-operation and typical supervisory techniques were mutually incompatible'. See vol. 1, p. 104.

5. An especially friendly commentary is provided in J. Madge, *The Origins of Scientific Sociology*, Tavistock Institute of Human Relations, 1963, ch. 6.

6. See A. V. Cicourel, *Method and Measurement in Sociology*, Collier-Macmillan, 1967, ch. 3.

7. Roethlisberger and Dickson acknowledge the advice of the anthropologist W. L. Warner. But once again it is extremely difficult to assess the real degree of his influence.

8. H. A. Landsberger, *Hawthorne Revisited*, Cornell University Press, Ithaca, N.Y., 1958, p. 22.

9. Roethlisberger and Dickson, op. cit., pp. 391–2.

10. ibid., pp. 578ff.

11. Madge, op. cit., though providing some useful introductory criticisms is brief and somewhat uninformed on key matters.

12. Landsberger, op. cit., p. 64.

13. ibid., p. 67.

14. See J. L. and H. L. Wilensky, 'Personnel Counselling: The Hawthorne Case', *American Journal of Sociology*, 57, 1952, p. 266n.

15. Landsberger, op. cit., p. 86.

16. ibid., pp. 96–7.

17. ibid., p. 99.

18. Roethlisberger and Dickson, op. cit., p. 568.

19. ibid., p. 553.

20. T. N. Whitehead, *Leadership in a Free Society*, Harvard University Press, Cambridge, Mass., 1936.

21. T. N. Whitehead, *The Industrial Worker: A Statistical Study of Human Relations in a Group of Manual Workers*, Oxford University Press, 1938, vols. I and II.

22. *The Industrial Worker*, vol. I, ch. 16, covers operator 2's initial impact.

23. ibid., p. 127.

24. ibid., p. 233.

25. ibid., p. 161.

26. W. L. Warner and J. O. Low, *The Social System of the Modern Factory*, Yale University Press, New Haven, Conn., 1947.

27. In particular, W. L. Warner and P. S. Lunt, *The Social Life of a Modern Community*, Yale University Press, New Heaven, Conn., 1941.

28. W. H. Whyte in *The Organization Man*, Penguin Books, Harmondsworth, 1963, p. 42, quite wrongly states that Warner devoted only 'a couple of sentences to the logical, economic factors' behind the strike. This kind of misconception of Warner's work is typical.

29. Warner and Low, op. cit. p. 65.

30. ibid., pp. 172ff.

31. ibid., pp. 188–9.

32. ibid., p. 195.

33. ibid., p. 196.

34. ibid.

35. See W. L. Warner, *American Life: Dream and Reality*, University of Chicago Press, Chicago, Ill., 1953. Needless to say, however, at the end of the day Warner is a better analyst of 'dream' than 'reality'.

36. W. L. Warner, *Black Civilization: A Social Study of an Australian Tribe*, Harper & Row, New York, 1937.

37. See especially the chapter 'Individual Opportunity and Social

Mobility in America' in *American Life: Dream and Reality*.

CHAPTER 14 *pages 147-60*

1. P. W. Bridgman, *The Logic of Modern Physics*, Macmillan, New York, 1928.
2. G. C. Homans, *Sentiments and Activities*, Routledge & Kegan Paul, 1962, 'Autobiographical Introduction'.
3. C. M. Arensberg and S. T. Kimball, *Family and Community in Ireland*, Harvard University Press, Cambridge, Mass., 1940.
4. E. D. Chapple and C. M. Arensberg, *Measuring Human Relations: An Introduction to the Study of the Interaction of Individuals*, Genetic Psychology Monograph No. 22, Journal Press, Provincetown, Mass., 1940.
5. C. M. Arensberg, 'Behavior and Organization: Industrial Studies' in J. H. Rohrer and M. Sherif, *Social Psychology at the Crossroads*, Harper & Row, New York, 1951, p. 345.
6. Homans, op. cit., p. 37.
7. E. D. Chapple, Editorial, *Applied Anthropology*, 1, 1, 1941.
8. See review of Mary Parker Follett's *Dynamic Administration*, *Applied Anthropology*, 1, 3, 1942.
9. O. Collins, M. Dalton and D. Roy, 'Restriction of Output and Social Cleavage in Industry', *Applied Anthropology*, 5, 1946, 1-14.
10. M. Dalton, 'The Industrial Rate-Buster: A Characterization', *Applied Anthropology*, 7, 1948, 5-18.
11. C. M. Arensberg, Editorial, *Applied Anthropology*, 6, 1947.
12. R. F. Bales, *Interaction Process Analysis*, Addison-Wesley, Reading, Mass., 1951.
13. Compare E. D. Chapple, 'Applied Anthropology in Industry' in *Anthropology Today*, A. L. Kroeber,

ed., University of Chicago Press, Chicago, Ill., 1951, with C. M. Arensberg and G. Tootell, 'Plant Sociology: Real Discoveries and New Problems' in M. Komarovsky, ed., *Common Frontiers of the Social Sciences*, Free Press, Glencoe, Ill., 1957.
14. For example, *Organizational Behavior: Theory and Application*, Irwin, Homewood, Ill., 1969.
15. Homans made one or two minor contributions to industrial sociology, was once widely regarded as the inventor of interactionism, and figured prominently in critiques of human relations (see C. Kerr and L. Fisher, 'Plant Sociology: The Élite and the Aborigines' in M. Komarovsky, ed., *Common Frontiers of the Social Sciencies*, Free Press, Glencoe, Ill., 1957). He is currently best known as an 'exchange theorist'.
16. W. F. Whyte, *Street Corner Society*, University of Chicago Press, Chicago, Ill., 2nd ed, 1955.
17. *Organizational Behavior*, pp. 18-19.
18. W. F. Whyte and B. B. Gardner, 'Facing the Foreman's Problems' and 'The Position and Problems of the Foreman', *Applied Anthropology*, 4, 1945, 1-28.
19. ibid.
20. W. F. Whyte and B. B. Gardner, 'From Conflict to Co-operation', *Applied Anthropology*, 5, 1946.
21. W. F. Whyte, *Pattern for Industrial Peace*, Harper & Row, New York, 1951.
22. W. F. Whyte and B. B. Gardner, 'Methods for the Study of Human Relations in Industry', *American Sociological Review*, 11, 1946, 506-12.
23. W. F. Whyte, *Human Relations in the Restaurant Industry*, McGraw-Hill, New York, 1948.
24. W. F. Whyte, 'The Social

Structure of the Restaurant', *American Journal of Sociology*, 54, 1949, 302–10.

25. ibid.

26. W. F. Whyte, 'Small Groups and Large Organizations' in J. H. Rohrer and M. Sherif, *Social Psychology at the Crossroads*, Harper & Row, New York, 1951.

27. W. F. Whyte, *Money and Motivation: An Analysis of Incentives in Industry*, Harper & Row, New York, 1955.

28. ibid., pp. 208–9.

29. ibid., ch. 6. Whyte relies upon Dalton's work here. See M. Dalton, 'The Industrial Rate-Buster: A Characterization', *Applied Anthropology*, 7, 1948, 5–18.

30. Whyte, *Money and Motivation*, p. 227. Whyte's italics.

31. ibid., p. 233.

32. Whyte, *Money and Motivation*, p. 260.

33. Especially M. Dalton, L. Sayles, O. Collins and A. Bavelas.

CHAPTER 15 *pages 161–67*

1. See H. Feldman, *Problems in Labor Relations*, Macmillan, New York, 1937.

2. R. Lippitt, 'An Experimental Study of the Effect of Democratic and Authoritarian Group Atmospheres', *University of Iowa Studies in Child Welfare*, 16, 1940, 43–195; R. Lippitt and R. K. White, 'An Experimental Study of Leadership and Group Life' in G. E. Swanson *et al.*, eds., *Readings in Social Psychology*, Holt, Rinehart, New York, 1952.

3. K. Lewin, 'Group Decision and Social Change' in G. E. Swanson *et al.*, eds., op. cit.

4. L. Coch and J. P. French, 'Overcoming Resistance to Change', *Human Relations*, 1, 1948, 512–32.

5. For a friendly critique of the Harwood investigations see M. S. Viteles, *Motivation and Morale in Industry*, W. W. Norton, New York, 1953.

6. D. Katz, N. Maccoby and N. C. Morse, *Productivity, Supervision and Morale in an Office Situation*, Survey Research Center, University of Michigan, Ann Arbor, Mich., 1950.

7. D. Katz *et al.*, *Productivity, Supervision and Morale amongst Railroad Workers*, Survey Research Center, University of Michigan, Ann Arbor, Mich., 1951.

8. D. Katz and R. L. Kahn, *The Caterpillar Tractor Co. Study*, Survey Research Center, University of Michigan, Ann Arbor, Mich., 1951.

9. See M. Argyle, *Social Interaction*, Methuen, 1969, pp. 302–3.

10. F. C. Mann, 'Changing Supervisor–Subordinate Relationships', *Journal of Social Issues*, 7, 1951, 56–63.

11. C. M. Arensberg and A. B. Horsfall, 'Teamwork and Productivity in a Shoe Factory', *Human Organization*, 8, 1949, 13–26.

12. See Viteles, op. cit., for an exhaustive catalogue.

13. E. Seashore, 'Group Cohesiveness in the Industrial Work Group', reprinted in W. A. Faunce, *Readings in Industrial Sociology*, Appleton-Century-Crofts, New York, 1967.

14. Undoubtedly Viteles, op. cit., is the most outstanding example; a 'sociological' close runner-up is B. B. Gardner and D. G. Moore, *Human Relations in Industry*, 3rd ed, Irwin, Homewood, Ill., 1955.

15. C. Kerr and L. Fisher 'Plant Sociology: The Élite and the Aborigines' in M. Komarovsky, ed. *Common Frontiers of the Social Sciences*, Free Press, Glencoe, Ill., 1957.

16. C. M. Arensberg and G. Tootell,

'Plant Sociology: Real Discoveries and New Problems' in Komarovsky, op. cit.

CHAPTER 16 *pages 168–72*

1. For an account of how the particular circumstances of Britain favoured informal human relations ideology in management literature at this time, see J. Child, *British Management Thought*, Allen & Unwin, 1969, ch. 4.

2. G. C. Homans, *Sentiments and Activities*, Routledge & Kegan Paul, 1962, p. 4.

3. See E. Freeman, *Social Psychology* Holt, Rinehart, New York, 1936, pp. 323–66; R. S. Lynd, Review of Whitehead's *Leadership in a Free Society*, *Political Science Quarterly*, 52, 1937, 590–92; M. Gilson, Review of *Management and the Worker*, *American Journal of Sociology*, 46, 1940, 98–101.

4. C. W. M. Hart, 'The Hawthorne Experiments', *Canadian Journal of Economics and Political Science*, 9, 1943; D. Bell, 'Adjusting Men to Machines', *Commentary*, 3, 1947, 79–88; W. E. Moore, 'Industrial Sociology: Status and Prospects', *American Sociological Review*, 13, 1948, 382–91; H. Blumer, 'Sociological Theory in Industrial Relations', *American Sociological Review*, 12, 1947, 271–8; C. W. Mills, 'The Contributions of Sociology to Studies of Industrial Relations', *Proceedings of the Industrial Relations Research Association*, 1, 1948, 199–222; R. C. Sorensen, 'The Concept of Conflict in Industrial Sociology', *Social Forces*, 29, 1951, 263–7; E. V. Schneider, 'Limitations on Obervations in Industrial Sociology', *Social Forces*, 28, 1950, 279–84; J. T. Dunlop, 'A Framework for the Analysis of In-
dustrial Relations: Two Views', *Industrial and Labour Relations Review*, 3, 1950, 383–93.

5. A. Carey, 'The Hawthorne Studies: A Radical Criticism', *American Sociological Review*, 32, 1967, 403–16.

6. For example, R. Bendix and L. Fisher, 'The Perspectives of Elton Mayo', *Review of Economics and Statistics*, 31, 1949, 312–19.

7. Mills, op. cit.

8. C. Kerr and L. Fisher, 'Plant Sociology: The Élite and the Aborigines', in M. Komarovsky, ed., *Common Frontiers of Social Science*, Free Press, Glencoe, Ill., 1957; W. H. Whyte, *The Organization Man*, Penguin Books, Harmondsworth, 1963, Part 1.

9. C. M. Arensberg and G. Tootell, 'Plant Sociology: Real Discoveries and New Problems' in M. Komarovsky, ed., *Common Frontiers of the Social Sciences*, Free Press, Glencoe, Ill., 1957; C. M. Arensberg, 'Behavior and Organization: Industrial Studies' in J. H. Rohrer and M. Sherif, *Social Psychology at the Crossroads*, Harper & Row, New York, 1951; W. F. Whyte 'Human Relations – A Progress Report', *Harvard Business Review*, 34, 1956, 125–32; G. C. Homans, 'The Strategy of Industrial Sociology', *American Journal of Sociology*, 54, 1949, 330–37.

10. See M. M. Viteles, *Motivation and Morale in Industry*, W. W. Norton, New York, 1953; B. B. Gardner and D. G. Moore, *Human Relations in Industry*, 3rd edn, Irwin, Homewood, Ill., 1955.

CHAPTER 17 *pages 175–80*

1. See E. L. Trist, *et al.*, *Organizational Choice*, Tavistock Institute of Human Relations, 1963.

2. E. L. Trist and K. W. Bamforth, 'Some Social and Psychological Consequences of the Longwall Method of Coal-Getting', *Human Relations*, 4, 1951, 3–38.

3. See A. K. Rice, *Productivity and Social Organization*, Tavistock Institute of Human Relations, 1958; and *The Enterprize and Its Environment*, Tavistock Institute of Human Relations, 1963.

4. R. K. Brown, 'Research and Consultancy in Industrial Enterprizes' *Sociology*, 1, 1967, 33–60.

5. Trist and Bamforth, op. cit.

6. J. N. Morris, 'Coal Miners', *The Lancet*, 2, 1947, 341.

7. Trist and Bamforth, op. cit.

8. Trist and Bamforth, op. cit.

9. ibid.

CHAPTER 18 *pages 181–86*

1. C. R. Walker and R. H. Guest, *The Man on the Assembly Line*, Harvard University Press, Cambridge, Mass., 1952.

2. C. R. Walker, R. H. Guest and A. N. Turner, *The Foreman on the Assembly Line*, Harvard University Press, Cambridge, Mass., 1956.

3. G. Friedmann, *Où va le travail humain?*, Gallimard, Paris, 1950.

4. Walker and Guest, op. cit., p. 4.

5. ibid., p. 2.

6. ibid., p. 3.

7. ibid., p. 20.

8. ibid., p. 80.

9. ibid., p. 160.

10. ibid., p. 66.

11. ibid., p. 134.

12. ibid., p. 66.

13. ibid., p. 161.

14. ibid., p. 156. Italics in original.

15. M. Dalton, 'The Industrial Rate-Buster: A Characterization', *lied Anthropology*, 7, 1947, 323–32.

16. See Chapter 26 below.

17. See R. H. Guest, 'Job Enlargement: A Revolution in Job Design', *Personnel Administration*, 20, 1957, 13–15.

CHAPTER 19 *pages 187–94*

1. See D. Silverman, *The Theory of Organizations*, Heinemann, 1970, ch. 4.

2. See A. H. Maslow, 'A Theory of Human Motivation', in V. H. Vroom and E. L. Deci, eds., *Management and Motivation*, Penguin Books, Harmondsworth, 1970.

3. Maslow's ideas have been propagated least cautiously of all by Frederick Herzberg, who is more optimistic on this score. See F. Herzberg, *Work and the Nature of Man*, Staples Press, Granada, St. Albans, 1968.

4. Maslow, op. cit.

5. D. McGregor, *The Human Side of the Enterprize*, McGraw-Hill, New York, 1960; and 'The Human Side of the Enterprize' in Vroom and Deci, op. cit.

6. R. Likert, 'New Patterns of Management' in Vroom and Deci, op. cit., p. 322.

7. See especially C. Argyris, *Personality and Organization*, Harper & Row, New York, 1957.

8. C. Argyris, 'Understanding Human Behavior in Organizations' in M. Haire, *Modern Organization Theory*, Wiley, New York, 1959, p. 115.

9. ibid., p. 119.

10. ibid., p. 120.

11. ibid., p. 145.

12. See C. R. Walker and R. H. Guest, *The Man on the Assembly Line*, Harvard University Press, Cambridge, Mass., 1952; and W. Baldamus, *Efficiency and Effort*, Tavistock Institute of Human Relations, 1961.

13. A. Kornhauser, *Mental Health of the Industrial Worker*, Wiley, New York, 1965.

14. See Baldamus, op. cit., and Part v below.

15. See R. Blauner, 'Work Satisfaction and Industrial Trends in Modern Society' in W. Galenson and S. M. Lipset, *Labor and Trade Unionism*, Wiley, New York, 1960.

16. M. Dalton, 'The Industrial Rate-Buster: A Characterization', *Applied Anthropology*, 7, 1947.

17. T. Burns and G. M. Stalker, *The Management of Innovation*, Tavistock Institute of Human Relations, 1961.

18. See H. J. Leavitt, 'Applied Organizational Change in Industry: Structural, Technical and Human Approaches' in Vroom and Deci, op. cit.

19. Silverman, op. cit., pp. 87–8.

CHAPTER 20 *pages 195–200*

1. L. R. Sayles, *The Behavior of Industrial Work Groups: Prediction and Control*, Wiley, New York, 1958.

2. Sayles even writes at some points that technology *moulds* group phenomena: op. cit., p. 4.

3. ihid., p. 39.

4. ibid.

5. ibid., p. 42. Sayles's italics.

6. ibid., pp. 58–9.

7. D. Lockwood, *The Black-coated Worker*, Allen & Unwin, 1958.

8. Sayles, op. cit., p. 70.

9. ibid., p. 93.

10. ibid., p. 94.

11. ibid., p. 135.

12. ibid., p. 156.

13. With some sarcasm; see for example ibid., p. 170.

14. ibid., p. 166.

15. ibid., p. 163.

CHAPTER 21 *pages 201–5*

1. J. Woodward, *Management and Technology*, H.M.S.O., 1958; *Industrial Organization: Theory and Practice*, Oxford University Press, 1965.

2. See Woodward, *Industrial Organization: Theory and Practice*, pp. 245ff.

3. Woodward, *Industrial Organization: Theory and Practice*, p. 40.

4. ibid., p. 50.

5. ibid., p. 72.

6. ibid.

7. See J. Woodward and J. Rackham, 'The Measurement of Technical Variables' in J. Woodward, ed., *Industrial Organization: Behaviour and Control*, Oxford University Press, 1970.

CHAPTER 22 *pages 206–11*

1. R. Blauner, *Alienation and Freedom: The Factory Worker and his Industry*, University of Chicago Press, Chicago, Ill., 1964, p. 6. Blauner's italics.

2. ibid.

3. ibid., p. 15.

4. ibid., p. 24.

5. ibid., p. 26.

6. See D. McLellan, *Marx Before Marxism*, Penguin Books, Harmondsworth, 1970, pp. 213ff., especially.

CHAPTER 23 *pages 212–17*

1. E. L. Trist, *et al.*, *Organizational Choice*, Tavistock Institute of Human Relations, 1963, p. 6.

2. Quoted in ibid., p. 6.

3. ibid., p. 8.

4. ibid., p. 278.

Notes

CHAPTER 24 *pages 218–23*

1. The term 'technological implications' was first applied by J. H. Goldthorpe.

2. See A. Etzioni, 'Industrial Sociology: The Study of Economic Organizations', *Social Research*, 25, 1958, 303–24.

3. See D. Silverman, 'Formal Organizations or Industrial Sociology: Towards a Social Action Analysis of Organizations', *Sociology*, 2, 1968, 221–38.

4. See T. S. Kuhn, *The Structure of Scientific Revolutions*, University of Chicago Press, Chicago, Ill., 2nd edn, 1970, chs. 2–5.

5. In particular, W. H. Scott, *et al.*, *Technical Change and Industrial Relations*, Liverpool University Press, 1956. Though all Liverpool studies tended to remain relatively untheoretical the foregoing work is consistent with 'technological implications' theory.

6. D. Bell, *The End of Ideology*, Collier-Macmillan, New York, 1961. Despite its own clearly ideological flavour, this work contains two interesting chapters specifically on industrial questions.

CHAPTER 25 *pages 227–31*

1. See M. Weber, *The Methodology of the Social Sciences*, Free Press, New York, 1949.

2. See P. S. Cohen, *Modern Social Theory*, Heinemann, 1968, chs. 3–6.

3. M. Dalton, 'The Industrial Rate-Buster: A Characterization', *Applied Anthropology*, 7, 1948, 5–18.

4. E. Chinoy, *Automobile Workers and the American Dream*, Doubleday, New York, 1955.

5. ibid., p. 133.

6. See F. Parkin, *Class Inequality and Political Order: Social Stratification in Capitalist and Communist Societies*, MacGibbon & Kee, 1971.

7. A. W. Gouldner, *Wildcat Strike*, Harper & Row, New York, 1965; *Patterns of Industrial Bureaucracy*, Free Press, New York, 1964.

8. A. W. Gouldner, 'Cosmopolitans and Locals; Toward an Analysis of Latent Social Roles – I and II', *Administrative Science Quarterly*, 2, 1957–8, 281–306, 444–80.

9. M. Dalton, *Men Who Manage*, Wiley, New York, 1959.

10. See J. C. Abegglen, *The Japanese Factory*, Free Press, Glencoe, Ill., 1958; C. Kerr and A. J. Siegel, 'The Interindustry Propensity to Strike – An International Comparison' in C. Kerr, *Labor and Management in Industrial Society*, Doubleday, New York, 1964.

CHAPTER 26 *pages 232–42*

1. The most important discussions are J. H. Westergaard, 'The Rediscovery of the Cash Nexus' in R. Miliband and J. Saville, eds., *The Socialist Register 1970*, Merlin Press, London, 1970; and G. Mackenzie, 'The Affluent Worker Study: An Evaluation and Critique', Paper presented to the British Sociological Association, April 1973.

2. J. H. Goldthorpe, D. Lockwood, F. Bechhofer and J. Platt, *The Affluent Worker: Industrial Attitudes and Behaviour*, Cambridge University Press, 1968.

3. See J. H. Goldthorpe, *et al.*, *The Affluent Worker in the Class Structure*, Cambridge University Press, 1969, ch. 1, for a survey of these speculations.

4. J. H. Goldthorpe and D. Lockwood, 'Affluence and the British Class

Structure', *Sociological Review*, 11, 1963, 133–63.

5. D. Lockwood, *The Black-coated Worker*, Allen & Unwin, 1958; J. H. Goldthorpe, 'Technical Organization as a Factor in Supervisor–Worker Conflict', *British Journal of Sociology*, 1959, 213–30.

6. See J. H. Goldthorpe, 'Attitudes and Behaviour of Car Assembly Workers: A Deviant Case and Theoretical Critique', *British Journal of Sociology*, 17, 1966, 227–44.

7. Compare Goldthorpe, 'Attitudes and Behaviour of Car Assembly Workers', with Goldthorpe, Lockwood, Bechhofer and Platt, op. cit., pp. 175–8.

8. See H. Behrend, 'The Effort Bargain', *Industrial and Labor Relations Review*, 10, 1957, 503–15 for an exposition of this concept.

9. See Goldthorpe, 'Attitudes and Behaviour of Car Assembly Workers'.

10. Goldthorpe, Lockwood, Bechhofer and Platt, *The Affluent Worker*, p. 183. Italics in original.

11. ibid., pp. 146–7.

12. ibid., ch. 7, p. 167 especially.

13. For an illustration of the risks see G. K. Ingham, *Size of Industrial Organization and Worker Behaviour*, Cambridge University Press, 1970. An even more blatant example is my own *Computers, Managers and Society*, Penguin Books, Harmondsworth, 1969, chs. 7 and 8 in particular!

14. Bechhofer, op. cit., has since gone some way towards rectifying any such misconception.

15. See W. W. Daniel, 'Industrial Behaviour and Orientation to Work – A Critique', *Journal of Management Studies*, 6, 1969, 366–75.

16. See A. W. Gouldner, *Wildcat Strike*, Harper & Row, New York, 1965; and T. Lane and K. Roberts, *Strike at Pilkingtons*, Fontana, 1971.

17. See Goldthorpe, Lockwood, Bechhofer and Platt, op. cit., pp. 40–41.

18. These themes recurred in the (unpublished) proceedings of a symposium on the traditional worker held at the University of Durham in September 1972.

19. R. Brown and P. Brannen, 'Social Relations and Social Perspectives Amongst Shipbuilding Workers – A Preliminary Statement', Parts I and II, *Sociology*, 4, 1970, 71–84, 197–211.

20. See Mackenzie, op. cit.

21. Goldthorpe et al., *The Affluent Worker in the Class Structure*, ch. 6.

22. Goldthorpe, Lockwood, Bechhofer and Platt, op. cit., ch. 8.

23. See A. Glyn and B. Sutcliffe, *British Capitalism, Workers and the Profits Squeeze*, Penguin Books, Harmondsworth, 1972. Whatever the accuracy of these authors' analysis and prognosis, recent events have been such as to render them the subject of a debate unimaginable ten years ago.

CHAPTER 27 *pages 243–50*

1. For an introduction to subjectivism which brings out its strengths see A. M. Rose, ed., *Human Behavior and Social Processes: An Interactionist Approach*, Routledge & Kegan Paul, 1962; Houghton Mifflin, Boston, 1962.

2. See B. Hindess, 'The "Phenomenological" Sociology of Alfred Schutz', *Economy and Society*, 1, 1972, 1–27.

3. D. Silverman, *The Theory of Organizations*, Heinemann, 1970, p. 5.

4. ibid., ch. 2.

5. But see L. Haworth, 'Do Organizations Act?', *Ethics*, 70, 1959, 59–63.

6. This point is established economically in M. Albrow, 'The Study of

Organizations – Objectivity or Bias?' in J. Gould, ed., *Penguin Social Sciences Survey*, Penguin Books, Harmondsworth, 1968.

7. Silverman, op. cit., p. 14.

8. ibid., pp. 127–8.

9. ibid., pp. 139–40.

10. ibid., p. 172.

11. ibid., pp. 224–5.

12. ibid.

13. Other subjectivists have extended this principle to cover individual physical strength. See D. Atkinson, *Orthodox Consensus and Radical Alternative: A Study in Sociological Theory*, Heinemann, 1971, pp. 192ff.

14. Quoted by Silverman, op. cit., p. 138 from P. L. Berger and T. Luckmann, *The Social Construction of Reality*, Allen Lane, 1967; Penguin Books, Harmondsworth, 1971, p. 101.

15. For example, by Jennifer Platt in her review of *The Theory of Organizations*, *British Journal of Sociology*, 21, 1970, 466–7.

16. Silverman, op. cit., pp. 130, 132.

17. ibid., p. 134.

18. ibid., p. 216.

19. Hindess, op. cit.

CHAPTER 28 *pages 251–62*

1. A. Willener, *The Action Image of Society*, Tavistock Institute of Human Relations, 1970.

2. These models are utilized respectively in C. Kerr, *et al.*, *Industrialism and Industrial Man*, Harvard University Press, Cambridge, Mass., 1960; and H. Marcuse, *One-Dimensional Man*, Routledge & Kegan Paul, 1964.

3. A. Touraine, *L'Évolution du travail ouvrier aux usines Renault*, Centre National de la Recherche Scientifique, Paris, 1955.

4. For example, in C. R. Walker, ed., *Modern Technology and Civilization*, McGraw-Hill, New York, 1962.

5. See G. Friedmann, *The Anatomy of Work*, Heinemann, 1961.

6. Touraine, op. cit., p. 112; Touraine's italics; trans. M. R.

7. ibid., p. 181.

8. In particular A. Touraine and O. Ragazzi, *Ouvriers d'origine agricole*, du Seuil, Paris, 1961.

9. A. Touraine, *Sociologie de l'action*, du Seuil, Paris, 1965, p. 123; Touraine's italics; trans. M. R. *Dépasser* has no precise English equivalent. Like the German *aufheben*, it implies 'going beyond' some state or object, possibly after struggling with it, to reach a novel and superior state.

10. ibid., p. 54.

11. ibid., pp. 38–9.

12. ibid., pp. 133ff.

13. ibid., p. 134.

14. ibid., p. 143.

15. ibid., pp. 253–4.

16. ibid., pp. 338, 407ff.

17. ibid., pp. 16, 473.

18. Willener, op. cit., p. 106.

19. E. J. Hobsbawm, 'Karl Marx's Contribution to Historiography' in R. Blackburn, ed., *Ideology in Social Science*, Fontana, 1972.

CHAPTER 29 *pages 263–67*

1. A. Etzioni, *A Comparative Analysis of Complex Organizations*, Free Press, New York, 1961.

2. For a thoughtful critique see T. Burns, 'The Comparative Study of Organizations' in V. Vroom, ed., *Methods of Organizational Research*, University of Pittsburgh Press, Pittsburgh, Pa., 1967.

3. The best example is D. Atkinson, *Orthodox Consensus and Radical Alter-*

native : *A Study in Sociological Theory*, Heinemann, 1971.

4. A. Touraine, *Sociologie de l'action*, du Seuil, Paris, 1965, p. 15; trans. M. R.

5. Predictably, hardly any of these writers' work has been translated; but see A. Gorz, 'Work and Consumption' in P. Anderson and R. Blackburn, eds., *Towards Socialism*, Collins, 1966.

6. Besides A. Glyn and B. Sutcliffe, *British Capitalism, Workers and the Profit Squeeze*, Penguin Books, Harmondsworth, 1972, see A. Jones, *The New Inflation*, Penguin Books, Harmondsworth, 1973, for partial and backhanded recognition of these problems by a 'renegade' right-wing politician.

CHAPTER 30 *pages 268–77*

1. See T. S. Kuhn, *The Structure of Scientific Revolutions*, University of Chicago Press, Chicago, Ill., 1970, p. 15.

2. R. W. Friedrichs, *A Sociology of Sociology*, Collier-Macmillan, 1970; B. Ward, *What's Wrong with Economics?*, Macmillan, 1972.

3. See M. Rose, 'Sociology: Still No Improvement', *Cambridge Review*, 93, June 1972, 149–54.

4. A. W. Gouldner, *The Coming Crisis of Western Sociology*, Heinemann, 1970.

5. A. Dawe, 'The Two Sociologies', *British Journal of Sociology*, 21, 1970, pp. 207–18, examines this division but fails to demonstrate its real significance.

6. This is rapidly becoming more evident thanks to fuller examination of the neglected *Grundrisse*, which Marx himself described as a mere rough draft of his complete system. See K. Marx, *Grundrisse*, trans. M. Nicolaus, Allen Lane, 1973; Penguin Books, Harmondsworth, 1973: as the translator remarks elsewhere, this work 'throws into sharp relief the fragmentary nature of *Capital*, and it can serve as a powerful reminder that Marx was not a vendor of ready-made truths but a maker of tools'; see M. Nicolaus, 'The Unknown Marx' in R. Blackburn, ed., *Ideology in Social Science*, Fontana, 1972.

7. M. Shaw, 'The Coming Crisis of Radical Sociology' in Blackburn, op. cit.

8. See S. M. Lipset, 'The Changing Class Structure of Contemporary European Politics', *Daedalus*, 63, 1964, pp. 271–96.

9. See R. Miliband, *The State in Modern Capitalist Society*, Weidenfeld & Nicolson, 1969.

306